2-17-93

— RyB —

TIME CHANGE

An Autobiography
HOPE COOKE

SIMON AND SCHUSTER · NEW YORK

PUBLISHED BY SIMON AND SCHUSTER
A DIVISION OF GULF & WESTERN CORPORATION
SIMON & SCHUSTER BUILDING
ROCKEFELLER CENTER
1230 AVENUE OF THE AMERICAS
NEW YORK, NEW YORK 10020
SIMON AND SCHUSTER AND COLOPHON ARE TRADEMARKS
OF SIMON & SCHUSTER

DESIGNED BY EVE METZ
PHOTO EDITOR: VINCENT VIRGA

MANUFACTURED IN THE UNITED STATES OF AMERICA

3   5   7   9   10   8   6   4   2

LIBRARY OF CONGRESS CATALOGING IN PUBLICATION DATA
COOKE, HOPE, DATE.
   TIME CHANGE.

   1. COOKE, HOPE, 1940–   2. SIKKIM—QUEENS—
BIOGRAPHY.   I. TITLE.
DS485.S576C663   954′.167′00994 [B]   80-24916
                ISBN 0-671-41225-6

ACKNOWLEDGMENTS

I thank all at Simon and Schuster for their commitment to the book, particularly my editor, Alice Mayhew, and picture editor, Vincent Virga. I also thank many of my friends for their help, especially Marylin Levitt and Lenore Rey, who, each in her own way, helped me clarify many parts of the work.

TO MY FRIENDS

Beach plum. Pitcher plant. Joe-Pye weed. Spiked loosestrife. Spotted wintergreen. Partridgeberry. Solomon's seal. Hog cranberry. Wild sarsaparilla. Broom crowberry. Sweet goldenrod. American flowers. American names. The Rinpoche stands smiling in the dirt road leading to my house. From around the bend of the road comes the splinter of surf on the Vineyard's South Beach. "It makes me think of Tibet," he says. "Where I lived in the monastery, there were fields of flowers so colorful we had to make shields of yak hair to keep our eyes from stinging with the brightness."

The Rinpoche, a senior priest from Sikkim who spends part of each year in America teaching Buddhism, has been with me in Martha's Vineyard for three days now. Yesterday we went around the West Tisbury agricultural fair, where, to the appreciation of a gathering crowd, he dunked the West Tisbury fire chief in a tub of water by hurling a well-aimed softball at the proper mechanism. Today, his long red robes gathered around him, he went swimming in the ocean for the first time in his life.

I feel the various parts of my life come together, that again I am whole. Sitting around the kitchen table of the cottage I've rented for the summer, we talk. Outside, evening light washes over the meadow around the house. V's of geese fly by low over the ground. Inside, the music we're able to pick up from New Bedford scratches out from the radio. The fire hisses, and the water in the teakettle mutters, about to boil. I ask Rinpoche again whether Buddhism holds life to be impermanent or—my old sticking point—unreal. Unreal, he says; only in the sense that if we hold things to be permanent, that's illusory.

7

PART ONE

1

I AM THREE, I thought. I must remember this. I must feel this way hard. I shall always again want to remember how it feels to be three. I was standing in a corridor of my grandparents' apartment in New York looking at an old-fashioned bulbous doorstop screwed into the wall where I stood. Sunlight patched the piece of hall, brightening the rusts and blues of an otherwise dark Oriental runner. I wore a yellow dress and felt yellow like the sun stripes and the creamy yellow wall I was facing.

A year later I stood in front of the long mirror on my sister's closet door thinking, Now I'm four. Last year I remembered what it was like to be three, now I must remember being four. My plump white face hung with brown curls approached and receded in the mirror. Something was wrong. It didn't work. Adjusting my eyes, I focus. Brown ringlets, side part, taffeta bow, fierce hazel eyes, straight freckled nose, blue-and-white-striped dress embroidered with a circus train. They remained just a collection of details. Nothing came together—there was no intimation. It was sad, a little embarrassing too. Sheepishly I turned away from the mirror with a sense of loss for the experience I couldn't repeat.

My sister Harriet and I are in the bedroom next to my maternal grandparents' room in New York. It is dark and the aqua colors in the room hover between their own color and shadowy gray. Periodically, through the crack above the windowsill, lights from the traffic on Sixty-second Street knife across the room. Car noises shiver and hum.

I am in a bathtub being washed by a nanny, who is kneeling on the floor scolding and coaxing me by turns to come down where she can reach me more easily. I'm at the far end of the tub, and she has either to reach across the toilet or else stretch diagonally across the length of the

11

tub to get me. I'm slippery with soap, which makes her job harder. The pipes rattle and scare me. I'm afraid of going down the water drain in the front of the tub—also I'm angry. My grandparents are going to what I understand to be Hope Sound, in Florida, and leaving me. They are taking my sister.

These are my first memories. I must have been two. Before this I have no memory of anything. No memory at all of my mother or father or places I lived in before coming to stay with my grandparents in 1942. The lights and noise from the traffic must have occurred when my sister and I were first staying in New York, during the period my mother was setting up residence in Nevada for the purpose of divorcing my father. The bath must have been given me shortly afterward, when my grandparents went to Florida for the winter to recover from the blow of my mother's death.

Number 45, a ten-story brick building, where we lived on Sixty-second Street, was next to the Colony Club, between Park and Madison Avenues. The Fifth Avenue parades turned off here and marched a bit down our street, letting me know that it was important. Our apartment was big, full of Far Eastern furniture and paintings. The dining room had hand-painted wallpaper with Japanese men and women holding fans on verandahs, and dark mahogany furniture, including a Dutch table with twelve legs. As the youngest, I always got a leg. My own legs stubby, uncomfortably straddling. When there were more people than chairs, I got the piano stool. The Manhattan phone book sliding forward on the shiny mahogany, tipping me toward the table. Earlier, in a high chair, I'm being spoon-fed Cream of Wheat by my grandmother. "It's goody goody two shoes," she says in a sugary voice. I refuse the cereal, and she leaves the room impatiently, rustle of petticoat and whoosh of her silk-stocking-encased fat thighs rubbing against each other.

The living room has a vast blue Chinese carpet. It is like a sea. I am at one end in a sofa that is like an island. or a ship, a yellow ship bobbing at anchor with the big Chinese model junk on the bookcase. Across the carpet, by the fireplace, my grandparents sit silently reading or doing crossword puzzles. In the daytime my grandmother sits at the big drop-leaf table in the corner of the room making out checks and menus. Her desk is laid out with unchanging wonders. Ivory carvings and crystal balls from China on ebony stands, a sheathed silver letter opener and magnifying glass, Schrafft chocolate mints in a flower-sprigged box. A pile of New Yorker magazines, each copy stuck to the next.

My grandfather does his writing in the library at a desk covered with red leather. Around the room are shelves full of red and browny-gold leather volumes. They are very important. They are classics, he tells me. It is a long time before I realize the things on the shelves are books.

There is a small hall like a Dutch interior, brass chandelier and mirror, black-and-white tiled floor, which opens out to the corridor that leads to the bedrooms. A nurse stays in a rose-colored room nearest the hall. Silk gros-grain bedspreads that grate deliciously on the skin. A large picture of the Battle of Bunker Hill, dismembered bodies spilling out of the foreground of the painting. The room where my sister and I stay has two high single beds and a dressing table flounced in chintz. The dressing table in its paniered skirt looks like old-fashioned ladies in fairy tales. There are no toys. Nothing to make it a child's room.

Opening off a dressing room where my grandmother keeps her Bergdorf hatboxes, lavender with purple silhouettes of women marching in a circle, is my grandparents' room. Woven cane and painted-wood Venetian furniture, wispy flowers on the headboards of the beds, on the desk, dressing and bed tables. On the bed table is a yellow and green papier-mâché Kleenex box that my nurse tells me I made for my grandparents. I examine it each time, suspicious. The nurse must have made it and then got my sister to put on a finishing touch. Even at the time, I have no memory of making it. My favorite object in the room is a Russian lacquered box full of cracks, mysterious, painted with a sled pursued by wolves. Inside are pennies.

Aside from these bedrooms there are three more, small iron-bedsteaded rooms for the maids and cook, which open off the kitchen in the back of the apartment. Jean, the cook, when she is not working is like Marshmallow, the rabbit we have in the summertime on Long Island, that never comes out of her hutch; she stays all day long in her room, staring, the door half open. Even in the evening she doesn't turn on the lamp but sits in grayness relieved only by the dim light of the building courtyard.

After a year my grandparents buy the apartment across the hall for my sister and me, the governess, and another cook. The furniture is being moved in. I stand down near the 8B end of the hall and for no particular reason experimentally stick my tongue out at my grandfather, who is standing in the doorway of 8A. His expression warps in disgust. "Don't do that!" he exclaims sharply. After we are living in 8B my sister and I go across to my grandparents' apartment only on special occasions, for Sunday lunch, and, dressed for bed in navy bathrobes and red slippers, every evening at six to say good night. Leaving our governess behind, we pad along the tiled hallway dividing the two apartments, ring the bell, and wait to be admitted by their maid.

Twisting the buttons on the tufted sofa, we sit silently as my grandparents remain bent over their books or crossword puzzles, the mantel clock ticking. My great-grandfather's portrait over the fireplace, his eyes looking at me blankly over the marble chimneypiece. Facing me. Long oval face, big-eyed and bushy-bearded. If they are doing puzzles, from time to time my grandmother looks up: "Chet, what's a tribe in New Guinea that . . . ?" . . . "Well, Helen, what about a drink?" my grandfather says. Every night they have two old-fashioneds. My sister and I always get their alcohol-soaked cherries and several crackers with cheese. I love the Bel Paese because of its silver-map wrapping. At seven my grandfather switches on the big radio—its green light mysteriously flickering, an elephant's eye—for the news, signaling my sister and me to kiss them good-night. My grandmother's cheek dry and crepey, her hair feathery, full of big hairpins, my grandfather's cheek rough, abrasive, a contrast to the feel of his velvet smoking jacket. Occasionally, not thinking, mistaking them for my grandparents, I kiss the cheeks of their visitors, and stand rooted to the spot, cheeks burning with shame. As we leave, my grandmother calls after us, "Did you have chops for dinner?" She never quite trusts our cook to provide us with the food she ordered and paid for.

My grandparents rarely come to our apartment, maybe only once a month or so, and then only to my room to get a bottle of liquor from the locked closet in my room where they keep their wine cases. Even though I know what's inside it, the locked closet in my room scares me. So do the elevator noises at night. My room is next to the hallway, far away from my sister's and governess' rooms. The elevator stopping and starting like chains rattling. I am not allowed to leave my room at night to go to the bathroom. I lie on my bed listening to the noises through the wall. When I have to, I urinate in the smiling Toby jug on my bookcase and put it carefully back on the shelf until morning.

The first governess I remember is Miss Buchanan, a Scot. I don't remember anything about her except that she didn't approve of my going to see Michael, a little boy I had met in the park, because his mother was a painter and he ate ice cream with a fork. Miss Grant, another Scot, came after her. Before coming to us she had looked after Barbara Hutton's son and was always comparing my sister and me unfavorably to him. On days off, when she went to see him, she would return in a sour mood, full of the contrast between Lancy's and our behavior and,

14

no doubt, although she didn't say it, the relative shabbiness of her present position. Stripping me naked, she used to stand me in the bathtub and beat me with coat hangers when I couldn't remember the Lord's Prayer—"Let's try once again"—every word of the prayer flying out of my mind. "You're being deliberately naughty." One week, so frightened of forgetting my prayers, I wet my bed every night and am not discovered until the following washday, when the laundry hamper is shaken out to reveal not the expected one, but six pairs of identical striped pajamas. My sister and I never mentioned anything about Miss Grant to our grandparents.

She leaves during the summer soon after I've had my tonsils taken out. Something about the operation has gone wrong, and I lie in bed, swallowing mouthfuls of blood, surrounded by an impressive ring of grown-ups. After the others have gone downstairs Miss Grant comes back to my bedside and in cajoling but urgent tones begs, "Please don't tell Mrs. Noyes I beat you today." The idea hasn't occurred to me. Her suggestion makes me feel very important, although the odd way she is behaving embarrasses me.

As my grandfather has gone away to the war, there is no one to curb my grandmother's bad temper, and she is dictatorial and rude to the people who work for us. We are getting more and more governesses; they're not staying or my grandmother is firing them. One governess ties my hands to the bedposts at night. I am masturbating and there is blood on my panties. No one will marry you, she says. Why not? I ask. She doesn't reply. I am always frightened that I will be picked up at school by a different person. I don't care who it is, I want it to be the same one.

My grandmother has for some reason put me in a French nursery school on Eighty-fourth Street and Lexington Avenue in New York, called Toit des Petites. It has one big room, with tables of three-year-old children, four-year-olds, and fives. I sit at the pale green table with the four-year-olds, where I have two friends, Valer and Melissa. Both of them are blond and blue-eyed and look like angels. Valer has a fatter sister, Cecily, also blue-eyed and blond-haired, who sits at the three-year-old table. Cecily looks like a cherub. We are allowed to speak only French. I just know the word for honey—miel—which we are given at recess. I always think of Melissa when we have the honey and when I see the white pot on my grandparents' radio that has "MEL" printed on it. My grandfather has told me mel is Greek for "honey."

I am dumb most of the time in class and sit pricking out portrait silhouettes with pins, and knitting. We knit every day and always leave our work at school. When we return the following morning to our places at the table where we had left our ragged knitting, there are finished pairs of booties. "I didn't make this," I exclaim astonished, "I never made this." "Yes, you did," Mademoiselle assures me. "You certainly did." I am dumbfounded, impressed, ready to suspend disbelief. In good weather we practice dancing and singing on the narrow red-tiled roof that runs around two sides of the room. I am heartbroken because I'm assigned the triangle to play for the Maypole dance we will have in the spring. The triangle is a ridiculous instrument, absurd. I pine to play the tambourine, to stamp and shake.

When dancing is finished, we are allowed to run free on the roof, crashing into the brick-and-fine-mesh fence enclosure looking out over the squat wooden water towers on surrounding buildings. One day I wet my pants on the roof. Urine streaming down my legs into my shoes. Acrid stink. In shame I'm changed into a spare pair of Mademoiselle's bloomers, long, bright pink wool that come down to my knees. My governess is called to take me home.

By and large, being eager to please, I get on better with the governesses than my sister, who is more elusive and stubborn. Her confrontations with them often occur at meals, particularly breakfast. Harriet has a physical revulsion toward many foods, particularly eggs. She can sit for what seems like hours, a piece of egg she'd been forced to take bulging her cheek. I'm not allowed to leave the table until we are "all finished," and sit fiddling with the vitamin pills on the table. My sister has told me they are jumping beans, and if I try long enough they will hop. After that there is nothing to do but sit and watch Harriet with exasperation and respect. She never gives in. Sometimes it is funny, as when our grandfather clock stopped and it was found that the pendulum had been blocked with breakfast food stacked up over months. Sometimes it is horrible, as when she threw up and was forced to eat her vomit.

Physically Harriet and I are opposites: she has dark brown coarse hair, olive skin, and good teeth; I have fine reddish brown curly hair, fair freckled skin, and already many cavities. She has black hair on her arms, which upsets her, and I have golden curly hair of which I am very proud. "See that," I say, standing in the light to show my arm hair to best advantage, "see that." "I do, Hope," she says, her voice dripping with disgust. Although only three years older, she's much taller than me, her body as long and hard as mine is soft and round. My grandmother always dresses us alike, buying tailored clothes that suit Harriet's long

limbs, not mine. Aching to have organdies and sashes, I hate the plain
linen and piqué dresses my grandmother chooses, and at the same time
I envy Harriet her strong, athletic body. I can't do any of the things she
can—not even bend my legs to one side. If she sits on the ground, her
legs are always gracefully tucked under her. I can't figure out how to do
it and always sit with legs jammed out in front, feet sticking up, showing
their Indian Walk labels. At the same time, I'm less clumsy in some
ways. Because of her vagueness and an early mild bout with polio, she
has a tendency to fall over everything. Her knees are constantly bloody.
Except for an occasional heroic gash caused by a grand roller-skate fall,
I'm never scarred. I'm better also with my hands. Probably because,
earlier, her nurses had tried to change her left-handedness, she is clumsy
and can't tie packages or make things. The weeks before Christmas,
balefully watching my show-off dexterity, grimly holding exploding
paper together, are agony to her.

In temperament too we are opposites, the difference increasing with
age. Harriet's introspective, dreamy, aloof. I'm a chatterbox, pragmatic,
friendly, always willing to take anybody's hand. I always agree, Harriet
always argues. One day she even dares leave the table when my grandfather says, as a joke, "There are too darn many people in the world—
what we need is a good bomb." At an early age she refuses to go to
church. I go for seven years, with perfect attendance, receiving at the
end of each year a certificate and a hydrangea. Struck by the color and
spaces of the church and the chance to kneel and thank a God I do not
believe in, I love going. From childhood, Harriet is an intellectual, reading Niebuhr and Barth, while I stick to books on the Oregon Trail. She
chooses to go to Europe the summer I choose to go to camp. She is a
medievalist, in love with King Arthur, riding sidesaddle, to my dismay,
on the Central Park merry-go-round. I'm a "modern," always fighting
Redcoats or defending my Pilgrim cabin from Indians.

When I'm ten, a teacher, fascinated by Harriet's precocious love of
madrigals and Monteverdi, approaches me expectantly one day to ask
who my favorite composer is. "John Philip Sousa," I reply, looking
straight into her eyes.

I hardly see Harriet. We keep separate spaces, rarely playing together.

As the older, she has certain prerogatives—a later bedtime, a higher
allowance, a far bigger room in our apartment. My grandparents—my
sister told me later, when I was in college—also preferred her. As a child
I didn't or wouldn't realize it and put down any inequities in our treatment to the general injustice of being the youngest. All other things

being equal, and if my sister was correct, my grandparents possibly liked me less because of my mother's death. It was never, never spoken of, however. In our family we never asked questions. Anything painful or difficult or embarrassing was never alluded to. Growing up, I knew nothing about my father except that the charged silence about him maintained by my grandparents, made him one of several taboo subjects. I was terrified of him.

Through magazine articles about me I know that my mother, Hope Noyes, whose first marriage to Harriet's father, James Townsend, ended in divorce, met my father, John Cooke, when she was learning to pilot airplanes at Roosevelt Field in Long Island, where he was a flight instructor. They were married soon afterward, to the dismay, I realize now, of my maternal grandparents, as he was in their opinion socially untouchable, being Irish and fairly poor. So feared and detested was the secret of his origins that it was only by chance years later, after I myself was about to be married, that I learned anything about my father's background at all. In the short period of their marriage my parents—I don't know why they moved so much—lived in St. James (Long Island), Pebble Beach (California), and finally Palo Alto, where they had a house when I was born in a San Francisco hospital on June 24, 1940. Soon after that, I gather, my father left my mother. My clue to this piece of information, like everything else I know about my parents, came well after I was grown up, when my mother's sister, Aunt Mary, looking at some patchy jewelry odds and ends I'd inherited, snapped shut the lid of a man's watchcase saying, "That watch is jinxed for sure. That's what Hope bought your father just before he left her."

In 1942 Harriet and I came to stay in New York with our grandparents while our mother established residence in Nevada for her divorce. From Nevada she wrote us a letter about her love of flying, which, later, when I was growing up, made a strong impression on me. It seemed to me as if the stars and sky had had some powerful pull on my mother—that she had been caught between the gravitational spheres of earth and a galaxy where she remained spinning in space.

I didn't and don't know if they found any parts of her body or, if so, where she is buried. When I was a child this lack of information prevented me from feeling the finality of her death as strongly as I felt her permanent suspension away from earth and myself. A bird winging into space, frozen in place in the permanent act of disappearing.

At my grandparents' house in Huntington there were cardboard cartons in the attic filled with newspaper clippings. I couldn't yet read when I found them, but I was so impressed by the photographs of my mother, some only of her face and some at the side of her Piper Cub, that I told my grandmother of my discovery. The next time I went back they were gone, and I spent the afternoon riding on the old dappled rocking horse that had disappeared one day from my room and that I'd just rediscovered in the attic.

My mother probably killed herself. When my engagement was written up in the papers, a man who had known my mother, "an admirer although not a beau," wrote me a loving appreciation of her in which he suggested that it would have been in my mother's character to feel a great loss of integrity after the failure of two marriages and that this possibly caused a spiritual weariness leading to her death. I didn't get the point. After I'd married, when I read an article in McCall's purportedly "as told by me" to a writer friend of Aunt Mary's, who'd sat chatting with her and "getting background" on the plane from New York to Calcutta on my wedding trip, I still didn't get the point. I didn't realize until many years later, when another half sister, Hilary—my father's daughter by a subsequent marriage—wrote me that she'd met our father for the first time (she too had been separated from him since early childhood), and I was never again to write anything that would hurt him as the McCall's piece had. I read the article, "An American Princess: My Story," several times before I found an offending sentence. It stated simply that she had taken off that last day with an almost empty fuel tank.

My grandparents' anger—particularly my grandmother's—about my father's origins, and their indirect blaming of him for my mother's death, must have fired their hatred for my father and their determination that he should have no access to me. At some early point in my childhood my grandparents instituted legal proceedings to become my official guardians and keep my father at bay. On his part, for whatever reasons, he was willing to surrender responsibility for me, I'm told, after my mother's death. In fact, I've learned just recently, he tentatively considered allowing my mother's first husband to adopt me, a possibility cut short by James Townsend's death soon afterward in World War II.

I remember seeing my father only twice. I'm five, crouching under the grand piano in my grandparents' apartment, screaming in terror, "Go away, go away, go away!" Only his trouser legs show through the pedals and the piano stool. I don't see his face. When he has gone my grandmother says, "Well, I guess she fixed him." I'm heavy with relief he's gone and with guilt for having in some way been in league with my grandmother.

After that I saw my father one more time, that I know of. I'm about nine and have been invited to go from my grandparents' house near Huntington, Long Island, to Locust Valley to visit my half sister Hilary. My grandparents' aversion to my father extending to his other daughter, I'd met this half sister only several times, despite our proximity on Long Island during the summer and the good-natured efforts of her mother to get us children together from time to time. Once I'd seen Hilary when she was a baby, and once again, a few years before this visit, I'd seen her when she'd been brought over to my house to play. I had been so primed before her arrival with malicious solicitude for the poor child that I had made a large bundle of old toys for her. As the pile included a red vinyl Scotty to which I was still very much attached, I'd been non-plussed when Hilary, surprised, said, no, she didn't especially want the things.

This day my grandparents must have allowed me to go to Hilary's house because they could again afford to be magnanimous. My father and Hilary's mother are separating. Hilary, now a victim like myself, is no longer a threat. The day I go, my father has already moved out of the main house and is living in a smaller one on his wife's family estate. He's got no pride, my grandmother says.

On the drive to Locust Valley I'm numb with anxiousness. I first see my father's face from where I stand on the top of a flight of stairs. He takes the stairs two at a time, hauling at the banister, his face upturned eagerly. Dark hair, beautiful, lean, sensitive face, blue-gray eyes bright in anticipation of seeing me. "Oh, hello," I say in a cold, disdainful voice I'd never heard before, "Hello," watching the light die in his eyes. The beautiful kindled eyes. He makes no further effort that day to seek me out, and the rest of my time is spent safely among a large group of children as just another guest. My father driving us around a newly mown field in a red pickup truck, stopping at intervals so we can jump out into hay piles. As the afternoon wears on and it becomes clear I won't have to speak to him again, or look him in the face, that all I will see is the back of his black-haired head through the glass panel, I relax enough to enjoy the game, the rough-and-tumble risk unthinkable at my house.

I never saw him again, and only once or twice heard him mentioned. One day, rounding the ring at Captain Galeza's riding class, brown mud, horses hooves ooze down, pop free, heels down, toes up, knees in, elbows out, I hear my governess talking to another child's governess, probably soon after my father's separation from Hilary's mother. "Well, that's two fortunes John J.'s lost." Somehow I know she is talking about my father, but I can't understand. "What do you mean, Johnny?" I ask. "Lose fortunes how?" "Never mind, child, it's not for you." That evening I look up John Jay in the encyclopedia and find Jay Gould. My father John Jay's loss must have something to do with railroads, I decide. Several years later a friend in school tells me someone has seen him in the city showing slides, trying to get people to invest in a ranch out west.

I had some photographs of my mother, half a dozen snapshots of her as a child picnicking on the public beach in Seal Harbor, Maine, rubbing smoke-stung eyes, holding marshmallows on speared sticks, sitting brown-curled, direct-eyed, with my grandparents in a boat that flies the Seal Harbor Yacht Club pennant.

In the same album are two more pictures of her grown up. In one, holding my father's arm, smiling coyly, provocatively at the camera, wearing a forties summery dress that comes only to the knees of her muscular legs, she stands with a beige spaniel puppy in the crook of her free arm. In the other picture she sits, very pregnant with me, on the lawn of their Pebble Beach house, holding the same puppy.

The only color picture we have of my mother is the full-length oil in our 8B dining room. For the painting my mother has worn a décolleté shimmery evening dress and sits leaning slightly forward. Vivid heart-shaped face, dark curly hair, dark direct eyes, and a rather smug rosebud mouth. Her smiles in all the pictures distress me. They look cloying, falsely sweet, unrelated to the level communication of her eyes and the strong will and fierce honesty I've been told was her essence.

Because she is not there, I can imagine her any age. Usually I see her as a small child my age. When I see her this way, my grandfather is much older than she, about as old as he is now with me his grandchild. Partly I visualize this because, in the few times my grandfather talks of her, he likes to tell a story about my mother and him playing doubles in tennis which culminates in a voice from the spectators' pavilion singing out over their court, "Isn't that sweet, the dear little girl playing with the old old man." My grandfather, his lips curled, repeats the phrase in a fluting falsetto voice. " 'Isn't that sweet, the *old, old* man.' "

I see them. A formidable pair, both professionally in white—my mother, her long dark hair pulled back in a bow, my grandfather, his tennis hat jammed on the back of his balding head—leaning over their rackets, straining to anticipate the ball. My mother in childhood already showing the competitive spirit and determination that would later make her the twelfth seeded woman player in the country.

Occasionally I visualize her as a young woman, and see her this way chiefly in Maine, where we spend two months every summer. Just before we return to the city we always go as a treat to the lighthouse on the most distant of the three islands lying off Seal Harbor. The western side of the island is made of flat slabs of pink granite sloping toward the sea. I'm told they used to bring bands out when my mother was a girl and dance under the moonlight—my mother, pearls flying, Scott Fitzgerald dress, elbows and knees pumping wildly to brass music, tide foaming up the rocks.

My grandfather is back from the war, which makes me happy, as his humor blunts the edge of my grandmother's demands. He teases my sister and me. On his uniform he has a medal he says he got for being hit on the head by a telephone in an earth tremor. We have a celebration the day he returns in my grandparents' dining room in New York. Blue balloons are tied to his chair. It is like a throne. "How many Japs did you kill?" asks my sister. He's been in New Zealand directing ship movements, an assignment he was well suited for because of his position as president of the family cargo-shipping company. He is overage but had volunteered anyway, serving for a year or so with the rank of commander. During his time in New Zealand he'd sent back to my sister and me carved tikis and navy bathrobes, Harriet's embroidered with one more chevron than mine.

My sister and I are taken by our governess to a Trans-Lux movie theater to follow the progress of the fighting in the Pacific and are frightened there by the cartoons of Donald Duck, knees knocking against each other, creeping along jungle trails, Japanese soldiers, hiding in trees, pointing rifles at him. There are a lot of air raid alerts and blackouts in New York. A year before, still in a pram, I'd been caught with my governess at the zoo near the wildcat cages. When the siren began, she, cursing, pushed me to the nearest shelter, Temple Emanu-El, on Sixty-fifth Street and Fifth Avenue. In the darkness of the vast room a rabbi prayed for peace and began a lamenting song, his white, bony face and long white beard illuminated like a torch against the darkness.

The same year my grandfather returns, Aunt Mary comes home from North Africa; she wears cotton dresses, not the Red Cross uniform of her photographs. I've never seen her before. My grandfather says Mary's

22

impossible. She puts lobster claws on her fingers over her own long red nails and chases my sister and me, laughing. That summer we go on more picnics than ever before. She laughs and talks all the time, and her gold bracelets clang with charms. She rattles stones in a tin box and pretends they are candies. "Come, Hopie, try a chocolate." We go berrying together. Sweet smell of black oozy tar melting in the sunlight, crumbling away at the side of the road like fudge breaking off. She pushes my wicker carriage up the driveway through the pines. The carriage is just a convenience—I am too big for it. I'm in a pile of berry baskets—the real reason for taking the pram—some stiff, black and white, the others of sweet-smelling soft grass, bought from the Indians who come selling them at our house. The three of us sit by the roadside in the berry patch, sunlight on bronze leaves. I put handfuls of white berries and juniper berries into my basket. The little hard berries only as big as pinheads fall out through the cracks. We make blueberry pies with what we have picked. I squeeze out the wartime margarine we use for the crust from two tubes, one white, one yellow. Aunt Mary's teen-age children are staying at the house with us too, but we rarely see them. They are always off fishing with the chauffeur. When they come home in the evening they march up the driveway in their slickers, carrying oars over their shoulders, dangling the fish they've caught. Most nights they go to Cadillac Mountain with their friends to spot for planes. Brave to spend the night in the fog on top of the mountain. My sister and I stay home, playing dominoes on the rickety card table in the living room, safely shut in by blackout curtains.

One night in August there is a wild clamor of horns and buoy bells outside. Breathless, my grandmother enters my bedroom, where I'm almost asleep. "Hopie, Hopie! The war's ended!" She kisses me and gives me a mint candy—a treat, she says, for a special day. We go to see the warship anchored in Bar Harbor.

That winter, after we'd got back to the city, my grandfather took us to see the fleet of returning battleships down the Hudson River. Gray boats ploughing through the ice. "Remember this," he said, "remember this." My grandfather was a great fan of Churchill's. The greatest man the world has ever known. In the front hallway in my grandparents' apartment he'd hung a handwritten letter he'd received from Winston Churchill: "I thank you sincerely for your kind messages to me which I very much appreciate." The envelope, also written in Churchill's hand, was there too, and hanging next to it in the hall was a copy of Churchill's "We shall not flag, we shall not fail" speech. Every night when my

23

sister and I came to say good night, my grandfather, standing with us in the hall, made us recite it. We shall fight on the beaches.

That summer I learned to read from signs. When we go shopping in Bar Harbor, I sit in the wooden station wagon waiting for the grown-ups to return, the sun hot on the seats, my legs in shorts baking against the leather, sweat in the cracks behind my knees. "ICE CREAM" I read from the sign in the drugstore window I C E C R . . . Even after I've learned how to read by putting together the letters and pictures I see in the advertisements in shop windows, I still read "ICE CREAM" out in a loud, tremulous voice as if I'm just making it out. I've done it a number of times, but every time a grown-up thinks I've just made a breakthrough and brings me a cone as a reward.

I was proud to go to Chapin School in New York—where my sister had been for the last three years—already knowing how to read. Chapin, founded by Miss Chapin, a descendant, like Aunt Mary's husband, Selden Chapin, of Deacon Chapin, who founded Springfield, Massachusetts, was a conservative school, secure, undoubting in the classical Christian-oriented education that it gave us. Every morning began in the assembly room, repeating the Bible verses we had been assigned that week. "Lift up your heads, O ye gates; and be ye lift up, ye everlasting doors, and the King of glory shall come in. Who is this King of glory? The Lord strong and mighty, the Lord mighty in battle. . . . The Lord of hosts, he is the King of glory." Wonderful hurtled words, wonderful to be singing them out in a group.

Its student body, reflecting this orientation or inspiring it, was virtually all Christian. In our class I knew only one Jewish child, Vivian, whom we persecuted. There were no blacks and only two Democrats, one of whom was in our class and appalled us by voting against Dewey for Truman in the school mock election of 1948. In exchange for our "privileged" situation our headmistress, Miss Stringfellow, a spirited, straight-backed woman, demanded dedication to public service. The older girls were expected to work in neighboring settlement houses, and all of us were expected to develop strong, even stoic moral characters. *Fortiter et Recte*, carved over the stage, was our motto. We must be this at all times, particularly in adversity. "Don't forget, girls, you must finish in style," Miss Stringfellow enjoined us. "And remember, wherever you go, you carry the school with you." Although I knew something wasn't quite right, it was comforting to be a part of a group with such a clear, self-confident view of itself.

I liked social studies, art, reading, and writing. The summer before first grade I had written a poem:

> I was Noah in the time of the flood,
> I watched the great water rise over the mud.
> I was a caveman in times of old
> Who helped to fight the cave bears bold.
> Brave A. Lincoln freed the slaves,
> Now if you want more history, just come to me.

To my delight, it was published in the school poetry magazine. It was a beautiful poem. So beautiful it was frightening. I was even glad "Brave A. Lincoln freed the slaves" didn't sound quite right. I'd thought of changing it, but if I did, the poem would be too perfect.

I was not so good, I knew, in art, but loved the opportunity to imagine, and the feel of our art room in the basement—damp, cavelike, thick with the smell of poster paints, shriveled rubber cement, and sweet clay. Our art teacher, upset over the low quality of the paper and materials we were using, called us her poor war babies. What a fine expression. Repeating it often, I didn't understand my grandmother's indignant reaction. "Hope, you are not, I repeat, *not* to use those words." My grandmother didn't keep anything I made anyway, not even the glazed pieces that were especially good and had been fired in the kiln. The one thing she did keep, a clay candlestand, was pushed back in the cupboard in the library with bridge scorepads and stacks of elastic-banded checkbooks. After a while I didn't bring work home anymore. I left it under the bus seat or, spurred on by friends, threw it from the window at the roofs of cars.

Johnny, my new governess, who has come, is a friend of our first-grade teacher from summers in Newport, which makes me feel special. They even dress alike. Our teacher has an amethyst brooch just like Johnny's which tugs down the front of her dress. Johnny doesn't know I can read, and every day when I come home from school reads me the Mother West Wind story from the *Herald Tribune*—and they all went off to Asbury Park in a shoebox. I can read faster than she can, my eyes are almost at the bottom of the page. Impatiently I wait for her to catch up, her high English voice, toneless from her slight deafness, whining on. I love her so much I don't want to hurt her feelings. It is so cozy to be sitting there next to her, my hand on her crackled arm. It is freckled on top and white below, like mine, and her dress is soft and crepy over a hard waist. She has a corset underneath that she puts on every day. The cords attached to the bedpost, she strains forward, tightening the stays. After that she sits down and bandages her thin ankles. She is like a race horse, legs always in Ace bandages clasped with pins. I admire the way she deftly overlays them, coiling up and back down again. You can see them under her cotton stockings.

Most parts of Johnny are held together. Even her thin hair is meshed in place by a hairnet. The ridges made by the metal crimps she clamps onto her head every night poke through the net. Little strands of hair stick out under the elastic of the net and frizz over her forehead. The elastic leaves a red mark on her forehead. She has blond tufted eyebrows, China-blue eyes, a straight nose, and a long, faintly hairy crack of a mouth. When she stops reading to take a breath, her big bosom rises like a shelf. I love her so much.

On her pine bureau are pictures of her family in England. An oval sepia photograph of her mother, a white-haired, strong-looking character, a sainted woman, the photograph's faded tint making it like a memory of memory. Stuck in the mirror frame over the bureau are recent snaps of Johnny's nieces, Margaret and Christine. Christine is still studying but hopes to leave school to become a florist's assistant. "No, I always knew Margaret wouldn't come to any good. It's going to be Christine who saves the day in that family." Johnny and I are saving sugar lumps for her younger, favorite niece. On Saturdays, when we go to the new Howard Johnson's on Park Avenue and Fifty-ninth Street, we always bring back handfuls of sugar to put in the cornflakes box that Johnny keeps on her desk. We have sent two boxes to England already. "They'll be glad to have that, my girl. They don't see too much of that these days." In the evenings Johnny lets me count how many cubes we've got in the new row being formed and sometimes gives me one or two to eat before bed.

Pack up your troubles in your old kit bag and smile, smile, smile. What's the use of hurryin'? What's the use of worryin'? "Will you hurry up, child, you're going to be late again this morning." It's the end of the John Gambling show. I should have left the apartment by now for the bus stop. I can't get the buttons through the buttonholes of my uniform. Johnny has starched the linen so stiff the buttons are stuck. I have the stiffest dress and the tightest elastic in the linen bloomers that we wear underneath. It is so tight the elastic hurts, but I endure the discomfort with pride. Some children in our class don't have any elastic, and their bloomers droop straight down. What I don't like, what I despise, are my oatmeal-colored woolen knee socks. I want white ankle socks so much. Johnny says only nouveaux riches and Jews wear them.

When I come home it's always thrilling to meet her. Several blocks before Sixty-second Street, my stomach contracting, I start to get anxious that she won't be there, that she'll be replaced by some new face—that I'll jump off the bus, look up, and it will be someone different. Except on Wednesdays, when Kingie comes to substitute during Johnny's day off, it's always Johnny, however, and I straddle her tweed coat with my arms and grab her pocketbook-free hand and squeeze it, walking out of step until she gets confused, with Middy pulling the other way, and has to untangle herself from the leash. "Calm down, I never saw such a chatterbox." Johnny's hand is very fair, with loose skin like a glove and dark brown freckles. In cold weather she wears beige woolen gloves that never get stiff like mine.

I always want to go straight home and curl up in her room with one of the reading books I've brought back from school, but Johnny insists no. "A walk's good for you. Look at me, my poor feet, I've been walking around town doing errands for Mrs. Noyes all day and I can still manage." If her feet are really tired, we stop at Larimore's drugstore, and to my great embarrassment, giving me Middy to hold, she stands on the penny vibrating platform—hat, coat, handbag, everything jiggling.

We always walk toward Fifth Avenue, going past the stone-lioned mansion that used to belong to the family for whom Johnny worked before coming to us. "You should have seen the parties they used to have there, my girl, that was something." One time, when the Prince of Wales was invited, the daughters of the family had been kept in the bathroom all day so that the steam would make their hair curl. Now the mansion's interior, seen through the dirty windows, is unkempt, piled with dust. If there are bleachers up on Fifth Avenue for a parade, I run up and down the tiers, testing their springiness, trying to put off the moment when we will come to the zoo entrance, by the World War I monument. My heart is pounding that we'll be caught. I live in fear even after we exit safely from the park again at the Fifty-ninth Street exit. There is a sign right by the entrance steps, lettered with a large *NO* followed by a list in smaller print. At the top of the list is *DOGS*. We take Middy every day. One day we are bound to be arrested.

Afterward I lie in Johnny's room reading, enjoying its warm familiarness. Johnny's room is wonderful. All the furniture brown, with legs like roots—narrow brown bed, shiny varnished bureau drawers, a pigeonhole desk jammed with aerograms, and a night table with a biscuit tin showing Princesses Elizabeth and Margaret Rose, where she keeps her hair curlers. Johnny always sits reading in an upholstered armchair, the grease marks on its back gleaming under the floor lamp. I read in dim light lying down on a chaise longue, trying to move very carefully when I turn the pages so as not to crackle the tissue papers that Johnny keeps folded underneath the mattress. Sometimes she lets me polish shoes. Sweet, seeping smell of polish. "You're a good little helper, not like someone who shall not be mentioned." Harriet doesn't come home till later, and when she does, stays in her own room until supper, doing homework. On all nights except Thursdays we have what my grandmother has ordered, often lamb chops, which, my grandmother exclaims, have gone sky-high. On Thursday, our cook's night out, we have English food, bubble and squeak, which Johnny ate as a girl.

When we have returned from saying good night to our grandparents across the hall, I play checkers with Johnny in the living room or sit at the end of the room with my dolls behind the three-paneled screen, cut and painted to look like a house. Its door is so small that even Harriet can't fit, and if I let her enter, she has to pull out one of the folded sides. I prefer sitting there quietly, holding my dolls, doing nothing, to playing checkers, but I'm anxious not to hurt Johnny's feelings. At bedtime she listens to my prayers, which end with "God bless Granny and Gramps and Mummy and Daddy and Johnny." One day when I've been particularly naughty, Johnny says, "You might add 'and make me a good and truthful little girl,'" which is then incorporated, a permanent testament to my deceitfulness. Only very rarely will Johnny punish me by not saying good night. That is the worst punishment I could ever have. A nonperson listening to the elevator noises, I lie awake for hours, tears dampening my pillow.

Weekends were boring; there were no children in our building. All the apartments were owned by old people, so old that at Halloween we weren't allowed to go trick-or-treating for fear that they might suffer heart attacks. No school friends came to play or invited me. On Saturdays I read, walked, or played alone in the Mother Goose playground until noon, when, after lunch at Howard Johnson's, Johnny would take Harriet and me to the Plaza Theater or the Trans-Lux movie theater. War evacuees pushing carts along muddy roads, a cart stuck in a rut. An old man in a flapping greatcoat trying to drag the cart forward.

Sunday morning, until Harriet refused to go with us, my sister and I were dressed alike in gray woolen skirts and jackets and velvety gray felt hats, little clumps of berries pinned on the side, and taken to church—

Johnny's choice. St. James Episcopal, or Church of England, as she called it. "Dressing them up like English schoolgirls," my grandmother would harrumph, "and taking them off to a church that's almost Catholic." "Now, now, Helen," interposed my grandfather, who hated kneeling, "it's not the religion, it's just all the getting up and down that's pernicious." Granny would then turn up the sermon she was listening to a little louder on the radio and glare at both Gramps and Johnny.

At lunch, which lasted several tedious hours, Granny looked for ways to carry the argument further. "I beg your pardon," I say politely, having failed to hear a request to pass the stuffing. "You do *not* in this country, in America, beg anyone's pardon. An American does not beg," thunders my grandmother from her end of the table. Frozen quiet, eyes looking down, I trace the embroidery on the tablecloth, feeling the dark, shiny wood between the frets of lace, and pray for lunch to finish so we can escape and go listen to *The Shadow* on the radio in our apartment. Sometimes the fights go beyond endurance; my grandmother sits back from the table, her eyes like knives. I don't dare look at Johnny directly, but I can feel her aching. The saddest, the most terrible thing is that Johnny is all dressed up in her plum-colored dress and has on her amethyst brooch, which she wears like a Sunday badge. I bear down with my breath, trying to impale the room with my will for this not to be happening. If I use my power, my full power, this cannot happen, I think. Johnny, looking clumsy and frightened, her pink eyelids lashed with tears, leaves the table. For nights afterward I sit outside her bedroom door, watching the crack of light, and listen to her cry.

On some weekends my sister's relations took us out, and we'd be swept into a warm, loving, haphazard household. Harriet's father, a painter of clouds and a flier, had gone off to join the Royal Canadian Air Force before America entered the war and had been killed in Europe. He'd enlisted partly for moral reasons, people said, partly for grief over my mother's leaving him. His relations, instead of being bitter, however, took me and Harriet into their lives as often as my grandmother allowed. Bearing sleds, which we were not allowed to own for fear of dirtying our clothes, Harriet's great-aunt, Ros Sherwood, sister of the playwright Robert Sherwood, would come many weekends to take us to the park, encouraging us to get as dirty as she dared. Afterward we would go to Grandpa Townsend's shabby-chintz apartment uptown, where we drank cambric tea and Aunt Ros played ragtime on the piano while Grandpa Townsend's daughter Betsy, who was a dancer, showed me her ballet slippers and her sister Dooly teased me.

Aunt Betsy gave us beautiful engraved books from Scribner's, where she worked, and took us to plays. *Peter and the Wolf* made me sick with pleasurable fear and excitement, "Watch out, watch out, Peter!" I wanted to grow up to be like her and be on the stage. Some weekends we'd spend at the Townsend log cabin in Princeton Junction. Smell of pine burning. Rough feel of bark logs. Delicious anticipation of Harriet jumping awake too fast in the morning and bumping her head on the steep pitched ceiling. Like their New York apartment, the cabin was always full of relations, a big, loving Irish family. Irish in the only way acceptable to my grandmother, descended from Robert Emmet, whose picture, along with the other Emmet ancestors, stood on the chimney in 8B. I felt part of that family even though my sister's and my last names were different. At Christmas, Grandpa Townsend used to send us a new piece for the silver dresser sets we were acquiring. Each piece with the monograms twined HC or HT, the letters so curly it was almost impossible to make out the difference.

In early spring, on Saturdays, we'd start going out to Long Island to my grandparents' house on Young's Hill, in Halesite. Chicken sandwiches in waxed paper for lunch on the terrace near the garden, brick paving littered with twigs and leaves blown down during winter, goldfish pond choked with debris, big china pineapples on the pilasters streaked with dirt from rain. Then, the day after school ended, we'd leave our New York apartment to spend the month of June in Long Island before going up to Maine. Long Island was Granny's domain as much as Maine was my grandfather's. Enjoying her self-image as chatelaine, she lavished work and money on the beautiful pre-Revolutionary farmhouse and surrounding gardens, bringing olive trees from Greece and crab-apple trees from the Far East to add to the great oaks already there.

Dressed in my "pinnie," I was an extension of the idyll. A good deal of the day was spent doing needlepoint and listening to Johnny read poems about rooks under the huge trees near the rock garden. One poem, making tears start down her cheeks, ended "I wish the Lord had borne that breath away before the light of day." "What does it mean, Johnny?" "Oh, you'll know soon enough, child"—heaving her summery striped cotton body in a great sigh. On rainy days we sat with my dolls in the playhouse. Filling out and sending off box tops, cooking grape jelly over the stove, reading the shelves of books that had belonged to my mother and aunt as children. The little building with its porch and fireplace is my house. Here Johnny is a visitor, I the mistress.

Only occasionally were friends we'd met at the Piping Rock Club or the nearer Cold Spring Harbor Beach Club invited over. Usually they came just for my birthday, when, wreathed in tiny pink roses from our garden, attended by our nannies, we had high tea together. They were not as well-mannered as my sister and I, Johnny said. Not quite so well brought up. I used to cross-stitch their names in lists on my samplers.

Occasionally we were taken on walks to our German chauffeur's house down the road to play with his two handsome, blond children, who kept goats in a wire pen. But the walks stopped, after Harriet had polio, as someone thought the outings or the goats might have been responsible for the virus.

Harriet left in an ambulance and came back walking with a limp. The big canopied four-poster in her room was replaced, as someone said the canopy closed out the air and kept her from breathing easily. My room in Long Island was as pretty as hers, so I felt sorry for her, not glad, that they took away her good bed.

In the evenings, commuter trains throbbing by in the distance, Johnny, Harriet, and I have early supper at the lace-covered card table set for us at the end of the dining room by the French doors. "Keep an eye out for rabbits," my grandmother commands. "If you see a rabbit, up you get." I loved chasing the rabbits as much as I feared the way the gardener went after them. One day I'd seen him stamp a nest of naked, peeping, blind baby rabbits under his boot. He also set traps all through the garden, with dark, cruel, iron teeth, for moles. They didn't work well, and the garden was always ridged with tunnels, which made me feel slightly sick to walk across for fear that they might cave in and my foot would squash a velvet monster. The croquet ground was also hummocked with molehills. Each evening after supper as we played, we'd have to repeat shots as the ball sloped away, glancing off a ridge. "That doesn't count," Johnny would say firmly, repositioning her ball so that, mallet drawn back as far as it would go against her striped skirt, she could whack the ball to the stick.

I feel my mother's presence here more than in New York. There is a storehouse, an old icehouse, full of her belongings, near our barn. It is always locked. Sometimes, in the afternoon, planes dip down over our house and bank sideways. My grandfather says it must be her flier friends honoring her. I'm not athletic like her. I try to play tennis, but the racket is too heavy and my palm is burning and sweaty. "Just keep practicing against the backboard—you'll never be good unless you practice," my grandfather reminds me. I stand, sun glaring into my eyes, red sand gritting my sneakers, bored and uncomfortable. The whir of the lawn mower cutting grass near the court. It is easier to be like my mother indoors. I've found the account she wrote as a child for the Brearley School when she went to China with my grandparents to be present at the birth of Aunt Mary's first baby. She signs her name with a strong, bold-stroked H. I always think of things that begin with H. My sister's initial is H—H for Harriet, but mine is my mother's name—Hope.

In Maine it is the same way. Indoors in my room, peering out through the small, low windows my grandfather had carved for her when she was small so she could look out to sea, I am like her, but when I go out, I am not. One morning, in the meadow between Bracy's Cove and the Harbor Club, I try to catch butterflies, as she did. My room is full of her collection, everything neatly labeled under glass, intact except for their flattened heads. I'm repelled but fascinated. This morning I run through the stubby grass after a small, bright orange butterfly that is hovering on a devil's paintbrush of the same color. I steal up, throw my blue sweater on top of the insect, and, tears streaming down my face, pound the sweater with a stone.

I wait all year to go to New England. New York is dull, Long Island painfully boring. I hibernate, and come awake only when we go to Maine. My body tingling with excitement, I count the days till we go to the city to take the train. In our city apartment, swarms of dust dance in the sun shafting through the windows. The chandelier in the library makes rainbow refractions on the wall. Furniture like ghosts in white sheets. Ghost piano, ghost stool, ghost Granny's chair.

It is me in the space between the jump seats of the hired limousine. The youngest gets the crack. The windows are down and hot, gelatinous air seeps inside. Trucks surround us, men circle us like monkeys, yelling, pushing racks of dresses.

Inside Pennsylvania Station the beauty of the sun coming through the pillars is so awesome that I stand rooted among our piles of steamer trunks, in the way of the porters, unable to move. Granny is being helped into the wheelchair that she has been using since her heart attacks began. On her lap Dicky, our canary, cheeps from under his covered cage, which sits on top of Granny's hatbox of medicines. What if he should sing? I feel like singing. My sister and I scamper through the sky-reaching waiting rooms. We've got several hours before the sleeper to Ellsworth, the Bar Harbor Express, arrives from Philadelphia. Granny believes in being early.

The next morning it is almost too exciting to open my eyes. It is better to lie in my berth, eyes shut, waiting, anticipating the moment of looking out the windows at the pine forest and the lumber sheds on the outskirts of Ellsworth. My breathing comes in sharp pants of excitement. The air is crisp even though it's July.

As we drive up our long dirt road my head swivels to keep track. I know every pine on both sides, like children all grown a few inches taller. Some of the small pine seedlings of last year have grown up enough this year to have their branches shaken. I will walk down the driveway as soon as we've unloaded stuff, touching each pine in turn, holding their branches in my hand.

The first thing my grandfather does is take my sister and me out to the front of our house and check to see if we remember the names of the islands—Islesford, Big Cranberry, Little Cranberry, and, far away, Baker's. Gramps was one of the earliest summer people to discover Mount Desert and build a house in Seal Harbor. The point of land we live on is called Running Point because it used to be one of the way stations for the Indian messengers who'd traveled up and down carrying news along the Maine coast. My grandfather's been the world over, and always says, "It's very pretty, but not so pretty as Mount Desert." In a way it could be said that his family came from Maine; at least many of them lived there when the state was still part of Massachusetts. I wish we came from Maine, were not just summer people.

Mount Desert is an island most of the time. Crossing the narrows by the moccasin shops and lobster pounds is a magic crossing, you are in a magic kingdom. On the island the mountains come down to the sea, grassy pastures slope down to pink granite beaches, I'm about to burst with happiness and beauty. I know every root's shape. Like a dog circling his territory, I run along the paths through the woods. There is the chicken-claw-shaped root, the ball-of-twine root. Everything is the same; even the road gashed through the forest by the Rockefellers has mellowed and grown over. I'd twice pulled up the stakes, hundreds of them, on the point where their friends were supposed to build. They'd never built, and the road now is choked with blackberry bushes. The offerings are where I'd left them, piles of sweet hay stuck in the hollows of pines near our house. I'd put them there last summer on our last day. The chipmunk hole is still by the juniper bushes, and, by the smell of it, the skunk is still under our house. Only a few trees have blown over, and the dock is gone, blown away. Someone said that it had been washed up in Southwest Harbor. Piles of silver planks spiked with rusty nails have been thrown up on our land too by the cranberry bogs, fairly high above the beach. Either someone has moved them there, which would be odd, or the waves actually came high enough to float them up. For hours I sit imagining the ports to which my wrecked ship has sailed. Maybe it was a ghost ship like the *Marie Celeste*, which my grandfather's family owned.

When the outdoors has been inventoried, the next things I must check are the books in my room, which have been there since my mother's childhood. The Twin series, by Lucy Fitch Perkins, the Dorothy Dainty series, the Little Colonel series, the Brick House books, and the Little Maid books. I reread them every summer. The damp, musty pages clinging together, totally different from the sweet-smelling Chapin summer-reading books I've just finished on Long Island.

After the first few days of exploring the woods and beach around Running Point, I settle back in my rocking chair into being a bookworm. Smoke from the fire in the living room fireplace below gusts out of my fireplace, stinging my eyes. "Come, child, you'll ruin your eyes, and it's not often we get such a fine day as this. Be off with you now." Laggardly, reluctantly, I take my racket from the berry-basket cupboard and, slamming the screen door, go off to the Harbor Club.

The Harbor Club adjoins our woodland. If you listen, you can hear the balls banging against the backboard from our driveway. Sometimes on the path I meet my friends the Pyles from next door. They are the only children aside from the Rockefeller twins, Harriet's friends Mary and Michael, who live on our point. My other friends come down to the club from the hill across the harbor. Kit, tall, athletic, is our leader. We adore her, but she is too superior to us to be really close. Then there is Elizabeth, a red-haired child who lives in a huge Victorian house, where we go for pajama parties. Elizabeth has always been solemn, but her father's death has made her more so. Now she's the most grown up, often looking at us disgustedly, saying, "Don't be childish." Her brother, who smokes a pipe and is always off sailing, once showed her his penis. My best friend, even though I adore Kit, is Gloria. Gloria is mischievous like me and gets into trouble. Her younger sister, Margaret, who is prettier than Gloria, with flaxen hair, has a tumor of the stomach and is going to die. She has already had several operations. The child's a saint, Johnny says, a saint. One night, her nurse found her awake reading the Bible, and Margaret said, "Oh, Nanny, I know I'm going to die." Johnny says we must pray for her. Margaret is so good that I feel sorry for Gloria.

The nannies sit gossiping on the green-painted wooden slat benches by the pool. They all wear striped cotton dresses and white cotton sun hats. Earlier, there were no sun umbrellas over their benches, but Johnny organized the governesses to demand one from the club. "What do they think we are, just because we work for someone—animals?"

Even if it is very foggy, she shoos me out to the club "to get some air." I hang around in the tennis pro's cottage by the courts, practicing carrying balls on my arm and watching him string rackets. If my friends don't come, I go to the stone boathouse in the pasture above the Harbor Club dock and play being the Puritan twins defending my cabin from the Indians or the Scotch twins hiding with Rob Roy in his mountain cave. More and more I identify with Scotland over England—I love its virility and its rebelliousness and hate England for its imperialism. Johnny calls in Jean, our Scottish cook, one day to testify that Scotland became part of the United Kingdom voluntarily. Jean looks around the dining room anxiously, not quite sure what's being asked of her. "But why, Johnny, why should Scotland want to be part of England?" I cry. I always wear a sprig of pine in my hair, such as Rob Roy's followers wore in their bonnets.

At dusk, no matter what else we are doing later in the evening, Johnny takes Harriet and me up to the Unitarian Church we attend in the summer with our grandparents, to water the flowers. Accompanied by Middy on a leash, we walk up the hill to the church, carrying our china pitcher. In the dark piney evening, watching the water wash channels around the geraniums, I feel virtuous, which I confuse with feeling holy. In the church, whose door is open, I sit in the piney pews looking out the windows at the forest, wanting a revelation. One night I go up to the lectern and turn on the light over the Bible. My sister says I will be arrested. At home I fall asleep listening at the fireplace, trying to make out from the hum of voices in the living room below whether they are talking about what I've done.

Carrying our food in the berry baskets, we often have cook-outs in the evening on the rocks at our house or our friends'. I always bring my wooden boats to sail in the pools left by the tide. Our main treats, spaced apart over the summer, are excursions to Southwest Harbor for cinnamon toast, Baker's Island for a picnic at the lighthouse, and through the woods looking for Indian pipes, ambushing the governesses and pelting them with pinecones, to the Jordan Pond teahouse for popovers and strawberry jam. Every Thursday evening there is a dance at the Harbor Club, and we skelter about in and out of the clubhouse, our patent leather shoes wet with dew, throwing water in the tuba, dancing energetically with each other, and gawking in adoration at the older boys in their khakis and crew sweaters.

I am consciously happy. Even the scariness of coming home from the club each day doesn't daunt me, and the fear goes away as I draw level with the new bedroom that my grandparents have added on off the dining room; the heart conditions of both now prevent them from climbing the stairs. My grandmother calls, "Hello, Hopie, is that you?" I've been afraid to call out, afraid, coming into the house, that they might be dead in the dark new room. "Yes, Granny, do you want anything?"

My grandfather dies first. I'm in the fifth grade, home from school, sick in my bathrobe. We're having lunch in my grandparents' New York apartment when my grandfather keels over toward Johnny's chair. Later Johnny says, "Even in death Mr. Noyes was a thoughtful gentleman—he didn't want to frighten the child." I look at his body in the chair, looming out horizontally, his eyes staring. Everything in me stops. Johnny props him up in his chair, and I call my grandmother from the pantry, where she is on the phone trying to locate Harriet's flight from Panama. "Oh, Chet!" she cries, cradling him on the chair, "Oh, Chet!" I look up doctors in the telephone book. My grandmother might need one. Actually, I'm turning the pages because I have to do something mechanical. I have absolutely no feeling of existence and must do something to know I'm alive.

My grandmother is bereft at Gramps's death. Despite her tyranny, they had had a loving marriage. Even as old people, they still used to hold hands and dress for each other. Some days, when we were out walking, I would see them strolling hand in hand down Fifth Avenue, my grandmother wearing red, my grandfather's favorite color, and he a tie of her favorite color, yellow. The day he died, my grandmother, although still in mourning for her brother, who had died a few days earlier, was wearing a new red print dress. "I don't think your uncle would mind, do you?" she'd asked me that morning.

After Gramps's death, as she grew older, Granny became very beautiful. Before, she'd been stout; now her flesh tautened, defining her handsome bone structure and classical Greek nose. Her hair, turned perfectly white, is so fine, her great metal hairpins are always clathering out of her bun. Her manner is softer, and she bothers, as she had always charmed her friends, to charm my sister and me more often. Only her resistance to Johnny, partly because of the new dependence she has on the slightly younger woman, is sharper. I'm in constant fear Johnny will leave. On Johnny's day off, to make sure all her things are still there, I search her closet and then lay out her bathrobe and slippers by her bed with a note, "I hope you've had a good day off. I've been a good girl. Much love, Hope." The note, the goodness, and my love, a magic to force her return, just as in the past I'd used my magic to stop my grandmother's attacks on her. One day, at the bottom of her closet, I find a big leather case packed. For the next days I live in terror, but Johnny returns, and nothing seems to change.

Our apartment 8B is up for sale and we will move into my grandmother's apartment. Long Island also has to be sold. Aunt Mary says so. Something about helping to pay the death duties. Aunt Mary's inherited Maine, my sister and I, Long Island. I feel gypped. Maine is my house. I love it. Aunt Mary is never there, always away in Europe. I hate Long Island but am angry that it should be sold under our noses. My sister and I are asked to pick out things we want to keep. I keep barrels of children's books, the paintings of my great-grandfather's boats, and the beautiful early American furniture from the guest room, some of it dating back to Newburyport, which my grandfather's family had settled. "Why do you want that furniture? Whatever will you do with it?" I love the touch of it. I love to feel it all together, lace pincushion, ivory comb-and-brush set on the satiny wood dresser. "I like it, I want it," I say stubbornly.

Prospective buyers come to look over the house. My grandmother flies at them, driving them to the door, demanding they get off her property. Many phone calls later from our lawyer, my grandmother still is not reconciled to the idea that possible purchasers may come just because the property is for sale.

Harriet is going off to boarding school, Garrison Forest, in Maryland. She talks now only about horses and boys. She has had her period. From the box she keeps in her closet behind the water pipe I take her Kotex to see how it feels, enjoying the hard lump in my crotch. It was good she was going off to boarding school, everyone said, it would be more normal for her. In New York I move into her room, inheriting her paintings of Man o' War and Native Dancer. For a time I collect trading cards of horses.

At school I'm happy. Always at the evolutionary point of our social-studies syllabus, identifying my whole being with whatever we are studying, I'd progressed in successive years from bees to dinosaurs to Peter Stuyvesant. From old New York to Vikings to Greeks to Middle Ages to the American Revolution. Aside from social studies, I continue to love writing, both the making up of stories and their transcribing in the ink-splattering steel-nibbed italic penmanship demanded by the school. Most of my stories, different from those of the other girls, are about loss. Their stories are like the white keys on the piano, mine the black.

As pleased as I am with my facility in writing and with my friends in school, I'm discovering there is a whole new group of people with whom I can't communicate, haven't a word to say—boys. I've hardly even seen any males. Once, some years ago when I was little, a teacher had asked me to draw a picture of a man, and after a long time I'd finally drawn a figure of someone in a striped T-shirt, a top hat, and a briefcase. She'd looked at me puzzled, and I'd felt ashamed for not knowing. Now, in tongue-tied agony I sit on the frail gold chairs of De Rham's dancing class in the Colony Club, next door to our apartment building, yearning for the floor to swallow me up, for the wall to open, permitting me to scramble back to the safety of my apartment. I can't think of a word to say, and furthermore, if I could, there is no one to say it to. We have to sit with one empty chair on each side of us so that, as Mr. De Rham says, we won't frighten the boys. Crimson with embarrassment, hunched on my chair, trying to think of something to say if someone should ask me to dance. It is worse than being stood against the gym wall to wait for one of the team captains to pick you from the last knot of unchosen girls. At least, there you finally have to go to one team or another, even if you are met with groans and sighs. Here you can stay all night, isolated in your chair. On their way upstairs for dinner, the grown-ups stop in the doorway to look at us, proudly affectionate. My body is rigid—I see Mr. De Rham pushing a boy toward me. He is fat, with yellow teeth. He is shaking his head no. A girl wearing stockings, from my class, is dancing with Arthur MacArthur, the general's son. All the parents want their daughters to dance with him. He has black pomaded hair, slicked back, and a large turquoise ring. When he comes to church with his parents, there is always a huge crowd on the steps to watch them go by. A few girls in our class want the general for President. Most, including me, like Ike. I don't want to dance with Arthur MacArthur. I could go to the bathroom and sit there, pulling the chain.

My friends and I spend all the time on the school bus drawing anatomical graphs and, bemused by the first dictionary definition of rape as a kind of seed-yielding turnip, looking up all the dirty words we've heard. That summer I get my period in Maine and throw all my stained panties and Kotex pads in the woods so no one will know.

Harriet wants to come back to Chapin. The girls at boarding school are all jocks, she says, all they think about is horses. She is getting even more high-strung than she has been. The summer I get my period she goes to a modern dance camp taught by a Chapin dance teacher. Something terrible happens.

Granny is talking, bent over the phone. "When did it happen? When did it happen?" she repeats, her voice breaking. "It's the fault of that woman getting the girls so airy-fairy, always churning their emotions up," she later says viciously. "And also it's that blessed Ron's fault for what he told her." Ron is Aunt Mary's new son-in-law whom my grandmother doesn't accept. Granny goes to get Harriet and brings her to Seal Harbor, where she stays in her room in bed for several weeks. Every day a doctor comes to see her. Afterward, even until today, Aunt Mary always talks about "what Ron told her." When I finally understood the insinuation about my mother's death in McCall's, I thought maybe I'd finally learned what Ron told her.

Things are falling away from me, but a new independence, a new feeling of life being centered in me, makes it seem that it is I shedding them. Middy, our blind, blundering dog, has been put to sleep; 8B and our house on Long Island have been sold. Johnny is divided by her wish to return to England and Granny's increasing dependence on her. I don't feel anything. In an unconsidered way, I want to go away to school, out of this lonely, boring household. I've been reading vintage books on mysteries solved by sixth-formers in British boarding schools, how the Head untangled everything in the bell tower and the entire form celebrated by holding a midnight feast. Aunt Mary takes me down to Virginia to see her old school, Madeira, and I'm seduced by the beauty of the school's setting on the great falls of the Potomac River. Dogwood-covered hills stretching back as far as one can see. I enter in September.

At least half of the student body are southern. One of my roommates is from Virginia, the other from North Carolina. Physically and socially they are ten years more mature than I. They wear makeup, high heels and tight cashmere sweaters. At night they stay up whispering about French-kissin' theah pillows. I still curtsy and wear "vests," and also brown lace-up oxfords, which they throw out onto the roof, where they lie for the remainder of the term, out of reach near the water drain.

Our freshman class has only twelve girls. Most students come in at age fifteen, sophomore level, when the class triples. Our class of early starters comes from homes even more problem-ridden than those of the usual children of divorced or troubled parents who tend to make up the major constituency of boarding schools. For the most part, the girls in our class *have* to be there, have no other place to go. A depressed, bored mood hangs over the third floor of the main building where we live. There is a total absence of any civilizing influence of people, books or textures. The lessons, except for some English and history classes, are as bare as the walls and corridors of the buildings. We never read books, only assignments, in which, with utter lack of curiosity, we stop at mid-page or mid-sentence if the instructions allow. Although we are only fifteen miles into Fairfax County from Washington, D.C., we never read newspapers or pay more than hypocritical lip service to current events. Teachers and students never talk about anything going on in the Capital. On the alternate Saturdays we are allowed into the city, we are permitted to go, with our chaperones, only to F Street, the main shopping area, where we shuttle back and forth between Woodie's, Garfinckel's, and the one movie house.

Only the day students from Washington, although they don't enter much into school activities, provide a small sense of normality and civilization. I like imagining them at their homes, in carpeted dining rooms, eating decent food, talking with their parents about what is happening in the world. We mechanically do our homework, eat like beasts—unless it's the week before vacations, when we eat nothing—are chilled and humiliated on the hockey field, and, if we can, gang up on each other, exercising our power through student government, an institution that legitimizes our hierarchies and grudges.

Many of the girls relieve the misery, the days of boredom, by mooning around the telephone exchange on the long chance of a call, or rhapsodizing endlessly about Woodberry Forest and University of Virginia boys. My fantasy reprieves are twofold—conceiving and organizing elaborate campus pranks, and acting. Since the second grade, when during rehearsals I'd escalated by stealth my part in the Christmas play from a sheep to a silent shepherd to a very voluble one, I'd been struck by drama, and had written and starred in numerous plays. Despite a paralyzing attack of pubescent self-consciousness that made my already thin voice thinner, I'd recovered enough voice to earn the lead in the freshman Christmas play.

I feel the miracle of the Nativity through me, am touched by the holiness of Saint Luke's story. A babe is born. I'm thrilled by the lonely, splendid event. The holy family isolated, shining, magnificent. Mary giving birth, so alone and splendid, the baby born out of his mother, so alone, a miracle and splendid, and the shepherds keeping watch in the fields, so alone and yet so united by the dark blue sky. It is the only time the two planes, earth and sky, join. It takes my breath away. In the dark blue early morning the school carolers go from house to house singing "Angels We Have Heard on High." Shivers run up my body.

It is jarring and loathsome to be torn out of this sky-and-earth meeting, this mystical identification, and be put back at my grandmother's for the vacation. Johnny has gone, I feel probably for the best, as she was beginning to embarrass me with her buffaloed look and presents of molded china ornaments that were cheap and inappropriate. Harriet is not home much, since she has a circle of admiring boyfriends, all of whom have given her their long striped college scarves She wears the black-and-orange Princeton one. It is practically like being engaged. She seems successful, much happier, even worldly, sweeping out to coming-out parties with a pack of tuxedoed escorts. In contrast, I suffer, mortified, under the pressure of having to think up even one boy to ask to the dreaded society dances. Still, she is often odd and moody, saying dark things that amaze and worry me. One day I find a poem written on the back of three envelopes, the meter thoroughly marked out with strophes, that goes, "We are waiting for a death in this house, we are waiting. The little Irish maid is waiting . . ."

My grandmother dies in Harriet's arms when I'm beginning my junior year at Madeira. The day before she died I'd dropped her weekly letter to me, written in round, difficult-to-read script, with a clang into my metal scrap basket. The next day when the headmistress came to my room to hug me, to my embarrassment, and tell the news, I felt bad about the noise the letter had made in dropping. Even so, her death seemed redundant.

School continues, bleak and pointless despite the fact that I've achieved a measure of success, having through blandishments won the presidency of the sophomore class the year before and produced and written the class play. Increasingly I feel different from the preppy, narrow-minded girls, the freshmen with their gold circle pins and the seniors with their diamond rings, which, to clean and show off, they forever dip on threads into glasses of water and bicarb. I'd entered the election only to test my "popularity" against a group of girls whose conservative Wasp values I didn't share or respect, in fact hated.

I still know no Jews, and the only blacks I've seen have worked as Madeira's janitors and maids. I am subject to an accrual of folklore provided by the southern students. Having no idea what it means, and having heard him constantly referred to as such by the North Carolina girls, I've actually addressed our janitor as "Zombie." Even so, although ignorant, I have a strong feeling that the so-called privileged life I endure is gravely at odds with the rest of the world and my being. Only a few friends rail with me against the pretentious snobbery of our system and the barbarism of the girls. Taking refuge in our intellects, we one-up each other with our English SAT scores, study literature avidly with the one or two good teachers in the school, and pour carmine poster paint down our throats to ensure that the infirmary nurse will excuse us from field hockey.

As bad as school is, it is at least safe, and provides for me. The imminence of vacations is threatening, as Aunt Mary and Uncle Selden, officially my guardians since the death of grandmother, are now posted in Iran, and no precise arrangements have been made for my vacations. Every free weekend and short holiday brings apprehension and shame as I scrounge among my classmates, trying to put enough invitations back to back to fill the time.

Harriet is off at Bryn Mawr and increasingly involved with her Princeton boyfriend, so we rarely meet. She doesn't come at Christmas, which I spend with her Aunt Dooly Townsend, now in late life, married in New Jersey. The night before Christmas I lie awake on my tear-soaked pillow, sobbing because I won't get a stocking. Even past Christmases, cheerless and tense as they'd been, Johnny crying in her room while listening on the radio to the queen's speech and Granny by the tree for the third time commanding the maid to rehang an ornament, seem secure and good compared to this vacuum. In the morning, waking to find a filled stocking, I know I will forever be grateful to Aunt Dooly for realizing how much at fifteen I still had a need to believe in my childhood.

2

FROM MY FIRST MEMORIES of her in Maine, pulling off red lobster claws only to reveal shinier red nails underneath, I had been awed by if not entirely respectful of Aunt Mary, my new guardian. She always seemed to be swooping, racketing in on our dull, bourgeois life from some exotic place or situation. When I was seven we listened to her and Uncle Selden broadcast on the radio about conditions in Hungary, from which they'd just been thrown out for giving asylum to Cardinal Mindszenty. On their return to New York thousands of cheering Catholics had met them at the dock, and Cardinal Spellman had even invited them to breakfast. "No son-in-law of mine will be elected Pope," grumbled my grandfather.

Subsequent returns from various postings, although not so publicly dramatic, were, as Aunt Mary rattled on, telling funny stories about diplomatic pratfalls, equally disruptive of our household. Even from abroad she continued to regale us, sending small presents from countries they visited—charms to my sister and me, Parisian sweaters to my grandmother, and letters and clippings of all they were doing: what a pest Perle Mesta was, how Queen Juliana had lent a coach and six white horses for her daughter my cousin Helen's wedding in the Hague, how the violinist who'd fallen in the swimming pool at the soirée had, treading water, continued to play.

Aunt Mary and Uncle Selden, although they'd met before in Washington, had become interested in each other in Harbin, China, where he was posted as a young consul. She and a Barnard friend were junketing through the civil war-torn country on a trip to be written about later in a book, *Peking Picnic*. Afterward she married Uncle Selden in Peking in a ceremony witnessed by my grandparents and mother, who had traveled overland and by sea for six weeks from New York to China, carrying five wedding cakes given them by friends at stops along the way. In the early morning, in Tokyo harbor as their ship lay at anchor, my grandfather had taken my mother, then about twelve years old, up on deck, where together they'd solemnly thrown four of the cakes overboard. "There were too damn many," my grandfather said.

From China, Uncle Selden and my aunt had gone on to serve in many posts, including North Africa, where my uncle worked with de Gaulle and the Free French; Paris, where he reopened the American Embassy after the war; Holland, during the first Marshall Plan years; and Panama, where he had been signatory to one of the treaties about the canal. The personal experience Uncle Selden had undergone in Hungary, a country he adored, when the Soviet Union first moved to consolidate its eastern bloc in 1947, had left a profound impression on him. "And I asked Rákosi, if the Soviet Union effects a truly Communist state in Hungary, as opposed to a Russian-dominated state, will that be enough for Russia? Will they stop there? And he looked at me and said, 'I think, Mr. Minister, we had better change the subject.'" Uncle Selden told this story all the time. "It's not communism but Russian imperialism," he would thunder. His conservative—in the best sense—nature and the inescapable cliquishness of the diplomatic corps and the elite of the country it served, made him seem rather rightist to my youthful, arrogant eyes. So did his Gallic appreciation of good food and wine. (He and his sister Lydia—later married to Admiral Alan Kirk, the hero of the Normandy landings—had been brought up in Paris.) "A great meal is as high an art as a good painting," he would say, at which times I would owlishly peer at him across the table, resolving to show my liberal superiority by passing up seconds of our Italian chef's cuisine.

The Damascus airport, when Harriet and I flew out in 1956 to spend the summer in Iran with the Chapins, was a tin-roofed shack on a patchy airstrip. My first sight of the beginnings of Asia. Crowds of traditionally dressed villagers who had come to watch the airport phenomenon sat picnicking around the field; Arab music poured out of tents surrounding the tin terminal, and the night air was thick with the smell of export apricots left out all day for loading. Sight, sound, and smell. I was fifteen about to have my birthday, growing up. Time and place came together in an explosion.

Planes always land in Teheran at pre-dawn—the sky the stained-glass luminous blue of the Christmas skies that held me in thrall. Moon-surface craters, bare mountains circling the high plateau. In summer, even at this hour, the lights of Teheran and the upper villages of Gulhak and Shamiran, just below the Elburz range, still shimmer with the heat of the previous day.

Time change. Our first day here everyone at Ali Mansour's pool party is checking us out. (Our host was later to be Prime Minister and later still assassinated.) "My nieces. My nieces." Aunt Mary introduces us. Intricately coiffed women, glitteringly overdressed in brocades, stagger about on stiletto heels on the gravel paths of the garden. A good deal of the elaborately laid out rose garden is gravel, recalling the floral motifs banded by geometrics on many Persian carpets. I like wild English gardens pretending to be nature. The water here in the canals dividing the garden is static, muddy, greenly reflecting the roses and my face. The buffet is delicious—piles of long-grained rice topped with crisp buttered rice from the bottom of the pan, mounds of chello kabob. Odd, rather sweet spices. Yoghurt and cucumbers, Uncle Selden is picking at the yoghurt and leaving most of the other things. Yoghurt is supposed to be good for settling your stomach. Everyone is admiring the tapestries depicting the struggle between Ormazd, god of light, and Ahriman, Satan, that Ali Mansour has just brought back from the bazaar in Isfahan. Uncle Selden is looking at the Mansour's French paperback library to see if the pages have been cut.

Our life is a whirl of parties. At the upper end of the spectrum, imperial parties given at one of the Shah's palaces—either the old yellow-tiled Gulistan or the vulgar but dazzling mirrored palace in town —in honor of a visiting head of state. At the other end, barbecues of stateside—"Just flew it in today, sir"—steaks at the U.S. military attaché's or Point Four chief's house. In between are constant galas: buffets and dancing at the houses of Iranian or diplomat friends, poolside lunches, which we ourselves give every Sunday when knots of diplomats and their opposite numbers in the foreign office hash things out in mild sets of tennis, and large embassy bashes, including those on the various national days of the fifty or so countries accredited to the court of H.I.M. Shah Mohammed Riza Pahlevi. Teheran is known as about the most party-giving post to which anyone can be assigned.

Sometimes, to show my identification with the *real* people of the country, I go on long neighborhood walks around the temporary American Residency, where we live in a suburb of Teheran, and wander, yearning to know what's going on inside the mazes of walled compounds, which belong, I finally realize, to government officials and middle-class industrialists only a shade less wealthy than the Iranian elite we meet at parties. Often I conveniently shelve my feeling that these elite are unrepresentative of and unresponsive to the mass of the population that support them ("I'm so angry—one of my villages was washed away today," said a guest at a reception, to revive a lagging conversation) and that we, the diplomatic corps, through our cultivation of the elite, connive in furthering the imbalance.

At any of these gatherings, if I should meet one of my slightly radical friends, such as Sherin, the Radcliffe-educated daughter of a senior government official, I can even enjoy the party and give vent to moral indignation at the same time. Together, in our party dresses, we stalk the fringes of the crowd who've come to greet the visiting head of state or luminary, and mutter darkly, like a Greek chorus that has wandered into a Chekhov play, about the revolution sure to come. Sally, Aunt Mary's new social secretary, is even more priggish than me. The previous secretary, golden-haired and merry, who'd run off with a Spanish diplomat, had frankly enjoyed the parties, but Sally, a New Englander, also, like Sherin, from Radcliffe, is in moral agony. Finally she compromises by going to all the parties in a dress made out of maroon silk curtains from her room next to mine at the Residency. "It's curtain material," she says loudly, smiling defiantly at any gallant Iranian or diplomatic swain attempting to compliment her. "It's curtain material."

I'm being treated like a grown-up. An identity. It's not only my age, being visibly almost grown up, but also something about the East, which, not so much interested in process as product, looks at one from the outside and formulates its own definition of character and role about one's being. Obviously too, living in a foreign country sharpens my interior sense of values and self. Time change forces examination. It is noon under my sky, 2:00 A.M. under America's. I am awake, traveling in a jeep to find some trees by the banks of the Darband stream so that we may have our picnic in the shade. My boarding-school friends are lying on their lumpy dormitory mattresses, with five more hours to sleep before the first bell rings to call them for breakfast in the cold, noisy dining hall. Both are real.

The second year I returned to Teheran I felt I'd come back to my home. Aside from Aunt Mary and Uncle Selden, who remained patiently affectionate despite my young arrogance, I felt, in the deepest sense, at home among some of my Iranian and American friends here. I'd never before been with real families, with mothers and fathers and children. I was enchanted with the novelty, the luxury. My first summer I'd loved an American family so much, the mother letting me braid her hair and tuck in flowers when she went out to parties, that I'd had strong fantasies of being adopted by them. They'd since left, but there were several more families I was becoming close to.

Beyond the individual friendships I had, I also had a feeling of belonging to the American Embassy family, of being—as Secretary of State John Foster Dulles reminded us in an outpost-of-empire speech on his visit to the downtown embassy—a representative of America, among those often serving in adverse and lonely stations. "Yeah," a voice behind me had muttered. "Sometimes even our swimming pools freeze over." I couldn't dispute the cynicism. We were vastly privileged, well provided for by the U.S. government, and courted by the Shah, who several years after Mosadegh's overthrow, was still consolidating his position. Even so, I felt a thrill of service, of common purpose.

I couldn't go back to Madeira, to the bleak-tiled dormitories of stupid girls. The idea was horrifying. "Please let me stay. I need a home." Even if, in the strictest sense, I didn't mean just Aunt Mary and Uncle Selden, with whom I pleaded, I was telling a deeper truth.

Life settles into a satisfying routine. Going to school gives an added dimension of rootedness and authenticity that my vacationing life, joyful as it was, had lacked. Housed in an old mission hospital built of unbaked bricks in Persian missionary style, the Community High School, in which I enroll, is set in a compound in South Teheran, the old section of the city, the only quarter where donkey carts are still allowed and the narrow roads roil with street life. Having been to two sedate, blazered and bloomered schools, I've no preparation for a school like it. I find its Americanness, not its Iranianness, startling. The only exposure I'd had before to a co-ed truly American high school was lying on the porch on Long Island listening to *Archie Andrews* and *Our Miss Brooks* on the radio. Here the student body, composed of Iranians, Americans, Iraqis, Jews, Armenians, and several other nationalities cast adrift in Teheran dress and behave like larger-than-life Archies and Veronicas. The boys Levied and duck-tailed, the girls crinolined and cinch-waisted, we hang around the auditorium listening to Elvis Presley.

Being the niece of the ambassador, and possessing a degree of spirit lacking in many of the girls brought up in co-ed schools, who've been taught to "hide their personality," I'm elected to many offices. Head of the Committee for Designing Letter Sweaters, head of the Selection Team for Cheerleaders, Valentine Sweetheart of the senior class, vice-president of Student Government, and, at the end of the year, along

47

with a quiet, studious Iraqi boy, Most Likely to Succeed. I'm gratified but amused by my easy successes, my infiltration into rock 'n roll. Inside I know I'm an impostor and am shy. Sometimes before going into school dances, to delay the moment of arrival, I ask our chauffeur to keep driving around. For an hour or so, stopping occasionally to buy smoking-hot beetroot from corner vendors, we cruise the empty boulevards listening to the car radio.

It's fun being at school with boys. I realize that except for Matt, my friend in New York who played jazz, was good at math, and wrote me weekly witty letters to boarding school, up till now I haven't known a single thing about what a boy thinks. Their succinctness—all verbs and nouns—in speech and writing and the other-directedness of their concerns intrigue me. Also, I love their brash humor, of which at least once I am the victim. I think it out of character, quite amazing, when the boys as a body demand we name our class newspaper and yearbook *The Trojan*. We need something classical, something dignified and historical, they say. How odd, I think as, having painstakingly researched Trojan dress and decor, I draw the illustrations for our yearbook, how very odd.

Work in school is much easier than at Madeira. At boarding school I had toiled dully, doing well only in English and history; here I sail along free of the excruciating homework that filled our evenings at Madeira, and have infinite time left over for myself. Since Aunt Mary and Uncle Selden have decided that during weekdays, except for very special occasions, I shouldn't accept invitations, this gives me many, in fact most, evenings alone. Sighing tiredly, adjusting his bow tie, Uncle Selden takes Aunt Mary's arm to go off to do duty at yet another dinner party, leaving me to eat by myself in Uncle Selden's library, off the white-and-gold embassy china.

Uncle Selden, it seems to me, is just shy of the most important things of life. Instead of paintings he adores fine sixteenth-century maps; instead of baroque music he adores symphonies, operas, and operettas; instead of Greece he admires Rome; instead of D'Annunzio, Napoleon. That isn't really fair, I know. He has an extensive library, which he takes with him to all his posts, reflecting an appetite for every aspect of political and intellectual history of Europe. Nonetheless I'm bemused by the fixed points in his interest represented by the library wall decorations, records, and shelves of thirty thousand Napoleonic model soldiers, molded and painted by himself, perfect down to the last button on every gaiter. Not only Napoleon's French troops but all his European and African auxiliary troops as well. He's passionately involved with them.

The only time I've ever seen him angry is the morning after a big and particularly destructive reception when, purple with rage, he keeps repeating, "Someone's stolen my Marshal Ney, someone's pulled up my Marshal Ney by the boots." For myself, I resolve to have no special interests, to learn everything. To the noisy background of Beethoven and Aïda, I begin to work my way alphabetically through my uncle's Random House Modern Library. If only I can manage it, I will be complete, a Renaissance triumph.

Life is full to the brim, overflowing. Even waking up to the sound of the fountain outside is a spilling-over. Every minute is precious, lapidary, like the very art of Persia. Aside from my school life and evening reading, I'm up to a hundred things after school: painting murals in the orphanage run by the diplomatic wives; taking Persian-miniature lessons at a trade school in town, practicing with tiny strokes to draw the folds of a turban and a bulbul on a wrist; ski bumming to Ob Ali with my friends, arranging the grapes and wine to cool in snowbanks for our post-skiing feast; picnicking, listening to Nautch girl sing with Farhad in the Shamiran Hills; sitting around the brass foot stove at Parvin's house eating sweetmeats, and at Mina's listening to her mother tell rueful tales of her marriage at the age of fourteen.

Chastely courted by the men and accepted by women as a sister, I no longer fantasize about adoption by a family. Two American women in particular are my friends. One day when we're together we realize how curious it is that we're so close, since we're exactly ten years apart—sixteen, twenty-six, and thirty-six—stepping stones. What would each of us be ten years from then?

As the youngest, I feel safe and happy to be included by them, enjoying the inclusion and the fact that they are pathfinders, I the follower. Not having a mother, I've lacked a model. A good many of my mannerisms and self-images still retain a mixture of wise, overly polite little girl and imperious old lady. Gradually, however, some new formation is coming together. Among other things, through playing with my friends' toddler children, I discover I adore kids, that in some ways, still arrested in childhood, still needing to complement my own depleted one, I've an insight into children that, coupled with growing womanhood, makes me a passionate nurturer.

John Bowling is my biggest influence. He loves me, which I accept graciously, callously. John, in his late thirties, originally from Oklahoma, still speaks, despite his many years in the Orient, in a high-pitched drawl, his language full of Okie expressions. His career in the foreign service had been spent in East and West Pakistan, India, Afghanistan, and Iran. He knows these countries inside out, having trod every inch of stone and trekked through every morass. When all the rest of the embassy people are gathered sybaritically around a Teheran pool, John is out, solitary in the mountains, slinging his knapsack, striking his way through canyons. He loves difficulties, hardship. Once he'd told me that he'd awakened one morning in the Hindu Kush to find himself being trampled by a herd of sheep as he lay helpless in his sleeping bag, the zipper frozen solid with ice. John takes us on picnics different from all the others. With John it isn't a question of driving through the desert for hours, as we usually do, until we find a tree; it is trekking to an exact teahouse that he knows well, where the proprietor, over bowls of water freckled with a few tea leaves, tells tales from the old epics so that the hills around seem peopled with Kay Khosraus and Rustams.

I've been on conventional trips to Persepolis, Shiraz, Isfahan and to the great northwestern city of Mashhad, near the Russian border, but John takes me on a journey into the heart of Iran, through the mountains to the Caspian. Mules trammeled in brass bells and blue donkey beads to ward off the evil eye, kelims rolled into saddles, muleteers carrying staffs trudging alongside. We leave from a caravansary in a small village several hours from Teheran. During the next days we ford rivers, cross drifting bridges, and, scrambling for support at gorse bushes, plummet down gorges. Nights we spend camped among the Sang-Saar nomads, who migrate here annually, and awake in the mornings to milk being slurped back and forth in sheep-bladder churns. Some nights we find caravansaries and have tea in the small mud-domed structures. The vaulted buildings beautiful but dark—the only candles near the samovar. I walk smack into the fat-backed mutton carcasses hung by hooks from the ceilings. Cold blubber in my face.

I've never been so happy. Traveling into the heartland. Each step adventure. The very words "silk route," "caravan" make my heart sing. Each day leads to new mysteries and delights—my first scrub in a village bathhouse, gorges with spiraling cliffs, hawks gliding in air drafts, suppers with feuding sheep-rustling landlords, and finally our destination, a little White Russian *pension* in Bābol Sar, a decaying town on the Caspian. I know this is close, very close, if not the exact route I want to be taking. I'm stormed by happiness, happiness for what I have and for the adventure I can't articulate, which I know lies just beside.

India! my heart explodes. Parrot colors—red, yellow, green. No black chadors as in Iran. Orange-flowered gold mohur trees, rainbow turbans, apple-red sports car of the American Embassy man, who collects us at the Delhi airport. I'm here for spring vacation with Aunt Mary in an air attaché flight junket from Teheran, casually, unprepared. My adventure is coming into sharper focus. Everything I see is sharply outlined, almost painfully illumined. Everything I hear twangs some consonant part of my being. My head is adrum. I'm so alive to experiencing my body feels skinned, the very air vibrates me. Everyone is pelting around town buying yards of Kashmiri crewelwork and armories of brass trays. Sheltering under parasols from the baking sun, we see the Taj in Agra and fly back to Benares.

In Delhi the embassy man and I speed down the older streets of the city, past the porticoed bungalows and the pipal trees, their lower trunks painted white. Dust flies up behind us. Pony-drawn tongas clip by. Not only is it the most beautiful place I've ever been but I can love it for its soul as well. Here's a place, unlike the Middle East, with a conscience. Also, very important, here people have not become so westernized that they've cut off their history. They're in touch with their past, drawing strength from it. There's less gap here between rich and poor, and there's a chance to work in community development that will uplift the whole country, not just the elite or the cities. Here is energy and cause personified by Nehru. The beautiful visionary man with a dreamy smile.

Back in Teheran, I pursue Indians with a vengeance. Who asked that little Pink to the party? asks Uncle Selden. I always add the name of my socialist friend Vivek to the party lists. Vivek, first secretary at the Indian Embassy, brings me Indian Government Development literature—illustrated pamphlets and also long tomes full of graphs and statistics. I read them all, even trying to remember some of the statistical tables. After college I'm going to be a village-level worker and dig latrines as Vivek has done. Even village education is secondary to sanitation and surviving in a relatively decent way. "What I can't stand about him is his voice!" Uncle Selden says. It is high and reedy. Aside from Vivek, I cultivate Sherzad and Kuldip, two Indians in my class at school, inviting them to supper to give them the Hindu miniatures of Krishna chasing the Gopis that I've brought them back from Delhi. Although Sherzad turns out to be Muslim and Kuldip a Sikh, they thank me very politely.

John Bowling, although amused by my ardor, continues to lend me books on Indian religions—the Upanishads, including the Bhagavad-Gita from the *Mahabharata*. I'm transfixed at the idea of keeping one's soul after death, at the same time merging into the Great All. I talk about the

Great All a lot, inviting the ridicule of our missionary teachers at school in our compulsory Bible class. "You mean you think the soul's a little drop of water in a bucket?" our teacher asks me with scorn. "In a bucket?" I don't debate with him, but when shortly afterward, in Decision Week, they draw the curtains of the auditorium and play "By the Light of Burning Martyrs" ominously on the piano as the school principal pleads with us in the darkened room to sign cards deciding for Jesus, I stir in embarrassment.

I must stay near India somehow. Maybe go to college at the American University in Beirut, but that's off the point. Beirut is not India, not even Iran. It is itself pleasant, full of ice cream parlors, discothèques, and cobbled, hilly streets. Nice, but not for me. No, it's better to go back to America and study, possibly returning to India for graduate work. Uncle Selden is strong on this point too. "There's no better place in the world for education," he says. Still, I can't take the idea of college seriously even though I've sent off to Sarah Lawrence a picture of me holding the baby lamb given me by an Iranian friend, and have filled out essay forms on the person I admire most, Albert Schweitzer. Schweitzer? Even the side of me that yearned to be a village-level worker knew I had to be kidding.

My former roommate is writing me disconsolate, envious letters from Madeira. "Are you dreading college? God, I'm dreading it. I know very well that's the wrong attitude, but somehow I can't help it. School is so nauseating, I'm just coldly dreading going back. All that phonily dignified graduation mess. My mother said she couldn't even remember her graduation (Ethel Walker), and I hope I will be able to say the same someday. I wish I knew where in the hell I will end up (perhaps end down is more apt). All they talk about here is getting into college. Last Saturday just about the whole senior class decided to take a Saturday in town, and as we were about to climb aboard the gaseous bus, we suddenly got word that Miss Maynard wanted to see all of us in her office. Well, all the senior class went running in, and there stood old Thundercloud herself in the hall. She was clutching a great list and looked menacing. She was just furious at so many people going in to town and had made a little list of us and our weakest subjects. She said malicefully (what the hell is the word anyway?) that she would regard with interest her list when people were or were not accepted by their colleges. Not only bastardly but juvenile. If she felt so strongly about it, why didn't she make an announcement sooner?"

I can't go back to it. It's unthinkable. I want to hug every friend here to me and not let any go. I want to go on forever waltzing and stomping through the high plateaus, every friend clutched to me. I will fall in love with Alexei at our embassy. It is arbitrary. He is short and pale, with plump hands, and acts toward me with wary surprise. Still, I fasten everything on him, impaling myself on his being, a personification of all the places and people I love so dearly. I must be saved.

Aunt Mary and Uncle Selden have already left and flown to Europe. Uncle Selden, although valuing the importance of Iran and his post, is glad to leave the somewhat strained relations between the Shah and the U.S. (my uncle was one of the few U.S. ambassadors to stand up to the Shah's demands) and an area of the world he had never specialized in. Aunt Mary in particular is happy to be going back to the West. "I'm never going to eat mutton again as long as I live," she says.

My feelings heightened by all that I am about to lose, I'm racked by love for everyone around me. Three families give me birthday parties on my eighteenth birthday. I float back and forth between two loving households, one American, one Iranian. We spend all of my graduation day picnicking in Shamiran, picking cherries—cherries in buckets, cherries in bowls, cherries on every surface. I'm barely ready for the evening ceremony. All my friends have come—Dutch, English, Iranian, American— dozens. When I leave to join my aunt and uncle in England, they are all at the airport embracing me, pressing small gifts in my hands, enjoining me not to forget, not ever to forget. I move around, holding curled over my shoulder the wild sheep horn that I found on our mountain trip with John Bowling. Everything vanishing, the only thing I shall possess.

Later, in England, swollen with crying, I lie in the back seat of the Fiat Uncle Selden has rented for our three-week tour. "For heaven's sake, Hopie, sit up and look around you." This pretty green lake country is not my home. The East is my home. The wild bare steppeland and mountains. Oh, my friends, I miss them so much. On the boat coming back I stay in the cabin the whole time, not coming up even for lifeboat drills. My body is heavy and torpid. I can hardly breathe for the sadness.

3

Sarah Lawrence isn't real. Even allowing for geographical distribu-
tion, the student the postcard says is to be my roommate, Robin
Brooks, White Bear Lake, Manitou Island, Minnesota, must be invented.

"Hi, I'm Robin"—bouncing. "I'm Robin." Red suit, pop-it pearls,
black patent leather pumps. Sitting back on my bed, ratlike over Maxim
Gorky's *My Childhood*, I watch balefully. She has white skin, wide
green eyes, and black hair like Snow White. All she talks about is the
White Bear Lake Snow Festival. At night, crackling stealthily, she eats
Kit Kats and stores the silver papers under the bed. Robin talks a lot
about her angst, which she pronounces in her chain-saw Midwest voice.
We are always competing over whose angst is greater. Robin gains immediate cachet by claiming, somewhat to my skepticism, that as an infant
she'd suffered the trauma of being pulled back by her Scotty from the
brink of a crevice during an earthquake. I, however, aside from my unhappy childhood, had had an unfortunate aunt who'd been burned to
death in a fireplace in infancy—which always makes me win.

We stage tableaux vivants. Robin, clutching her T. Anthony suitcase
that her mother has given her and wearing her padded bra on her forehead for goggles, is often Amelia Earhart disappearing. I prefer epics—
Wagner's *Siegfried* excerpts at top volume. I battle around, holding my
Persian wild sheep horn to one side of my head, my Spanish drinking
cow horn clamped to the other. Sarah Gay, a very tall girl who plays the
Weavers and Odetta very loudly, constantly, wears my Persian cymbals
as breastplates. She and Robin have an act that they do together for the
good of the college. Sarah Gay stands at the top of the Tudor staircase in
the main administrative building, where we live, and balances Robin overhead, making menacing noises and faces. After waving Robin around
several times in the air, she dashes her to the landing floor, where Robin,

54

moaning piteously, rolls to the very door of the admissions office, lying curled and wounded as we cry out in consternation. We are doing it to keep the balance favorable. Sarah Lawrence is trying to attract, we hear, more preppy types, probably to help their financial problems. It is our duty to stop or at least keep down the circle-pin set.

As the only sister of four brothers, Robin is very athletic. Late one night, when we have gone to visit my sister Harriet, now married to her Princeton beau and living in Cambridge, Robin climbs up the wall to enter their apartment through the open window. I have not informed them of our arrival, and this course, we reason, is better than provoking my brother-in-law's short temper by ringing the doorbell at such an hour. "Keep the bags," Robin yells confidently, her spirit soaring at the challenge. "You look after the bags, I'm a human fly." She is off, up the dark ivy-covered walls of the old frame house, then disappears. From below I can hear crashing and banging as of metal or pots. Suddenly the floor is ablaze with lights and I hear Robin calling out repeatedly, "Do not fear, Hope is below, Hope is with me, I am a friend of Hope's." Further alarmed by the mention of more accomplices, the young householders clutch each other in fear. Finally it is established that Harriet and her husband live in the apartment upstairs, and I bring up the bags.

All of us are so loving with each other. On the first afternoon, sitting on the floor, we have tea together in Robin's and my room. Angelica, resolute, intellectual, antischool, engaged to be married; Clover, artistic, fiercely honest, with delicate sensibilities; Ellen, perceptive, funny, fey, her felt hat shot through with an arrow; and the three Susans: Sue Mack, a passionate girl, spirits so abundant she simplifies life by keeping her room cell-like, with only a few possessions to meditate on; Sue Fennelly, brassy antiestablishment, brilliant, half self-parodying, half genuine rock-'n-roller; Sue Hambleton, gallant, kind, boomingly funny. We are all temperamentally so different from each other and yet so connected from the start. We will learn something new to tell each other every day, I propose, and never fight or bitch. Maybe memories of wasted, unhappy boarding-school days stay in other people's memories as well as mine, maybe it's just a marvelous coming together. For whatever reasons, we become fast friends, a group bound by extraordinary bonds of feeling that have lasted until today. Our mutual tolerance and collective sense of silliness are amazing even to ourselves. Leaving aside Ellen and the three Susans, even our names—Angelica, Clover, Hope, and Robin— underline the uncanny, almost seraphic quality of our friendship.

Most of us are deeply involved with either fantasies or realities of men friends: Robin with a Minnesotan writer at Princeton, who, like his famous predecessor F. Scott Fitzgerald, is in the process of getting kicked out for roustabouting; I with perverse attachment to Alexei, who's been reposted in Berlin. Still, our center of being is the group.

During my sweltering summer in Washington at Fort McNair, where Uncle Selden now serves as deputy commander of the National War College, I'd spent every day reading my way through Turgenev, Lermontov, and Gogol, a book a day, in memory of my *amour lointain*, acquaintance, Alexei, whom I'd picked on to personify my welter of loves for Iran. I'm pleased now to have a real zest for learning return to me. The Russian books I'd been reading over the summer were just to numb me. I'm spun around by the intellectual possibilities at the college. I take French poetry with a professor who can spend an entire session on a few lines, each poem an epiphany, but based exactly and only on what is in the text. "The text, you must only use the text—you girls with your theories up in the air, look at what is inside the poem!"

Each poem is a microcosm, a separate life existence for me, something that touches my center and then vanishes, leaving me no further stored with knowledge, no heavier. Where I feel safer and more rooted is studying history. Each revealed level of time and event is like a further underpinning of my being. If I can learn everything, I will be a tower, a pyramid.

There's no Asian history open to freshmen, so I take European history, and through the Sarah Lawrence system of conference courses—in which, as well as classwork, the students work individually on projects with their professors—bend the course to suit me, writing papers on India and its independence movement.

Studying overwhelms me, becomes the realest thing in my life. Aside from the sheer amount of time I spend reading, the contents of the books, especially those on Hinduism and Buddhism, which I continue to read along with my course readings, also remove me further from the world. There is no line of time or space, all happenings are concentric circles going from and returning to an unreal me. Only my readings in history restore some vertical sense of myself and offer the possibility of past, present, and future. Even here, however, I'm blessed and cursed by my yearning to know everything—a Renaissance appetite but no corresponding sense of self. My strong imagination takes me into any era, any coloration. The questing I do becomes a kind of Weltschmerz, which, instead of shoring up my identity, allows me to merge in whatever happens to be my immediate intellectual or physical surroundings.

New York City is a good background for this kind of identity process, or disintegration. Within ten blocks one can lead ten lives, be poor and vagabondish and minuet elegant, stand waifish, orphaned, nose pressed to Bergdorf Goodman's window, and then enter to be courted (however sourly) by salesmadams. My childhood upbringing, which always made me eager to please and agree, makes me easily assimilated by any person encountered. My odd mish-mash accent, which has always been all things to all people, enhances the ease with which I assume form after form. To immigrant cabdrivers I'm anything from immigrant Scot to Slovak to Australian; to more pretentious people in fancy shops or hotel lobbies I'm a rarefied and vulnerable Englishy la-di-da something or other.

Growing up, I'd always been ambivalent about freedom versus rootedness. Now, as a young adult "free" of family supervision and structure, lacking any constraints or responsibilities other than my studies, I engage in painful and potentially dangerous testing of my boundaries or lack of them.

Some evenings, after leaving the public library on Forty-second Street, I sleep on the hard wooden benches of the ladies' waiting room in Grand Central Station, my coat pulled over me, my sneakers for a pillow, like a tramp. On several occasions, the money from my grandparents' trust providing me funds with which to explore my existential loneliness in expensive places also, I check into hotels near the station, alone among the noisy crowds, and spend the night in the bare box rooms, anonymous, with no reason to be there, unreal.

Hair up in Brigitte Bardot bun wagging loosely on my head. Eyes blackened in Persian houri style, dark eyebrow pencil and Acnomel hollowing out my cheeks to give me interesting shadows under my cheekbones. I possess, aside from my sari, three outfits—my Iranian sheepskin leggings, jacket and cartwheel hat, too hot now for spring, my dirndl, and a tent dress I wear on special occasions. Frightened sometimes my spirit will vagabond into oblivion, I dress up in the tent dress and go out, a lady, into midtown.

My lack of care about clothes and external appearances is not a cult, the faddish statement that it became with the hippies and flower children, but the result of a real and painful lack of belief in my identity.

Except for spurts of buying outlandishly sexy party dresses in Iran, I'd always been uninterested in dress. Now I grow vaguer and vaguer about clothes and am hardly able to assemble any reasonable outfit. On one occasion I take my grandmother's sables I'd inherited to a twenty-four-hour Martinizer, and leave them there forever. On another occasion I check my sneakers and coat, which I'd worn every day for several years, into a Grand Central locker and lose the key, never to retrieve them again.

Aside from formlessness and shabbiness in dress, my general living also is unstructured and unhealthy, a situation allowed to exist by the very latitude and respect for each student's privacy that Sarah Lawrence affords. For months I skip every meal in the campus dining room and live only on ice cream, delivered in a truck at any hour by the Bronxville druggist. (Later, after graduation, they send me an outstanding bill for $11.83, which the college forwards to me c/o the Palace, Gangtok, Sikkim, Tibet, which goes through to Lhasa and is returned to me in Gangtok covered with Chinese characters indicating addressee unknown.) Our room is a litter of old junk. Even by our floormates' not very tidy standards, Robin and I are adjudged to be like the Collyer brothers. Our floor littered with books, newspapers, pennies, unopened bank notices, underwear, old lemons, and teabags waiting to be used again, it gets to a point at which I have to lie and think in the morning how to get out of bed most safely. Robin by now, as much as I, has abandoned her establishment Midwestern norms and dress and wears only a tattered pair of jeans, her bare feet paint-splattered from work in the art studio. Episodically, however, her parents come into town, and she searches out her red suit and pop-it pearls from some recess and goes off into town.

I have no such family structure to serve as boundaries, as Aunt Mary and Uncle Selden are absorbed in making a new life on their return to the United States. In measure with their many responsibilities, they extend themselves to me. Uncle Selden, although not a wealthy man or a snobby one, even insists on giving me a fairly expensive "coming-out" party—"Although you don't think so now, at some point you might regret not doing it, or the man you marry might regret your not doing it." On the whole, however, I feel left out, the only attachment, connection, I have is to my vanished life in Iran in the form of Alexei.

Poor Alexei, who quite naturally hasn't answered any of my letters, becomes an obsession. After the Washington coming-out party, I resolve, instead of going to New York for a further series of coming-out parties to which I've been invited, I will fly to Berlin, where he now works, to find him and throw myself against his total rejection (rejection is too strong

58

a word; nonrecognition) of me and his inability to restore our time in Iran.

West Berlin itself as a metaphor intrigues me. Isolated, entirely bordered by a hostile country, the city itself bordered into zones. I will test my own borders. The Christmas season makes my testing seem even more masochistic, poignant. Christmas music from the churches and restaurants along the Kurfürstendamm underscores my quest. "Wo ist die Clay Allee?" I have his address. The trams lead all over the city. There is as yet no wall, and sometimes I'm afraid, exquisitely afraid, but really scared too, that I will wander into the wrong sector. "Wo ist die Clay Allee?" I've been back there twice. The young Marine guard kissing his German girlfriend in the sentry box. No one knows anything about him. Tears running down my face, I tramp the city, from time to time keeping warm in small basement cafés. Looking up through the glass door, I can see feet walking by. Outside once again, puffs of steam form and disappear from my breath. I have been past the ruins of the old Reichstag, a Christmas tree pluming its broken dome, through the Brandenburg Gate, down Stalin Allee, down the streets of cement-box houses built by the state, yards of rubble stretching away behind. In the refugee camp on New Year's Day I've met some of the hundreds of thousands of refugees who've crossed from the East Sector to the West. Some came; some stayed. I've no sense of politics, of real happenings. Everything's confused in my head. After New Year's I meet a man at the mission—white, lumpish face, small hat jammed over oily forehead—who looks at me curiously and says, "Don't you know he's on his honeymoon?"

Sarah Lawrence is a relief, a homecoming; I've done my goose chase, my mourning for my days in Iran. Even at the time of chasing Alexei, trying to pummel my longing for Iran into reality, I was both inside and outside the situation, seeing my ridiculousness and yet impelled to continue. I'm back to reality. My friends on our floor racket around with me. Everything seems funny, less fraught. Robin and I are supposed to be the funniest students on campus. We get a letter from the alumnae committee asking us to entertain at a fund-raising dinner. Depending on our spontaneity, we are unprepared and wander on about wildebeests. Many people don't contribute because of the low level of the entertainment. Our friends and faculty members nearby applaud warmly. I feel applauded all the time here, I'm the apple of the faculty's eye. I love it and give back to them what they expect of me. I love the whole college, even the ugly pseudo-Tudor Bronxville architecture. I remember with horror how the physical beauty of Madeira had seduced me. The very ungainliness of the small Sarah Lawrence campus reminds me inversely of the value placed here on spirit and thought. Damp, sodden leaf paths. Mud spring smells. Waking, I go buoyantly to class.

For her cartooning Robin has won a junior editor's job for the summer at *Mademoiselle*. It is rumored they expect visiting women editors to wear stockings, high heels, and a girdle. Robin smiles enigmatically. I'm going to spend the first part of the summer in Russia with a group of Sarah Lawrence students led by our European-history teacher, and the second part in India.

I'm pleased; both trips seem an extension of my being. I'm going to Russia for my own sake, not for Alexei's, but to round out and substantiate my own studies. India has always been my own. India is the one area of my life and studies that doesn't owe anything to a man. Everything else, even if, like Russia, I afterward make it my own, originally came into my heart through loving someone. I'm proud of loving India independently, underivatively.

Robin has typed some Indian itineraries for Aunt Mary to see. We have thought up very English-sounding hotel names, often adding Victorian or Albertian touches to embellish their propriety. Once or twice, for day trips, box lunches are provided; also there is a party of twenty.

I enjoy Russia for its limitations. It seems to me an end product, not a transmitter or processor of thought and civilization, like a European country or India. This is restful; I don't mentally and physically have to scamper about learning, understanding everything and how it affects me. In terms of music, Russia seems like opera—baroque, colorful, amusing, essentially unnecessary.

A treat, a divertissement—I sit back and enjoy it, knowing in a month I will be in India, my nexus. We are in Leningrad in June during their long white nights, bright until three or four in the morning. Sylvia, my new friend from Columbia, and I stroll with some Leningrad students along the banks of the Neva. The students play the balalaika; Sylvia does her trumpet bellow imitation of Louis Armstrong, the local musical hero. Afterward, passing by the old stuccoed palaces, we go with the students along canals, down Dostoevskian alleys, to their apartments. There we talk about God, and one of them asks the old Russian question, "Where is the soul?" In the nineteenth-century manner, a medical student quite seriously informs us that in the course of his examinings he's yet to find one. Before leaving we talk politics. Sylvia's uncle is a trade union leader and she knows a good deal about American institutions. My readings in Russian history complement her understanding of America, enabling me to make parallels or contrasts to Russian history, so we make a good team, representing America as best we can.

The students are eager, thrilled to have some contact with America, which they admire—love, really—in an emotional way. Everyone here is demonstrative; Sylvia and I almost crack up one night when a bemedaled drunk soldier embraces Didi Dupont, the chief capitalist member of our group, on the street corner and tries to tear off his medals to pin on her. Sylvia and I are befriended not only by the Russians we meet but also by the Algerian National Liberation Front soccer team, who have come to the U.S.S.R. on a softening tour to prepare the way for future political relations. Sylvia, a Zionist, and I, the niece of a rather well-known anti-Communist, are bussed out by the Algerian team to the Leningrad Sports Arena on the outskirts of town, where, to music of the Red Army Band and the applause of the packed stadium, we release dozens of white doves in the center of the playing field.

Wherever we go—Leningrad, the Black Sea or Georgia—the Algerian team is always with us in our hotel, along with a Danish soccer team, a Bulgarian soccer team, the Harlem Globetrotters, a group of American governors, and Norman Cousins. The Harlem Globetrotters are reluctant sightseers, to the annoyance of their Soviet hosts, who are determined to show them everything, particularly anything that might have to bear on traditional Russian love of blacks. In Moscow, in the lobby of our Hotel Ukraina, the Globetrotters shuffle their feet in the free shoe-polishing machine and mutter wrathfully about another early morning trip to another Pushkin shrine to hear yet another anecdote of Pushkin's Moorish ancestry. The Globetrotters are fed up with the Russian demand that games be a serious affair. The Russians are appalled by their playfulness. We joke a lot and sometimes go out together to see things.

It is through Wilt the Stilt that we get to shake hands with Khrushchev. One day, while we are standing in line at Lenin's tomb in Red Square, a big Zim limousine slows down and Khrushchev, probably not knowing who Wilt is but impressed by his enormous height (accentuated by a white hat worn at a jaunty angle), jumps out of the back seat to shake hands all around.

Despite many developmental strides, Russian leaders today are exactly like the old regime—state officials directly descended from the old czarist bureaucracy, who rule with the same cruelty tempered by ineptitude.

I have mixed feelings. In some ways the czarist continuation in this so-called modern state is laughable. Moscow, the third Rome, Russian communism, as Uncle Selden said, the new imperialism. Even the luxury items so sought after today—newly made chandeliers, champagne, brothel-pompommed lamp shades—are the identical symbols of the good life under the czarist regime. The ingenuousness of the continuity of taste and form depress and delight me. Aeroflot, the flying parlor car. Somehow, though, in the final analysis, there is something reassuring about the stasis. Even as man (despite the sweep of such great ideas as communism) remains a prisoner of himself, he also can't become abstracted, more or less than his own humanity.

Unlike Russia, which seems to me long ago to have ceased being idealistic and, ironically, remains interesting only for its national character, India is aflame with ideas as well as national spirit. Among all the world leaders only Nehru seems to keep all values together: a respect for the past soul of India and its continued vitality today, a profound dedication to the physical and economic uplift of his people, and a crusade for the freedom and dignity of people everywhere. It is an honor to be going there even briefly to witness India's past and the great strides being taken toward its future. My heart quickens as we fly down over the heartlands of central U.S.S.R. toward Tashkent and eventually Delhi.

At Palam Airport in Delhi everything is wrong; I'm dazed. First, on the tarmacked airfield at the ramp of the plane itself stand five of Aunt Mary's friends—my old friend with the red sports car, the economic councillor from the American Embassy, the Colombian chargé, his wife and son and someone I don't know, all clutching copies of the itinerary Robin and I had sent Aunt Mary. All of them look over my shoulder as I descend the ramp, searching for the group of twenty accompanying me. "Where is the group?" the economic councillor asks, I think unnecessarily, for even as we stand there, they are rolling away the stairs and it is clear there will be no further debouchement of passengers. "Oh, er, you know, ah," I say vaguely, waving my hand generally planeward as if I had carelessly stowed them someplace. "Ah, y'know." Oh, my God, not only that, but the whole of Sherzad's family, my Indian friends from Iran, with whom I'd intended to stay, also seem to be at the airport. But not to meet me—they seem to be going someplace. Had I cabled them I was coming? I couldn't remember. Dozens of little girls running around, their hair braided up in ribbons like pinwheels. Sherzad and her father and mother garlanded in marigolds literally up to their eyes. They're going to America. Oh, God, what about me? What will happen when Aunt Mary finds out? Where can I find a group?

I choose to ride into town with the Colombians, since they seem the least suspicious of me. The economic councillor is still looking at me, eyes narrowing till his pupils seem to be on the bridge of his nose. In the Ashoka, the vast warren of a government hotel where Aunt Mary and I stayed a couple of years ago, I sit on the floor of the cupboard (raised off the floor against insects and moisture) and keep incanting, "God, God, God." I've never been caught before in such a spot. No quick falsehood will save me. I don't even have a copy of the itinerary—never made one. Oh, my Lord, where will they expect me to go next?

I stay closeted in my room, going out only once or twice at the insistence of the baffled Colombians. After a few days the phone rings. I know it must be the economic councillor. I know what he is going to ask. He's not bringing it up. Be alert, Hope, careful. "Well, Hope," he finally says after a pause, "well, Hope, I know you're off today." Ha, that is a slip. I have learned something. "Yes," I say cautiously. Ah, yes, maybe he will say something more. I am silent, waiting. It is awkward. Finally he says, "Well, I'm glad you're staying at the Windemere—the Everest is pretty run down now." The Windemere—of course, the most Englishy hotel we'd found in the brochures, but where the hell is it? "Yes, in Darjeeling, you're certainly best off there." Breathlessly I say with a rush of real warmth, "Oh, I know I'm going to love it." Out of relief I add quite gratuitously, "I'm sure the group will too when we meet up." Off the phone, it takes only minutes to dash to the lobby and buy a first-class railroad ticket to Darjeeling. The tourist agent insists I go to Kashmir instead. "No, no"—by this time I am almost shouting—"Darjeeling."

It's such a relief to be on the train and headed in the right direction that at first I don't notice the boy with the jagged broken bottle. The windows of the compartment will not shut completely. They are open eight inches. In whichever corner I sit down, he is there. He circles the outside of the car, holding on with his one free hand. Whenever I look up, he is scowling at me, brandishing the jagged glass. Sometimes he puts the bottle under his armpit and reaches his skinny hand in the window, reaching for my throat, making choking gestures with his fist. As I have unwisely bought a first-class ticket, I am alone. No other ticket-holders get on this carriage; they are all cozily and safely ensconced in the crowded security of the second- and third-class compartments. At night I lie on the floor of the compartment to avoid the hand and also the eyes of the people at the stations. There are no shades, and at each stop gaunt faces press against the windowpane, eyes staring, intense, expressionless. The bedding I've rented is damp, the railroad curry rice hawked by uniformed vendors full of stones, the countryside outside my window khaki (an old Indian word for dust-colored), bleak and flat.

We pass nothing but treeless mud villages, unadorned except for an occasional whitewashed temple. The dirt roads round the hamlets stream with rivulets caused by the monsoon rains. The skies when the rain stops periodically, however, are beautiful: scudding silver clouds. On the third day, when the train reaches Bengal, the landscape changes from the barren browns of the northern states to brilliant green. Bright, almost electric green fields banded by silver piles of cut jute left out to dry. At Calcutta some students from Calcutta University get into my compartment. They are in a cheerful fraternity-house mood and make me the object of their fun, pinching my fanny and breasts, tossing me about the compartment like a football. I know it's nothing more than boisterousness, but the detachment, the dehumanizing aspect of it after the day with the bottle-wielding youth makes me want to cry. To my relief, toward daybreak we have to leave the train to ferry across a river to be picked up again on the other side by the narrow gauge train that will take us up to North Bengal.

I sit on the open deck with my baggage near an old Bengali lady who looks grandmotherly. We push off into the sun-sheeted river from the southern shore, the boatmen using long bamboo poles. A feeling of peacefulness, contemplation, returns to me. The very Sanskrit word yana ("ferry") has been built into Hinduism and Buddhism. Hinayana ("smaller ferry"), mahayana ("greater, or more encompassing, ferry") —vehicles to take us from one level of understanding to a deeper consciousness. I'm contented, happy to be there. Neither the departed shore nor the shore we're traveling toward in sight.

Siliguri, the railway-junction town, connects the main part of India with Assam and the northeastern frontier states, which lie eastward, north of what was then East Pakistan. It serves also South Bengal and North Bengal and by extension Sikkim, which lies above. Its railroad yards are busy with the Assam and Darjeeling mail trains. From Siliguri also leaves the two-foot-gauge toy train that has been taking travelers up to Darjeeling since the 1880s. Brass fixtures, gleaming, a delight. Passengers, impatient with its slow progress as it inches forward and backward along the many cutbacks, get off periodically and jog along the side. My spirit is whistling, like the train. The air, unlike the heavy humid blanket of the Indian plains, is tangy and sharp. When the sun comes out from behind the clouds, the tea bushes, related—I've just learned—to camellia plants, which also grow here, shine, the light bouncing off the glittery leaves. In contrast, the light on the bamboo fronds seems to be absorbed in a way that makes the bamboo glow from inside. Almost every slope not planted with tea is terraced as rice paddy, the terracing carefully shored up with neat walls of stones taken from the site. Some of the carefully maintained patches are tiny, hardly big enough for a buffalo to stand on, let alone plow.

One can begin to pick out—since the train goes so slowly—more and more signs of the labor needed to keep the fields viable. Networks of bamboo aqueducts conduct water from one level of terraces to another. Sunk into the ground at each level of terracing are bamboo shunts to draw off the excess water. Some slopes are too vertical even for ingenuity, for hard work; here the loose earth of the hillsides is held down by mixed forest strips of bamboo, Himalayan karch, and tree ferns. Occasionally there is a bright patch of orange flame of the forest. In some places people have been too ambitious, tried to terrace on too steep slopes, or else simply cut down trees for wood, and here huge landslips—narrow at the top, descending in ever-widening gashes—deface the mountain. Sometimes, only yards away from landslips flanking it on both sides, a little house juts out on a spur. Occasionally there are the half remains of houses built too near the edge.

There is no one at the train station from the hotel, so I give my bag to a rosy-cheeked Sherpa woman porter. I know she is Sherpa because of the photographs I've seen showing the way they tie striped aprons behind their backs as well as the ones they wear in front like the Tibetan women. Leaning forward, she puts my bag on her back, carrying it by a strap on her forehead. Slightly appalled, I hurry to follow her quick gait up the road from the station to the Darjeeling bazaar. I feel cheerful and at home. Nothing much seems exotic. The gray, cool weather seems familiar after the tropic heat of the Indian plains, as does the direct, rather bluff, manner of the people here, so different from the staring silence of the plainsmen I have just left. Also, despite unfamiliar languages and smells, the scale of the bazaar seems rather homey. The buildings are gingerbread English, and the shop windows full of signs offering Cadbury chocolates and tinned tea biscuits. Small children—girls and boys alike dressed in gray flannel, blue blazers, and striped neckties—file by, two by two, in procession. Pony boys, knitting sweaters as they walk, lead children dressed in the same uniforms on some rather scruffy little horses.

As we round the corner above the Planters' Club, a big verandahed build-ing, and get to the mall, I come alongside a little boy similarly attired. He is running to keep step with a young Tibetan man in a silver-but-toned blazer. "Hurry, can't you," the man says crossly, "she's getting away." Quite a few yards ahead a young blond woman clips along, out-distancing, despite her high heels on the uneven paving, the man and boy.

Seeing me, the young man sighs, gives up his chase and smiles. "I'm just taking the little fellow out for his half day," he says in partial expla-nation. Further conversation proves him to be the son of the Winde-mere owner, and apologizing for not having met the train, he steers the Sherpa porter and myself to the hotel on the ridge above town. Brass-polish smell, grandfather-clock chimes, logs burning in fireplaces, chintz covers on freshly painted furniture. Tea and a small bright cake brought at four in the afternoon. I know I'm going to stay here all summer. This is safety, a refuge. That evening, after a dry and stubborn English dinner, lying in bed with the hot water bottle the hotel has provided, I sink into my mattress, heavy with relief from the tension that had been building up in Delhi and on the train.

Life at the Windemere is warm, sedate, predictable. As most interna-tional tourists try to avoid India in the hot, rainy summer months, the majority of the hotel's few clientele are Darjeeling people, Calcuttans, or British Gurkha officers from a recruiting center in the nearby Nepal lowlands. The rates are modest, as the hotel makes most of its money from drinks. I'm the lead sheep. Every evening Kesang, the young man I'd first met, and his father, Mr. Tenduf La, exaggerating their disgust over whatever I'm reading (Malinowski's *Sex and Repression in Savage Society* is one that particularly upsets them), summon me to the bar in the lounge. There, near the fire, we chat about the day's events as the barkeeper, a turbaned Nepalese, putters about putting out the water-filled Air India ashtrays—an unnecessary ritual taken from the custom of the hot plains, where the ashes of cigarette butts, if unwaterlogged, are blown about the room by the overhead fans.

As the first people drift in, Mr. Tenduf La, his jacket pulled up, stand-ing in front of the fireplace, says, "Hope, what about a drink?" to which I reply, "Thank you, I'll have juice," and then he asks the firstcomers to have a burrah peg on the house. By the end of the evening, as more people come, the round of drink-buying is well under way, the unfortu-nate latecomers standing drinks of exorbitantly taxed Scotch to the full room of people. Occasionally, if there is a round-the-world traveler at the hotel—usually an elderly lady who has been traveling so fast she isn't quite sure where she is—we begin the evenings by listening to travel stories, generally atrocity tales about unscrupulous travel agents. The presence of a new face, an outsider, giving a chance to polish up the local stories that are told and retold every night—how such and such a tea planter had found fresh tiger pugmarks the size of a plate; how the rhinos in Nepal Terai and Bhutan are being poached for their horn, its aphrodisiacal reputation so great no sanctions can protect them; how you can drive away a howling jackal by pointing your slippers in a T shape toward the offending animal; and many ghost stories—Tibetan poltergeists that appear to Jesuit priests in dak bungalows, British colonel ghosts who review troops of Gurkhas on parade.

Darjeeling in some ways still seemed a Victorian bastion. The remaining English tea planters on weekends or ball nights, dressed up in Rhett Butler suits, still swept up to their virtually all-English Planters' Club, handing their ladies—some dressed in long gowns—out of their Land-Rovers. A picture of the queen still presided in the club's game room—where, jackets off, the planters played snooker under green-shaded lamps —and, more surprisingly, still hung beside pictures of Gandhi and Nehru in the more Indianized Gymkhana Club, at the other side of town. Alongside the increasing number of government local schools and colleges taught in Nepali, the six or seven European-run schools in Darjeeling were considered to be the finest in Southeast Asia and gave Darjeeling the number-one reputation as a school town in the subcontinent and beyond. In fairly recent years students from Calcutta and other parts of India, Thailand, Nepal, Sikkim, Bhutan, and Malaysia had by and large replaced the English children who used to be sent up from the plains for their health and education, but even so the staff and tone of the "European" schools remained Matthew Arnold British or, as a variant at St. Joseph's, Irish Jesuit.

The officers of the British Gurkhas who came to the Windemere for a rest from their jungle centers still recruited Nepalese tribal youths for the British Army. Although there was talk of pulling back to Suez, Britain still had a long-term treaty with Nepal promising to recruit a certain number of men (for which Nepal received valuable sterling) each year. Some of the old British Army men, who had officered Gurkhas during both world wars, still lived in Darjeeling out of love for the hills and because Darjeeling remained much the same, while the England they'd known had long disappeared. Colonel Mercer, a distinguished scholar of Himalayan anthropology and ex-British Army officer, was one. Ailing, he'd tried three times to leave, as he thought it proper to die "at home." Each time, as soon as he was well enough to travel, he was back in Darjeeling. One night, when we'd gone up to the Jelepahar recruiting station, built in Kipling's time, high above Darjeeling, to spend an evening of tribal dancing with the young hill boys being recruited into the Indian Army Gurkhas, he said to me emotionally, "These boys are my family. My real family."

The Windemere too had an English woman attached to it. Mrs. Brewster, so people said, had once owned a major share of the hotel. Now in her late seventies, reduced to a role as honorary manageress, she spent the day loudly counting the hotel linen at her corner table in the dining room and drinking tea with old lady friends who came up from the bazaar to chat. As much as Colonel Mercer and Mrs. Brewster stayed on in Darjeeling to end their days, probably to be buried in the small European burial ground of the Anglican church, Indians, also seduced by the old Anglo-Indian customs of Darjeeling, visited much in the manner of their English predecessors.

As in British days, Darjeeling remained the summer capital of Bengal. During the summer season, when the governor of West Bengal was in residence in the blue-domed Governor's Palace, or Raj Bhavan, "the season" continued largely unchanged from the way it had been in the last century. Visitors on ponies trotted around the road circling Government House, dutifully stopping at viewpoints. Races presided over by the governor were run at the Lebong Race Course—reputedly the highest and crookedest in the world—where, although in the dense mist all kinds of un-English practices (pulling horses, even switching jockeys) were employed, the general effect was still of the Raj. The same was true of the school soccer championships, the most passionately played events of the hills, where, before each game, the governor or presiding guest of honor would address the teams on the virtues of playing the game and stress that winning was not the important thing.

Even so, things were changing. The rector of a leading school had to be "sent home" because at one of the governor's garden parties he had taken a young woman by the hand down a path to the edge of the hillside, where, peering out on the lights of Darjeeling below, he had suddenly turned to her and said, "Come jump with me, my dear. We will end this life together." Less dramatically, other English teachers, finding it increasingly difficult to get the necessary residence permits required by the Indian government to live in the hill areas, also were departing, to be replaced by Indian masters.

The tea industry, although still preserving some old establishments, such as the Planters' Club, was changing too. Many tea gardens were being bought up by Marwari Corporations, which looked on the tea gardens as just another asset—to the fury of the old-time managers, who viewed everything about tea, from tea dust ("what you drink in America") to the three leaves and a bud (GFOP—Golden Flowering Orange Pekoe), as almost sacred. For whatever reasons and despite increased government protective regulation ensuring lodging, schooling, and medical services for the Nepali immigrant garden laborer better than those of the surrounding communities, there was increased labor unrest in the Darjeeling gardens. Several estate managers, both English and Indian, had been gheraoed, or surrounded in a state of virtual siege, for periods of weeks until workers' new demands were met. This, coupled with what the planters felt was an offhandedness on the part of the government in its general treatment of the tea industry, and a sour view that, as things were going, before long all industries in India, including tea, might be nationalized, caused many European planters to leave for opportunities opening in Kenya. Even the small package of tea I'd brought with me from Georgia (U.S.S.R.) was, to my surprise, enough to cause malaise. My Scotch tea-planter friend Billy Whisker, trying it, pronounced it good and went on to predict darkly that the modern techniques and new plants in the U.S.S.R., combined with the African competition, soon would put the old bushes and overworked soil of Darjeeling out of business.

Although still faithful to my first love, Hindu India and Nehru's socialist India, Darjeeling touched and fascinated me because of the two time zones, tremulous, overlaid, in which it existed, and the fact that as much as it existed in different time zones, it also existed in several space zones: the point at which the cultures of the Anglo-Indian south, the Nepalese immigrant west, and the Sikkim-Tibetan north converged. Although essentially not a caravan town like neighboring Kalimpong, from where much of the trade from Tibet had been conducted down to the Indian plains, Darjeeling, as the main administrative frontier town near Tibet, was as much Tibetan as English in character. Before the Dalai Lama's flight from Tibet it had been a town virtually poised between cultures and countries. Now, in 1959, with the Chinese consolidation in Tibet and the Dalai Lama's emigration to India in the spring before my visit, that geographic connection had snapped, leaving the Sikkim-Tibet border and the Tibet-Indian borders virtually sealed.

After the first waves of Tibetan refugee influx, only a trickle of connection remained with Tibet through occasional refugees or strayed herders and the one exchange of mail that continued at the Nathu Pass. Overnight Darjeeling had lost its nexus. Ironically, however, because of the refugee influx into the town, at the same time that Darjeeling lost its equipoise between India and Tibet, it was reinforced in its Tibetan identity through the number of new Tibetan exiles.

Evidence of the recent exodus was to be found all over town. Despite the upheaval, however—partly because of Tibetan dignity and basic healthy good looks and partly because a good number of the refugees were still rather prosperous—it was often difficult for my untutored eye to recognize, without Kesang's instruction, the refugees from the earlier Tibetan inhabitants of the town. Despite the hardships of exile and the separation of families that many were undergoing, the spirit of the refugees was extraordinary. In some ways, compared to the quieter Darjeeling people, they seemed almost boisterous. The men from eastern Tibet, swinging through town in their leather boots, hiked tunics, sword arm free in the manner of cavaliers, had particular panache—their style, Kesang said enviously, partly honed by frequent visits to the movies in Kalimpong. "They ride like Red Indians and walk like cowboys." Unfortunately, the insouciance made for bad as well as good. According to hearsay, which I understood only in a dim and fragmentary way, many of the Tibetan refugee elite who'd come with the Dalai Lama were even now, as exiles, carrying on old feuds and power plays that had divided them in Tibet, frustrating the efforts of various rehabilitation groups to bring the factions together.

I didn't know much about what was happening. The price of being treated like a daughter of the hotel was virtual compliance with the family's boundaries and perceptions. Although Kesang, interested in politics and a former student of political science at Williams College, in America, used to ruminate about the take-over in Tibet and its effects on Darjeeling, there didn't seem to be much contact between his family and either the old or new group of Tibetans in the town. Perhaps, aside from the traditional Tibetan arrogance toward nonaristocrats, the fact that Kesang was descended from Major General Laden La (the liaison man between the English and Tibetan governments during the first British expedition to Lhasa at the turn of the century, an expedition that established British influence in the country) caused a mutual feeling of ambivalence between the Tibetans in Darjeeling and Kesang's family. For whatever reasons, the Tenduf Las seemed to prefer a rather English way of life. Kesang used "Keith," his English school name given him by the Jesuits, as often as he used "Kesang."

Although sometimes frustrated by not being exposed to the more real —or what I felt to be the most real—aspects of Darjeeling, some inner clock harmonized with the rather boring limited routine we lived. Reading, occasional visits to tea gardens and the rain-drummed Bazaar Movie House, and weekend taxi rides (motor turned off to save petrol), down the hill to watch college soccer games filled my day. Only rarely, if Kesang was in the mood, did we visit any of the monasteries around the town. My docility, my acceptance of boundaries, surprised me and the Tenduf Las. "A simple girl," they'd say to their friends and hotel guests, "a homey girl, not like most of these girls nowadays."

As I felt it was not approved, I rarely left the hotel alone. Only occasionally, overcome by a ravening need to eat spicy food, I would dash to the local tea shop to wolf a snack. Even then, in order not to hurt the hotel's feelings, I would sometimes go to the length of trying to disguise my snacking by buying food for the local street urchins who hung around the mall. "I hear you've been feeding the local badmashis again," Kesang would say as fifteen minutes later, hoping my absence had not been noticed, I'd run puffing up the hill. "People will think you're mad." Although feeling somewhat shrunken in strength of character and vitality, I felt right being there. Glad to be part of the hotel family. Neither happy nor unhappy, but right.

The afternoon Kesang introduces me to the Maharaj Kumar, or Crown Prince, of Sikkim, I'm going off for tea at Mr. Bee's, the expatriate Australian who runs the dairy farm that supplies cheese and hams throughout East India. "Ah, Mr. Bee. Give him my regards," the Maharaj Kumar says. "Tell him I wish we'd get him up Sikkim way to show us how to smoke pork. I shouldn't say that," he adds, sighing. "Those poor pigs— my karma is getting worse and worse for all my sins. Still, we do need a good dairy farm."

The Maharaj Kumar, widowed two years earlier, had come to see his two sons at boarding school in town. "The little chap sleeps all the time, and my first son gets in trouble . . . He tried to flush his braces down the loo the other day in the dormitory, and there was a helluva row. He's like my elder brother, a born leader, but gets the boys to do all his badmashi schemes." Although it makes it difficult sometimes to follow, I like the Maharaj Kumar's habit of talking in the immediate, as if the

71

listener shares his reference. "And then they got him. They got Gyur-med's father. He had his tongue pulled out. Horrible!" By the end of the evening, at dinner and afterward in the lounge, I've pieced together some of the stories I'm being told, painful stories, mostly of the recent losses of various Tibetan relations and friends during the Chinese take-over.

"You must understand. Back in the early fifties when I tried to help Tibet, the only time they could be helped, your government let me down. Some pipsqueak in the Calcutta consulate told me, 'Your High-ness, you must realize that we with all our resources and intelligence have a clearer view of what should be done than you ever could.' We had everything lined up—pilots, supplies. All we needed was a few planes. A few planes. Now they're helping. They're helping this Johnny-come-lately crowd of Tibetan politicians—and what happens? The weapons all fall into Chinese hands and more Tibetans are killed. It had to be earlier. Now it is certain death to encourage the Tibetans to fight rearguard. Certain death."

I'm interested in the politics and anecdotes the Prince is telling me, but more than the words I'm struck by the sense of loss and pain that seems to run through him, by his sensitive face, which changes from sadness when he talks of the tragedy in Tibet to take on a half-courteous, half-puckish smile when Kesang and I contribute some relieving com-ment. Against Kesang's protestations he goes back to Gangtok the next morning. "All that chap does is sit up in Sikkim," Kesang says. "Stays up there for months at a time without ever coming out. He's got too much sense of duty. They don't deserve him. A bloody monk's life he leads."

Kesang hasn't brought up the Maharaj Kumar before his visit, but now he talks about him a lot, telling me with admiration of the Prince's efforts in all spheres to improve the country and his people's condition. "He doesn't put a penny in his pocket either. Not like the Indian princes." I think about Maharaj Kumar often—his rueful, droll manner, his obvious integrity, and his extraordinary, handsome looks: intelligent dark eyes, smooth bronze skin, sloping cheekbones, and sensual mouth. I imagine him in the countryside up the river in a pool of light. By chance, on the several previous occasions when we'd looked up across the Tista River to the foothills of Sikkim, the sun, as it tends to do dur-ing the monsoons in the Himalayas, had broken in a yellow burst.

The remaining weeks of summer pass quietly. I look forward to college, not unhappy to leave Darjeeling. "Send him a red vest like mine," Kesang says. "The Maharaj Kumar's always admired mine."

4

I WENT BACK through Teheran to see my friends, and then to England to see Johnny. I'd met her several times before in London when she'd come up to town for lunch, awkward, embarrassed in the fancy restaurants I'd chosen. This time I met her at her home near Epsom Downs. "You can't imagine how ugly I find these houses." She gestured toward the rows of brick houses, all alike, stretching away down the road. "When I was a girl this was all farmland." Poor Johnny, she'd left rural England in her youth and spent her years in America nurturing that idyllic picture—even Harriet and I dressed in our pinnies watering the plants were part of that image. Now she'd returned to a life of row houses strung together by superhighways. The people too, she complained, were impossible. "They don't understand me. They say I've an American accent! American accent—I'll American accent them!"

Inside, her house was shining, neat and cozy. Not sad, despite its load of memorabilia—an old hope chest full of embroidered linen, photographs, including many of Harriet and me, of all her dear children, and mementos of her posts. "Mrs. Noyes gave me this," she said, holding up a Victorian china dog with round, staring eyes that I remembered from her chimney on Long Island. "It was the one thing I wanted. Those days. Those days. They'll not come back soon again. Well, dearie, let me look at you. What a big girl you've become."

I'm acutely happy, acutely grateful. My Iranian years were the first time in my life I'd ever felt I belonged. Now, at Sarah Lawrence, by some miracle I'm again in the center of people I love and who love me. I love my studies. Each new class and book makes me high with anticipation. The work I feel to be my own, my career, I do in the course

"Cultural Frontiers of China," in which I try to prove through art and iconography that everything in the world has come from India. By sea the Pallava civilizations had carried the Kerala roofs, the horseshoe-shaped mandala window frames, the ornate set-back temple architecture to the Annamese Kingdoms and Indonesia. By land the forms of the Sanchi Gate·and stupas had been carried to China, and beyond to Japan. Not only had India been the source of culture for farther Asia but most things too in the West had come to us from there through the Middle East. Denis de Rougemont's *Love in the Western World*, suggesting that Eastern mysticism was the basis of troubadour literature and hence the Western romantic tradition, becomes my Bible.

In my "Cultural Frontiers of China" class I'm assigned a paper on stucco—the origin of the cheap medium and its role in spreading iconography through Asia. To chase the adoption of ideas and form from one country to another—what joy! I've never done scholarly research before. Increasingly often I go in on the train to the city's Forty-second Street public library. My work during the year is rewarded by fine reports, and my history teachers are urging me to think of going on to do graduate work in Oriental studies. Cantering up the flat, wide steps of the public library, I pause, awed, ennobled by the grandeur and endurance of the building. Repository of civilization. I am an inheritor. So are the sleepy policemen nodding over their books across the table in the main reading room. They are apparently boning up for some exam, which, if they pass it, will increase their pay. I sit in the vast room, ceilings a dream away, waiting for my number to come on the board. Sometimes I work clanged shut in the vaults of the rare-book division. Sometimes in the Oriental room, proud of being an accustomed face among the small gathering of readers.

Tiptoeing home through Grand Central, I enjoy the quickness and silence of my sneakered feet on the vast floor. If I go at rush hour, I love the feeling of slipping through and around the thickenings of commuters. If I leave at night, the huge space enveloping me makes all my movements a dance.

In the summer of my sophomore year I'd thought of returning to Darjeeling but instead had joined Uncle Selden and Aunt Mary in Peru, where Uncle Selden had been posted as ambassador. Although enjoying the beauty of Lima and the abundance of ancient sites that encircled the city, I'd remained essentially uninterested in the civilizations that produced them. Only in the highlands of Machu Picchu and Cuzco had

74

I felt touched—not by the intrinsic interest and beauty of the places but rather because they were so like the Himalayas: the geography, the terrain, the Indians themselves, the weaving and colors of their clothes. Despite the reproaches of Jane, an anthropology student and South America aficionada whom Aunt Mary had recruited from the recently graduated class of Sarah Lawrence as her social secretary, I'd spent most of my time reading books on East Indian art.

In the fall, returned from Lima to Sarah Lawrence and Asian studies, I knew I'd come back to my center. All night, many nights, I stay up writing research papers. When I'm not studying about the East, I'm experiencing it—or so I think—through Sherzad, my Muslim Indian classmate from Iran whom I've finally met again. Sherzad, whose father, Mr. Sayyid, is on assignment with the Indian Mission to the U.N., has been in New York ever since her family's garlanded departure from Delhi a year ago.

This year the General Assembly, where Sherzad's father sits with the Indian delegation, is like the Congress of Vienna. The city police are going crazy trying to protect the many V.I.P.s thronging the city. Every night brings stories on the news about police horses that after twenty-four-hour duty fell dead with exhaustion. Almost every head of state has come, including leaders who are not just heads of state but who have birthed their countries. Among others there is Hoxha, the Stalinist party boss of Albania, who is staying in the building where the Sayyids live, Marshal Tito, Emperor Haile Selassie, Pandit Nehru, Khrushchev, Queen Elizabeth, and a battle-dressed Castro. At the U.N. they all, even ranking foreign ministers, are awestruck and act like celebrity hounds. The day after we have seen Khrushchev hold the General Assembly spellbound by banging his shoe on his desk, we trail Mr. Khrushchev as he moves through the Delegates' Lounge, following a line of senior diplomats watching for him to do something noteworthy. Suddenly he turns outside the lounge, walks into the men's room, and, flashing a big grin, shuts the door in our faces.

Sherzad and I are in the Delegates' Lounge so often that it's taken for granted we have some role at the U.N. Even Krishna Menon, stalking angrily around the room, swishing his cane, stops and bows graciously as we swagger, vain with the self-importance of belonging, through the Delegates' Lounge. We're there day and night. Among other forums, the daytime provides the Economic Council, where there's a young Tunisian delegate, pale with melancholy eyes, on whom I've a particular crush. We always stay for the vote so we can hear him speak—"Abstention," he says in firm, resonant French; Tunisia having a policy of abstaining, we never get to hear him say "oui" or "non."

The evenings provide emergency meetings on the Congo, which we invariably attend. On only one occasion does the protocol officer challenge our right to guest tickets, saying all the delegation tickets are already used. "What," says Sherzad, stabbing her finger in the air, "are those on the table?" "You can't have those, they're for the Upper Volta." "I don't care where we have to sit," Sherzad says heatedly, confusing the Upper Volta with the third tier, "we'll take them."

Through batting around the U.N. with Sherzad I grow closer and closer to her mother, who often accompanies us. Increasingly I come in from college to be with them. She calls me her daughter, and by now I feel like one. Mr. Sayyid and the girls too treat me like one of the family. They have, as prescribed in the Koran, actually taken me, a near stranger, into their household and made me one of them.

Mrs. Sayyid, who has a classical background in Urdu studies but no Western education, charms me with her fervent wish to learn. "Oh, Hopie, there is so much I want to know. My English is so poor. You teach me, Hopie." Sherzad and I teach her such New York expressions as "Guhjas, dollink." "This saree is guhjas, dollink?" Mrs. Sayyid asks, looking at us doubtfully. "Ah, you badmash—tease—how can you tease your mother like this?" Within a few months Mrs. Sayyid, despite our mischief, has learned English well enough so that she can read fairly fluently. She is reading a translation of *Le Père Goriot* now. When I ask her why, she says, "Oh, I am like the mother in it—always preparing, always preparing for her daughter's marriage." She smiles mischievously, knowing the distaste and reproof her remark will provoke from me or her children.

When she's not studying English, Mrs. Sayyid is indeed often at Korvettes buying gadgets for her daughters' dowries. "Ah, Hopie, I can't help myself," she says each evening as I put down my book to help her through the doorway with all her new acquisitions. "I can't help myself. It is my duty."

Mrs. Sayyid thinks I'm crazy to sit indoors reading all day long. She has to be out doing things—her verve so great she sometimes makes several appointments for the same time. Each morning before she leaves the house, Mrs. Sayyid, a look of guilty uncertainty crossing her face, says to me, "Hopie, now, if the phone rings, you take it. It might be Betty. I think I told her to wait for me at Eighty-sixth Street subway line, but I've got to meet Mrs. Rand just then at West Side same time. Hopie,

76

you tell her something." Her qualms resolved, full of enthusiasm, she leaves for the day's adventures.

Mrs. Sayyid must have a friend, no matter what. If one friend leaves, she goes out deliberately to the supermarket to find another. Most of the women she collects are rather ordinary, even blowsy women. She brings all her friends home and invites them to all the official parties the Sayyids give. Despite her shattering of protocol, the U.N. people from top to bottom, even the Hindu delegates in the Indian Mission, who often suspect and condescend to their Muslim colleagues, adore her. "Mr. Secretary," she says, dragging the Secretary General by the sleeve, "Mr. Secretary, come, you must meet my friend Betty."

Mrs. Sayyid's ecstasy at being in New York is equally true of her family —even, despite her gloating over America's dilemmas in the U.N., of Sherzad. "Oh, Hopie, we were told such lies in India about the virtues of socialism and the U.S.S.R. America is paradise." At New Year's the two elder Sayyids hold prayers for the coming months. "Please, God," Mrs. Sayyid—who has the same innocent no-nonsense loving relationship with God that she does with everyone else—half entreats, half orders, "don't give me one more thing, but don't take one thing away."

Mrs. Sayyid is so fulfilled and happy here she is baffled by my obsession with India, though patient with it. One day, after I mail off a good deal of money to sponsor an obscure Tagore play whose main theme is the pupil of the eye and, of course, the Great All, she asks me, "Why, Hopie, you love so much India? Even at U.N. I meet people all the time who love India so much. India is a good country but . . ."

Sherzad and her sisters, Mimi and Ferdoz, also are amused by my Eastern passion. They themselves are entering further into American life. Sherzad, who keeps handing in the same two papers on caste and arranged marriages to various sociology professors at Hunter, has plenty of free time to explore the city. She has circles of friends and goes to parties constantly. Unknown to her parents, she has posted their names on the U.N. sign-up sheets of delegates who are interested in visiting areas outside of New York, and invites her friends over on the weekends her parents go away. By the time they return, all the evidence of the party has been cleared away. "These Americans are so hospitable," the elder Sayyids, exhausted from their four-hour bus trip back from wherever they've been, sigh wearily. "Too much hospitable."

Sherzad and Mimi are trying to share their new discoveries with me. To begin with, they try to get me to dance. Mimi, brandishing the hero sandwich she is always eating, directs me in the twist. I'm trying to get them to listen to classical music as well as the pop tunes from their favorite station, WINS, that fill the apartment. "It's no use," says Sherzad of my effort and, perhaps, hers. "It's like trying to educate a horse."

I've hardly ever watched television before; now I see it often. After supper, the elder Sayyids' attention riveted by a wrestling match, curry smells permeating the overheated apartment, we sit on the floor, leaning against the stiff Castro convertibles bought on their arrival. Sherzad recently has induced me to smoke, and we puff on mentholated cigarettes, dropping butts and ashes onto the Sayyid belongings. The tiny brass slipper ashtrays on the coffee table have long been filled, so, unscrewing the roof of a Kashmiri houseboat souvenir, we use that. When a wrestler is pinned against the ropes, Mrs. Sayyid bandies the throw pillow she has been holding in her lap and brings it down "thunk" on the carpet next to her leg—"thunk" again, she slaps it down. "Oh, Sayyid"—she turns to her husband, her eyes shining—"are you seeing?"

I've grown so used to the city from visiting the Sayyids that when, in the spring, Jane Milliken, Aunt Mary's social secretary, with whom I'd spent the summer in Peru, suggests I become a day student at Sarah Lawrence and share a floor in a brownstone with her and another student from Sarah Lawrence, Jane Alexander, I'm pleased. Getting off the subway, though, walking back to our house on West Eighty-eighth Street, I'm a little scared: fears bellying out, shoulders hunched forward, trying not to look at Puerto Ricans looking at me. The two Janes and I are the only non-Hispanics on the block. I've hardly been on the West Side before, never spent the night there. When I was little I thought the Grand Central building at the end of Park Avenue was the end of the earth, the place where nails flew out and ships fell off.

Jane Milliken, or Jane M.—as she's called to distinguish her from Jane Alexander, or Jane A.—is three years older than me. The previous summer in Peru, left alone when Uncle Selden returned to the U.S.A. for a medical checkup, we'd run amok. The two of us, partly because of the anomaly of the gorgeous palace we'd occupied in Lima and our lack of actual roles there, had lived like mischievous sprites wraithing the mansion. Now, to my eyes she seems to have become mature, even motherly. Every so often, red-faced, embarrassed, she comes—trying to avoid looking at my room, the surfaces burned by cigarettes, stained by glass rings, piled with abandoned clothes, records, and iron spring mattresses—to sit on my bed and politely give me cautionary talks.

Like Jane M., Jane Alexander, despite her involvement in a troubled romance and a career letdown, perversely following her recent success in the Edinburgh Festival, also seems adult and professional. Taking in her stride the indignities of occasional dog-walking jobs, which, she feels, are more honorable than unworthy acting roles, Jane remains sturdily resolved about her future in the theater. At home she shows a simple clarity and practicality in everyday matters which perplexes me.

After the rabbit someone's given me at Easter dies, and its body, stiff and ridiculous, remains in its cage for several days, both Janes start coming into my room when I'm gone to try to make some order there. They also try to improve and socialize my eating habits. Taking turns cooking, Jane M. makes Spanish black beans, from her South American years, and Jane A. baked beans, from her Boston childhood. I resist, continuing to eat odd things at odd times. One day, on the kitchen floor, I'm cutting up the remains of a watermelon on which I've subsisted for four days, when our landlady comes up to remonstrate about the way we, I in particular, live in the apartment. I gaze at her through the kitchen door in wonderment. We are trying, really trying. My foot, congealing in juice, is sealed to the floor. I'm afraid she will enter and remain stuck here with me.

Except for papers, which I continue to prepare conscientiously, and trips to college to attend classes, I have little sense of time or event. One Sunday, coming out of the dim incense-clouded meditation room of the Theosophical Society, I stand gawking in the sunny street, confused to see people wearing palm leaf crosses. I'd forgotten not only that it was Palm Sunday but that there was such a thing as Palm Sunday. I'm compensated, though. Although I have little literal sense of life or reality in which self, chairs, friendships stay in their places, intense images and moments dislodged from any ordering or distancing principle buffet my senses, making me feel acutely alive.

I'm suffused by the sun in patches in our living room, by Jane M.'s geraniums growing on the fire escape, by the Spanish music that comes through the open windows of all the houses on our block. I feel a rush of love between ourselves and the undershirted families sitting out on their front steps. "Buenas tardes, Esperanza." "Buenas tardes"—even the boys shooting craps in the permanent floating crap game on our pavement stop to greet me when I come home in the evening.

Some days when Sherzad and Clover, my closest friend from Sarah Lawrence, come over, when Jane A.'s old beaus come, bringing champagne, and Jane M. plays the guitar, I feel, we feel, so much happiness, so much love for each other, there is nothing we can do but dance wildly through our part of the house.

Often Emile is with us, my new and first boyfriend, whom I'd met through a friend of the Janes soon after moving into the brownstone. Despite dropping out of college in Illinois, Emile is an avid history and poetry buff, reading more than anyone I'd ever met. His entire life revolves around books. Walking streets past the deserted stock exchange, warehouses, rotting piers, and fish markets lit by oil-drum fires, we spend the cold spring nights talking about poetry and Asia. Sometimes we ferry back and forth to Staten Island, sometimes go out to Coney Island to sit on the damp beach under the boardwalk, Emile looking in the sand for the beer he buried long ago. Mostly, however, we just lie on the llama-skin rug in my room, laughing, smoking, and eating greasy pick-up suppers from the nearby Merit Farms on Broadway.

Emile stays too much, agrees too much, lends himself to my personality. Lacking my own definition, and finding none in Emile by which I can inversely define myself, I remain amorphous as ever but rather cheerful. Somehow, although Emile lacks outline, he has mass—a kind Midwest density that affects me. I felt when I was with him, a little more real, more solid.

That summer Emile and I planned a trip to Asia. After a stopover in London to visit the School of Oriental and African Studies, where I'd thought I might apply to graduate school the following year, and a subsequent short visit to Darjeeling, I proposed to backtrack and meet him in Iran. On some levels I believed I intended to do so. At other levels I knew that that plan, even the plan to go to graduate school at the School of Oriental and African Studies, was just a ruse to make me think that the rope road I traveled didn't unfurl out of myself into space with nothing holding it up at the other end. The thought of graduate school and meeting Emile was a shape, a weight, to fill up an abyss made more profound by the prospect of finishing Sarah Lawrence a year hence. Even when making the itinerary I knew I wouldn't stick to it but would probably stay the summer in Darjeeling. I'd said so out loud, although Emile, being a bit drunk on beer, had just laughed. I couldn't have gone to meet Emile. He had as little identity as myself. It would have been like the old story about Alexander traveling the earth for years and finally, at the end, climbing a mountain and meeting—himself. I needed a counterpoise. Someone connected, but a counterweight.

Some prompting in me, which, frightened, unwilling to acknowledge responsibility for, I understood as my fate, told me even that night on the fire escape that I would stay in Darjeeling until I saw Maharaj Kumar again.

Excerpts from Letters to Clover from Darjeeling:

I feel guilty about not meeting Emile. Was it unfair to have returned to Darjeeling? It's funny—except for him I wouldn't have come back here. It's Emile who's made me feel as real as I do—feel I exist, ready to connect. It's almost as if Emile unthawed or readied the attraction/love for Maharaj Kumar I'd been carrying around these last two years. What brought me back here? Is it me egging fate on? Or fate egging me? I feel scared thinking it's the first. Something impelled me, I think, to return to Darjeeling, to see Maharaj Kumar one more time. The joke was he, Maharaj Kumar, asked me to marry him, or rather would I consider marrying him, the first night we met again. I'd overheard "She's come back" in telephone conversations between Kesang and Gangtok since I'd arrived, but when we met, I had the feeling he didn't remember me. In fact, I had the impression he was confusing me with someone else—he said he'd thought the red vest I'd sent him from the U.S.A. had been sent by some stewardess or other. Why, then, the first night dancing at the Gymkhana Club did he ask me if I'd consider marrying him? If it isn't fate and if this is all coming from me, how did that happen?

. . .

So many things seem preordained. The first time I visited Gangtok, Maharaj Kumar (I still don't call him by his name, Thondup, as only unconnected Westerners call him this, and it would make me feel— which sounds odd—more distant, less close to him) sat with his little girl (she's about four) on his knees, and, looking over at me, said "Amala sarp," and the child looked across at me too. I understood it. *Amala sarp* means "new mother." I understood *Amala,* because that's what Kesang calls his mother, but how could I know *sarp,* "new"? In any case, what prompted Maharaj Kumar to say that to his little girl? His small sons too, in their stiff gray-wool uniforms—I'd always thought even when I was little that I'd have children who wore English flannel uniforms, and yet I knew they wouldn't be English.

Even coming through Calcutta this time wasn't frightening. I think that after being with the Sayyids this winter, nothing Asian seems exotic. But this is different. I feel attracted to, at home with this man in particular. Although I feel he has his own weight heavy enough to be a counter-

81

poise to anchor me—more important, we have a connection so close it's almost like a membrane joining us. Sometimes it seems that, in an almost Buddhist way, I've lost my ego and am becoming an undifferentiated part of Maharaj Kumar.

Paradoxically, however, just by loving him and his loving me, I've begun to stir up controversy, and so people are regarding me as if I'm an even more, not less, definite shape than I ever have been—and I'm ambivalent. In some ways, although I seek to dissolve and permeate everything, in some ways I welcome people's perception of me here as different, as "other"; it freezes, shrinks, reduces me into a solid, tangible object. It's a much stronger sensation than a sense of self-importance, although sometimes I feel that too. It's a growing sense that I am, stronger than I've ever felt before.

Maharaj Kumar's earthiness adds to this feeling of being solid. Aside from knowing about practical things, he can do them. He's literally engineered every bit of development in Sikkim (people's income here is twice as high as in the neighboring countries—Nepal, India, Bhutan) from the orange-juice factory to the Sikkim National Transport, which he also pioneered in a real sense. In the beginning he even used to take his turn at driving the trucks down to India to make sure all was going well. I've begun to love being with someone who doesn't buzz with words and abstractions. Without having to talk, he just is.

He can be, though, philosophical, even scholarly about Buddhist philosophy. He is head of the Mahabodhi Society of the Subcontinent and often represents the society abroad. When he came back just now from the World Buddhist Federation in Cambodia, the Cambodian papers said he was the ablest delegate, and he founded the Institute of Tibetology for the study of dharma when it seemed likely China would erase Buddhism in Tibet. Even so, he seems more in harmony with Buddhist tenets than an analytical thinker. He's often rueful, humble about himself. Thinks he should be a better Buddhist. Sometimes he makes wry jokes. There was a prayer wheel turning in the stream behind the old nuns' chapel, and he nudged me and said, "That's my hydroreligion plant." I think it's because he's an incarnate lama and had such strong training in the monkhood as a child (he never wanted to go into government, didn't consider it until his elder brother was killed) that now he feels a bit sidetracked, tied down by worldly matters.

It's a conflict. One night when we were up late in the little sitting room fooling around and dancing, he excused himself to go to do his offerings, and then came back singing some piece from a pop song.

An odd duality—philosophy and the workaday world. I don't mean superficial contrasts when he has to play different roles, as when on special occasions he puts on brocade robes over his khakis or whatever old trousers he usually wears. That's odd, but no odder than Sherzad's slacks-to-sari personality. In fact, Maharaj Kumar is less divided than Sherzad. She behaves differently when she wears slacks and when she wears saris. This is something more fundamental than just playing different roles. In his own self there are two strong bents—a foreground and a background, little middle ground.

It's his foreground I love, his immediacy. I'm embedded in his earthy side. It's so extraordinary what this man can do. Sikkim is a flower of his care, his talent for the practical. Driving back to Darjeeling after one visit, we'd taken a different road from the one we'd driven up and passed many settlements and government buildings I hadn't seen earlier. I hadn't known we'd taken the different road, so Kesang, teasing me, said, "Look, Hope. It's been six days. What do you think? Don't you know Maharaj Kumar is a dynamic leader and Sikkim a dynamic, growing place?" Silly, but in a way, I think, true.

Sikkim is the one thing of which Maharaj Kumar is really proud. It's a model country. When you cross the border from India, it's a different world—electricity, neat houses, clean bazaars. Although the main bazaar street in Gangtok is a little scruffy-looking—rather like a one-street prairie town, complete with saloons, in a cowboy movie—the rest of the town is beautiful. All the government buildings, schools, chest clinic, cottage industries, hospital, printing press, secretariat, etc., situated on spurs looking out over the valleys, are built in traditional Sikkimese curved-roof architecture. All have bright blue roofs, Maharaj Kumar feeling it worth a little extra money to give people a cheerful, cohesive environment. Perhaps it's the manicured look of the buildings, or maybe it's the fact all the buildings labeled neatly with signs saying what their function is, but somehow Gangtok gives the impression of being a model town in a social studies book.

. . .

For twenty years, Maharaj Kumar (his father, a semi-invalid semi-recluse, is virtually retired, spends his time painting and meditating) has been doing all the work, caring about every small corner, visiting (often on foot) every village several times a year, and knowing by sight just about everyone.

The same excellence is not true of his personal life. I've come to know (he's trying to let me change my pure image of him) of the areas in his own life where he has failed. Particularly, he's had a problem with women. Sometimes I feel frightened, overwhelmed that he should trust me, tell me things that are painful to him. I love the new man for his humility, contrition.

When we went down to Calcutta together we had a very emotional, revealing time. I'd never seen a man cry before, and was moved and shy. I'd been tearful, partly because the desk clerk had looked at me so lewdly, superciliously, as if I were a whore, when Maharaj Kumar asked for a room near mine. Anyway, when Maharaj Kumar, coming into my room, saw me crumpled up on the bed, crying, tears came into his eyes too. He looked so hurt and worried, and told me he'd hurt so many people, he couldn't stand the thought of hurting me. It was odd. Suddenly he was like a small wounded boy (he often even physically looks very little-boyish) and I was comforting him. He's vulnerable in a raffish way I find irresistible. Partly it's the sadness of his wife's dying so tragically (he always calls her "my late wife," never by her name) just as things were going better between them. (It had been an arranged marriage, and in the beginning she wasn't happy.) Partly, I think, it has something to do with his childhood. Like me—even more than me, when he was small he had a rather sad life—bullying from his older brother and neglect from his parents. He told me once that when he was little and living away from home doing monk's training with his uncle, a monk, he came back to the palace, and running into the chapel, found his mother praying, and she turned around and said, "Why've you come?" To which he replied, "Today's my birthday." "Go back," she said. "Your birthday's next week." And he did go back to his uncle's in a rickshaw.

· · ·

It's almost his vulnerable points I love best, his sad/funny, almost Chaplinesque loneliness. When he came here for the first time this summer from Gangtok with the band of Indian Army officers, driving all over the Windemere lawns, deep jeep tracks in the hotel flower beds, prancing about at the Gymkhana Club the night he asked me to marry him, he was like Peter Pan with the lost boys. I felt like Wendy.

· · ·

The house itself is so vulnerable, so lonely. All the dark guest rooms so barely furnished, dimly lit—bare bulbs, cobwebs—even by my standards his own room is dark, cluttered, cheerless. Only the little sitting room, full of music, bright with its rose carpet and fire, is an exception. And yet, during the holidays, when the palace is crammed with Maharaj Kumar's children, home from school, as well as his nephews and nieces, and every room is full of comic books, polliwogs in jars, firecrackers, what have you, the house sings.

I want a family so much. I want to fill this nest, make it a real home. When I watch Maharaj Kumar with his children, he's so tender that I almost burst with love. The last time up in Gangtok, when he and his little girl, Yangchen Dolma, were doing prostrations in the chapel, I watched as he, continuing his own prayers, gently showed her how to fold her hands. I was so overcome by happiness, longing, I just stayed kneeling, couldn't get up on my feet.

. . .

When Maharaj Kumar first said he'd make me Yangchen's local guardian at the convent in Darjeeling, I thought it crazy. Even though we had that weird feeling of connection and talked right away of marrying, he hardly knew me. He could have been handing her over to anybody. The mother superior at Loretto was surprised too, doing a double take when she saw me. Jenny, an alcoholic English guest at the hotel, had left out her pink tweed suit the night before, saying that the mother superior was going to be shocked enough as it was and I should put on respectable clothes. But something in me rebelled at the idea of dressing up in the middle-aged clumpy tweeds, and I'd stolen off for the early-morning appointment with Maharaj Kumar wearing a cotton skirt I'd made in Darjeeling.

To the surprise of the mother superior and other Darjeelingites, and justifying Maharaj Kumar's odd certainty, things have turned out curiously well, and we've settled into a good routine. Sometimes I go on pony back down the steep hill to the convent—voices of choir practice sounding through the tall pines around the school buildings—to pick up Yangchen. We ride up to the hotel, where she gets out of her stiff, bloomered, necktied Saint Trinian's outfit and into her comfortable Sikkimese robe.

She's called me Mummy for some time—in fact, repeating "Mummy, Mummy" in an excited, breathless sort of way, sometimes supplicating, sometimes demanding. Her brothers have just begun to. The last time I was in Gangtok the oldest boy, Tenzing, was showing me a comic, and he said, "Look at this picture . . . Mummy." I almost choked, he was so manly, courageous, trying it out. Right afterward he lapsed back into

"Miss." I felt so shy, so overcome by the trust he was vesting in me, I acted—and still do—a bit stilted.

Yangchen is different. I don't feel shy about her trusting me but enormously happy and grown up. Maybe it's because she's a girl, maybe it's because she didn't really have a relationship with her late mother, as her brothers must have had, but I feel perfectly at home with her. I could spend all my time with her. Indeed, Kesang and his parents are getting fed up with me as more and more I resist going down to the lounge and making small talk with the other guests before dinner.

Kesang's surprised at me. Surprised at how devoted I am, doing the hard parts as well as the easy ones. I've been trying to reform myself, keeping my room tidy as an example to Eloise (she looks and behaves just like Eloise at the Plaza) next door, as well as keeping her on the up-and-up, doing things good for her, not just spoiling her. The other day when we were coming back through Chaurrastha, the main square of Darjeeling, just below the hotel, where all the town grandees go to stroll, we passed a shop where they sell English toffee. I didn't want her to buy any candy (she always seems to get it from some place—I don't know where), so I put my foot down and said no, while Memeh, her ayah, a nice Tibetan lady who often gives in to Yangchen's demands, just stood there looking frightened as Yangchen went into a screaming fit. I've never seen anything like it. She just screamed and screamed and then lay flat down on her back in the middle of Chaurrastha and screamed until I thought she'd choke from swallowing air. I was, as you can imagine, unnerved, as I knew that within minutes the passersby would have a rumor going that the American girl was beating the little Sikkimese princess. Still I was steely, and felt good both for myself and Yangchen when we finally made it back to the hotel—I don't know how—without buying anything.

· · ·

I'd be so lonely without Yangchen. Aside from the trips Maharaj Kumar took to Cambodia and Europe, even when he's in Sikkim, he can't get down too often to Darjeeling. It's true what Kesang says, he really does stick to his job, and I can't go up to Gangtok too often (Kesang's advice) as it looks pushy. When he comes down here, life is wonderful. Otherwise it's pretty dreary.

I tried to take a class in economics at St. Joseph's, a college in Darjeeling, taught by an old Jesuit with a long white beard. The fog used to come in at the classroom window and make a white cloud over the old man. He was dressed in white too. Quite nice. But the actual classes were terrible. No discussion, all dictation—he even told us when to punctuate, everyone dutifully sticking in commas.

When I read my engagement announcement in the *Times* I really laughed. I'd written Uncle Selden (for years he'd been wanting me to learn to type) that I was learning how. I was too, in a desultory sort of way. When I get so bored I can't stand it, I go into Kesang's office and peck away at his machine. One finger, just fooling. But *The New York Times* notice said, "Miss Hope Cooke, who has been in Darjeeling studying typing . . ." No wonder people think I'm a C.I.A. agent. What a cover, especially if they could see the way I type. That's one of the scariest things—the people I meet now and what they're saying about me. Right now my only friend is Kesang, and although he can be an angel and very supportive, he can also—aside from being a tease (he goes around singing "We Live in Two Different Worlds"—be a manipulative bully. (I don't mean just the way he is always forcing me to dress up, put my hair up, etc., but really manipulative.) Sometimes more than feeling just bored or lonely, I feel almost scared. I miss you, Clover, and Jane and the Sayyids—all my safe, loving people—so much. Jane's mother came up for a few days and I almost cried from homesickness and release of tension to see her. She'd brought out the new Joan Baez record too, so I had the enjoyment of playing that all day on Maharaj Kumar's record player the next time I went up to Gangtok. I think maybe it's because of Maharaj Kumar's record collection (he's got lots of my favorrite classical records—we have music all day long) that I feel so much more at home there than here in Darjeeling.

Here I feel quite vulnerable. Some people come to the hotel just to check me out. The other day a Bengali tycoon and his wife came and looked at me so closely I thought they were going to make a written inventory. Apparently some Tibetans are spreading rumors I'm a whore. The other day two Indian military police pushed in the unused door (there was a cupboard in front of it, but it wasn't locked) between my room and the one they were in and left a rude note inviting me to eat dinner with them. Can you imagine that? Me?! Bluestocking Hope! Asian men are ridiculous about American girls. I think because they've seen so many American movies they think we all must be loose. Before I was engaged, when I went down to Calcutta with Maharaj Kumar, some dreadful boy at a party, a maharaja's son who thought he was a big shot, kept asking me if I was booked—*booked!* I said yes, and he got so angry that he put a glass on my chair, hoping I wouldn't notice and would sit down on it. When that failed, he spilled a full glass of some liquor on my lap, and to top it (he was in a wheelchair with a broken ankle), he kept kicking me with his good leg when I was saying good night to our hostess.

Even Maharaj Kumar sometimes treats me like a sex object—but quite differently, in the very nicest way. I would compromise equality, I think, for roses (long-stemmed)! I feel I could be an Asian wife. I really like obeying people I love if I'm protected and tenderly treated. Also, it's not as if Sikkimese women have the same situation as in India. They're much more independent, sort of buoyant. In the beginning I felt a bit denatured, corrupted, setting my hair with beer, dressing up in the sheath dresses that I've had made in the bazaar, high heels, etc. (I fall down a lot, especially on these bumpy roads in Darjeeling, dragging Yangchen down with me if she's holding my hand), but in some ways now I enjoy the French-perfume aspects of life.

. . .

Worse than the gossipy whore rumors are the political allegations. Although the C.I.A. cover joke concerning my typing is funny, it isn't completely a joke. Some people here would do anything to unseat Maharaj Kumar politically—and if he goes, so does Sikkim. I love Maharaj Kumar and Sikkim too much to jeopardize them. I can just see them using me as a wedge to help destroy his rule. It's a squeeze from all sides. China might think I'm a U.S. presence and that my next step would be a strategic air base here. (The Bhutanese are so concerned not to upset China, they won't allow the Peace Corps to work there.) India also has been hurtful, imperialist, to Sikkim in the past. Even now Indian Army trucks rip around Gangtok as if they're an occupying force, and if Maharaj Kumar ever complains, rumors go back to Delhi that he is anti-Indian. Although apparently Nehru was nice about the idea of our engagement when Maharaj Kumar went to see him in Delhi, fundamentally they won't like this assertion of independence from Maharaj Kumar and could use it to hurt him.

Worse still than China or India's views will be the local problems. The chief problem Maharaj Kumar says is a woman called Kazini in Kalimpong (it's odd, because she's not local but British, or rather of Belgian extraction, with English papers), an Indian border town, married to a Sikkimese politician. For years she's been causing problems, trying to get the Sikkimese Nepalis (they're in the majority) to make trouble. Some British journalists she has in tow write frequent articles about

88

Maharaj Kumar, calling him the Lumumba of Sikkim and saying Nepalese opposed to the regime are tied by their necks and thrown in sacks into the river. She seems to make trouble for its own sake as well as to be politically ambitious for her husband. In any case, Maharaj Kumar is pictured as a most despotic, miscreant ruler, and the Nepalese are urged to overthrow him. On top of this there is a problem with the Bhutia Lepcha community of Sikkim. A traditional council of Bhutia Lepcha monks and village elders is meeting soon to discuss the marriage. Everything in Sikkim works by consensus, and it's important that Maharaj Kumar have their agreement. The royal family is of Bhutia Lepcha stock, and therefore their backing is important for continued political support. In general, they're the most conservative force in Sikkim and are used to the King's marrying someone from Tibet who is a Buddhist.

This last reservation about me—about my not being a Buddhist—I find particularly ironic, as for the past years I've felt so Buddhist, so nonattached. But now the formal conversion to Buddhism seems out of the question, as it would seem merely expedient and not genuine. The other irony is that the very contention brings me into sharper focus, makes me more body, less spirit, less Buddhist.

. . .

Although the Sikkimese, particularly the elders, seem reserved, Maharaj Kumar's family is being quite warm to me. I was so touched by how loving and open-minded Maharaj Kumar's father, His Highness, was when Maharaj Kumar asked him for his consent to marry me. Instead of bringing up difficulties, he just said, "Do whatever makes you happy." Even his sister Cocoola is being sweet, although sometimes I get the feeling she is just being kind to me for her brother's sake, that she too thinks I'm a beatnik eccentric, possibly an adventurer. I'm in awe of her for several reasons; first of all, she is so strikingly beautiful and sophisticated that often I feel boorish. I had a disaster at the palace the very first time I went there. People had been drinking a lot. (People drink too much here—sycophants are always pushing drinks at Maharaj Kumar— "Just one more, Prince, just one more!") Many toasts in my honor. Maharaj Kumar's brother drinking champagne out of my scruffy shoe. Anyway, as I don't drink as a rule, I threw up in the hall as M.K. was getting out the car to take me back to the guesthouse. Threw up! Can you believe it? And there was no one to apologize or explain to. I lay awake for hours in agony thinking of what I'd say next morning. When I did meet Cocoola the next day, I shuffled out an apology. "Er, er, Your Highness," I blurted out, "I'm very sorry about last night." She took my hand, and, gazing straight in my eyes, said in this silky voice, "Oh, that's all right, Hope La. You must treat this house as if it were your own." I didn't know what to say—"I don't throw up in my house, only in others' "? It was mortifying. I couldn't take my hand back.

Anyway, she is a fantastic lady. She's in charge of the Tibetan refugees here and single-handedly directs all the work, taking into account even the minutest detail—from distributing supplies to designing the grippers (they're made from old Indian Army cartridge shells) of the silver hair clips the Tibetan artisans make for sale.

Maharaj Kumar's second sister (actually he's got one more, but she's very shy and doesn't come out much), Coola, doesn't do as much, partly as she lives—not too happily—in Calcutta, but she is just as beautiful and intelligent. (She was the top student in all of eastern India and Sikkim the year she took exams.) The sad thing is that the landlords here, who are jealous of the royal family, to prevent her from going to college, finishing her education, more or less insisted that she be married to a Tibetan noble and go off to Lhasa. Coola (their English governess gave them all these names—Maharaj Kumar's brother George is named after the King) has been particularly kind to me. She and her husband have been so accepting, so loving, I feel almost shy. She's always attentive, always trying to make one feel more comfortable, at ease. I really want to be like her.

Of the two sisters, Cocoola seems more like her mother, as does Maharaj Kumar too, in manner and looks. Both George and Coola are more like their father—delicate, high-strung. The mother, Her Highness, is a presence—earthy, solid, even in the dim, rather shabby room where I met her. As she's been separated from the maharaja since Maharaj Kumar was a child and lives some way from Gangtok, she didn't come for the engagement, since she doesn't come to the palace.

· · ·

The Engagement! We left Darjeeling in a Land-Rover—Kesang, Yangchen, her ayah, and I. We were so jammed we sat on our suitcases. All of us holding on our laps huge bags of radishes the driver had bought to take back to Gangtok. As the hotel family had given me a white scarf for luck before I left, which I was wearing round my neck, I must have looked an odd sight—groceries and scarf! We were all singing Christmas carols very loudly—Yangchen Dolma joining in, "Jinkle bells, jinkle," from time to time. Little face pinched up in the babushka she always wears when we travel. Darjeeling town still full of marigolds—baskets of them, like treasure. In the Dewali festival, the Hindu festival of lights, just over, there were jeeps in town filled to the brim with marigolds, and even animals were festooned.

It's a beautiful time of year here, the most beautiful. The rice paddies, about ready for harvest, are bright chartreuse. The cherry trees are in blossom, and the snowy mountains finally clear after the summer's rain. It's like all four of Vivaldi's seasons played at the same time.

On the Darjeeling side you pass through tea gardens—or rather, up and down through tea gardens—the roads mostly lined with cryptomeria. (Some trees are being cut back, though, as the road is being widened for troops, to be rushed up to the border in case of a Chinese invasion.) After you cross the Tista, the river dividing Sikkim and India, at this time of year no longer muddy from the summer monsoon but clear green, you sign in at the Sikkim Police Checkpoint. (For "Purpose of Visit" I wrote "Tourism," Yangchen yelling "Handzup" all the time at the police.) Here the landscape changes. Much sunnier and more tropical, many orchids along the roadside and quite a few families of monkeys— Yangchen always delighted when we spotted them! Everything looks trimmer here, more cared for. The farmhouse always well thatched, and many more tin roofs (even painted—a real sign of wealth) than you see in Darjeeling. The few towns there are also much better planned and kept. There isn't an extreme of rich and poor; everyone, by Asian standards, is relatively provided for, no one rich. Things fit into scale. The royal family, although it owns a good bit of land, mostly mountain peaks, is not at all wealthy—even the palace is just a big bungalow.

Darjeeling, in contrast, because of the ugly Anglo-Indian architecture and overcrowding, is a mess. It's a social hodgepodge too—like a mule, bastardized and sterile. Sikkim is coherent; it has its own entity, and you can feel this. Partly it has to do with being its own country, not just a border area. It's funny, now I want to belong to a definite place, not be on an edge, on a frontier, as I was in Darjeeling.

The engagement ceremony was simple—only His Highness, Maharaj Kumar, the Dewan, and a few other people in the big sitting room. Everyone exchanged scarves. Maharaj Kumar giving me (embarrassing) a diamond ring. I preferred the first part, when Maharaj Kumar came down to the guesthouse to fetch me—bright sun pouring in, sound of the river down below the hill—and sat with me, changing the bandages on my fingers, teasing me about having to make sure there was space, or indeed a finger, left for the ring. (When we were in Calcutta, he actually took me to a doctor to have him examine the finger sores I'd developed over the summer, they'd gotten so bad and I'd neglected them.) Anyway that was a very tender time; and very like him—concerned with such practical, small things as the bandages, and protective. Also sweet, because he really doesn't like very manicured people. (He says American women with big hands and varnished nails somewhat appall him, and he likes my hands because they're small, even if they don't conform to the standard type of beauty.) He really is simple, not ratty sophisticated, and likes natural people, even though sometimes I see him looking at my nicotined, bandaged fingers, wondering how he's going to make a lady out of me.

Afterward there was a press reception and picture-taking. The palace dhobi had taken the corduroy skirt I'd made in Darjeeling and pressed pleats into it, so I looked like an open cardboard box—flaps sticking out stiffly in each direction. Talking to the press (all Indian journalists) was misery. First of all, I fear they're going to write on the Ah, Wilderness theme, and I want, if they must write about the engagement, to use the occasion to get favorable attention for Sikkim—to let people know that every child lives within two miles of a free primary school, that the per capita income is one and a half times that of neighboring areas, etc. I was shy and rather asinine talking to them, going on and on about Johnny to some stringer for an English paper who asked me if I had any "U.K. connection," telling him that I had had a nanny who lived near Epsom Downs who was something of a bookie (Can you see that headline?!), and then, worse, to another man, who'd asked me if I was going to convert to Buddhism, saying that conversion was actually un-Buddhist, that in Buddhism names or categories are really an illusion, and that it's a philosophic and psychological framework rather than a formal belief system. Kesang, trying to intervene, afterward told me I wasn't writing a paper for Sarah Loony College, and I should just have said it was being considered. Kesang's always trying to save me from myself, "preserve your dignity," as he calls it. He says that I mustn't talk too much, must be aloof, otherwise everyone will take advantage. Even at the reception the next day I had to wear what Kesang and his mother called "proper clothes"—my high heels, a sheath dress, and Mrs. Tenduf La's sweater, gloves, and handbag (big and clumsy).

Anyway, it wasn't the worst it could have been, and afterward we went to a lunch party for the wedding of Jean La (the quiet third sister), which by coincidence, or rather astrology, was on the same day. I felt rather bad, as, in a way, our engagement took away from her big day, but it was fun and relaxed, and afterward we came back to the palace and played hide-the-shoe with the children, and a kite-tail game in which everyone hangs onto someone else and eventually onto a leader (me), and the leader tries to curve and whip back and forth until the tail person is thrown off. I felt so happy with them (I hadn't seen the boys for some time)—really one of the happiest moments of my life. I felt like Mrs. Sayyid praying at New Year's—Please, God, don't give me anything else—but don't take anything away.

5

MY SENSES had never been as alert, nor my powers of denial as high. From the start I'd noticed every nuance, every threat, and at the same time had repressed every negative conclusion. Kesang wrote me at college, where I'd been for several months after returning from the engagement, "Don't ask me why I'm writing you this, Hope, but make it a point to come back as soon as you can next summer. He really loves you, so do this." I knew. It was easy to put together. I'd had a letter at the same time from Maharaj Kumar, written also on Windemere paper, saying his sister Cocoola had introduced him to a Mrs. Donnell, or rather, as she called herself, Grace Baines ("seems husband and wife don't get on"), from Wilmington and Brussels, who was something of a trekker, mountain climber, painter, and bullfighter.

When he wrote in May that if my college work permitted he wanted to fly out to see me, even if just for a few days, I felt anxious; he was coming to reaffirm something he doubted. I didn't say anything, however, when he came. Neither did he. At a record shop in the city he hummed the "Toreador Song" as he bought *Carmen*. My anger and fear turned supercilious. *Carmen!*

A month later he flew again to the West, this time first to England, to look over prep schools for his sons, then to the U.S. to collect me and Clover and her father, who were coming to Sikkim for the summer as my chaperones. It was clear to me from various slips in transatlantic phone conversations that Grace Baines was with him. Double sting. Now she was also usurping my role as stepmother. I couldn't bring myself to tackle him about the deepest wound; I tackled the second: "I would have liked to have gone round the schools with you myself." "How could I presume," he replied, "to ask you to do that kind of chore before you're my wife?"

1

My grandparents, mother and nurse in Seal Harbor

2

My sister Harriet by my mother's plane

3

My father and mother

4

Our house on Long Island

5
Showing my Indian Walk shoes

6
Harriet being graceful

7

Johnny, my governess,
Harriet and I in Apart-
ment 8B

Harriet and I with Aunt Dooly
Townsend

8

9

Sulking as Harriet poses with her first fish

10

My grandparents with Aunt Mary, Uncle Selden Chapin, their teenage children, Harriet and myself

SEAL HARBOR

12

Maine picnic

11

My domain—our play-house on Long Island

13

14

Harriet grown up, married

15

16

Making a globe for UN Day at school in Iran

Spring vacation 1954—boarding school friend and I working the locks on the Panama Canal

17

Spring visit in 1957 to India

Listening to Secretary of State John Foster Dulles' Outpost of Empire speech at the American Embassy in Teheran

18

19

Trekking with friends
through the Elburz mountains

20

Insouciant Uncle Selden, informally dressed, showing the
American fleet to H.I.M. the
Shah

21

Loving Chapins and scowling self at my
Teheran "coming out" party

22

23

24

Clover at Sarah Lawrence

Sad departure from Iran, carrying my ibex horn "the only thing I shall possess"

25

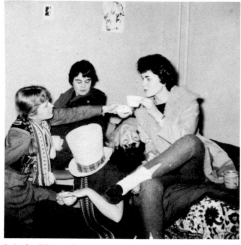

Mad Hatter's tea party at college with Clover, Ellen, Hester, self in hat, and Robin as guest of honor

26

Hope-doing one better than Leggett?

Robin's rendering of me returning from freshman summer in Russia and the Himalayas

27   SIKKIM:—Engagement day with Wongchuk, Yangchen and Tenzing

28

The Two Janes, Jane Alexander and Jane Milliken, at our engagement party in New York

Wongchuk and Tenzing

29

30 *Kanchendzeugna*

31

Pemayangtse lamas

32

Detail from monastery door

33

Terracing in western Sikkim

34

The palace

Eastern view of Gangtok showing the palace and royal chapel on lower hill and Tathangchen village below

35

36 The wedding

38 Chogyal and I in state robes

37 The coronation

39

Mothering

Hope Leezum

40

41 Sunny day lunch at the palace

Chogyal with Palden

42

Friend modeling one of my designs
at fashion show

Palden at village school

43

44

45

Meeting villagers in
North Sikkim

46

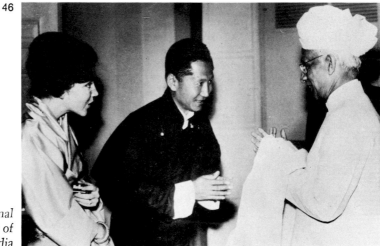

Presenting traditional
scarf to President of
India

With Prime Minister Indira
Gandhi of India

47

48

"My dear woman, there's a lot more to Far
East foreign policy than the former Hope
Cooke!"

Post-Troubles New Yorker cartoon

49   Crowd burning a picture of Chogyal and me during the Troubles

50

On the "Today" show, appealing for Chogyal's safety following 1975 attack on the palace

51

Self, Ellen, Susan, Robin, Suzie, Clover

FRIENDS AT RAINY DAY
PICNIC NEW YORK
1980

52

Kesu, Joyce, Daniele and
Alice

53

54   Cavorting in Central Park with Palden and Hope Leezum

The following week a telegram came to him from her, care of me in New York, giving the date of her arrival in Wilmington from Europe and suggesting a time for a visit. A letter followed, in which, reading it against the light, I could make out the assurance that the telegram had been so worded as to be perfectly safe if opened by someone other than him.

The Baineses had been relieved to meet me, he told me after our requisite trip down to Wilmington. "I think they feared I was marrying some little chippie." Some little chippie?! Who the hell do you think you are? Who do you think they are? Some interloper's dreary family making judgments on me! Aloud I merely said primly that I resented the presumption. "You're right," he said. "It was stupid to bring it up."

At the end of the summer, when Maharaj Kumar accompanied Clover and me back to Paris on our way home from Sikkim, Grace flew into Paris on the day I was supposed to have left for college—a precious extra day I'd wrung out of Sarah Lawrence to surprise him with. I took off from Orly crying until I felt my body was falling apart. Maharaj Kumar flew over to New York a few days later. (I think he flew back to be with her again on his way to Sikkim after he had left me.) "It was terrible to watch you leave like that. I hope you were crying not because of Grace but because you were leaving me. I love you, girl. You're my woman." I told him I hated Grace, that I couldn't stand it. Later I wrote to him in Sikkim to apologize for my anger. "Don't feel badly," he replied. "In many ways it showed your love for me and that you're a real woman."

All day long in the Sayyids' apartment, where I'm staying since lending my apartment to Cocoola's daughter, who has come to study in New York, I cry and cry. Jealousy consumes me. It's a stronger emotion than love. I can't get Grace and Maharaj Kumar out of my mind. Almost every place I have been with Maharaj Kumar, she has been with him too. There is no longer any safe place to let my mind rest. She and Maharaj Kumar fill it with their embrace.

Mrs. Sayyid is worried and loving. "Ah, Hopie." She hugs me again and again.

Sherzad, brought up in newly independent socialist India, hates the Indian princes, and comforts and needles me by turns. "I told you about the maharajas. They can't help it, Hopie. It's no good." "He's not an Indian maharaja. He's Sikkimese and he's simple and hardworking—he's not one of your damned playboys." "Never you mind Sherzad," Mrs. Sayyid says. "She is jealous. She loves you so much, and you think so

95

much of Maharaj Kumar, and she is worried too about her own marriage."

Sherzad has been crying also, not noisily in the daytime as I do when my mind wanders off the books I'm reading for college, but quietly at night, little sucking indrawn breaths. Her parents have arranged a marriage for her when they return to India, which will be soon—January or so. They're already making arrangements to sell things. Sherzad lies on her bed, her body rigid, refusing to talk. Occasionally she blurts out, "I love him so much." I've met her young man, an Indian student with whom she's been going out for some time. I don't know what to say. I know Sherzad's parents are liberal; they don't want her unhappy, they're just trying to do what they consider their duty. "Speak to them," I beg. "Speak to them." Sherzad lies looking straight ahead. "No, Hopie, I cannot help it. It is my kismet."

As much as she accepts her situation as beyond change, Sherzad is fierce in urging me to stand up to Maharaj Kumar. Letters and more letters come from him urging me to be happy, to be confident. For some time I don't answer. One day he telephones, anxious. The line, as usual, is terrible—beepers, static, teams of operators, whishing noises. I feel too emotionally exhausted and angry at the core to talk. On the other hand, as all our calls are usually disconnected at least once in the course of a conversation, if I just hang up, it will be a futile gesture. "Shout bang," Sherzad says, making a gesture of slamming the phone down. "Shout bang in his ear."

That fall, every day during October the newspapers carry front-page stories about fighting in northeastern India between Indian and Chinese troops. Sikkim is only a couple of hundred miles away. Fear interrupts my jealousy. During the weeks of conflict, sick with worry, barely able to work at even rudimentary studies, all my feelings concentrate on willing support and safety to Sikkim and to the Maharaj Kumar. I just manage to drag myself to school.

For different reasons, Sodenla, Cocoola's daughter, and all the Sayyid family except for Sherzad's sister Mimi, who's still bouncing around as usual, are unhappy, as restless as I. Sodenla is homesick—so far away from home for the first time—and overwhelmed by work at the design school she attends. Also, she is angry at me for returning to Sikkim and the center of the family just as she's left. Her anger is complicated by loyalty to her mother, who, according to Sodenla, has some long-rooted bitterness, even rivalry toward Maharaj Kumar. Although I am lending her my apartment, Sodenla treats me with furious contempt, even to the point of telling friends that I'm the maid. I'm scared of her. She has her mother's haughty anger. At the same time I sense her vulnerability and feel sorry for her.

Mrs. Sayyid is as heartbroken as Sherzad to leave New York. "Oh, never again, Hopie, will we be alone together, living like a family free from troubles." When they return, Mr. Sayyid, as the oldest brother, will face a battery of dependent relations, who will force the family into the rigid roles they will be expected to play. Even here I get hints of how circumscribed their behavior will have to be. As if she were rehearsing her mother in role-playing, Sherzad one day turns on her for her "childishness" in throwing a snowball.

Ferdoz, Sherzad's other sister, is refusing to go, threatening to get a job, run away, never leave the city. "Talk to her, Hopie," Mrs. Sayyid says, "she listens to you." I know Ferdoz' chances for getting a good job are small, her expectations of jobs, men, life in general much higher, more glamorous than is realistic. "Just try it, Ferdoz," I say. "Just try it. Your parents swear they won't marry you off if it's not what you want, that you can choose the kind of life you want to lead." She glares at me like a cornered animal. "I've done it. I'm never going back, never."

At night Sherzad and I go up on the roof to smoke and eat ice cream. Looking over the drive, the traffic a moving lasso of light, she shakes her head numbly and asks, "Hopie, how can you leave all this?"

When the Sayyids go, one of Sherzad's American boyfriends and I drive back to the city, saying nothing, sad, the car radio still on station WINS, Sherzad's constant voice.

Back in my apartment, now that Sodenla's moved to the Y.W.C.A., I discover she's destroyed several art books and my Persian miniatures— the glass and frames broken and the pictures gouged. "Just tracing them," she says in a frightened voice on the phone.

My center is gone. The Sayyids were the realest family I've ever had. I am, as Mrs. Sayyid said, her daughter. All the familiar things and people in my life here seem to have receded. My friends are helping me—one has offered to begin shopping for the things I want to take to Sikkim (100 blotters, 30 flower holders, 20 notebooks, other small objects)—but even they seem shadowy. When a professor gives a pregraduation party for me at college, I can hardly think of a single friend to invite and am embarrassed by my hostess' confusion.

I've talked to a few people, telling them of my feelings of jealousy and doubt about getting married, my unhappiness, but my talking rattles like a stone in a can. Jane M., who's lived in South America, says philandering is part of life. None of my friends seems to have any standards or advice or to know much more than I do.

I don't want to go. I've got to go. So much machinery is in force. Hundreds of invitations have been mailed out, elaborate plans have been made for the ceremonies and festivities in Gangtok. Half New York, it seems, is asking me what to pack. Every mail brings a new account or schedule of lunches to be given, presents to be exchanged, customs to be observed. Even the press here has started bothering me. Some magazine wants me to dress up like a bobby-soxer so they can photograph me at college "before and after."

At Christmas I go to Sikkim. Maharaj Kumar and I still don't talk. I've a feeling Grace's just been with him in Gangtok. He says no, not elaborating. We spend much of the time outdoors as the weather is sunny and clear, celebrating the Sikkimese New Year, which falls on Christmas this year. There are crowds of people. All the kids are back from school, Yangchen with the Dutch doll I'd mailed from New York. Life is easygoing. The opposite of the grim, fearful border situation I'd been worrying about all fall in New York, where the tiny *New York Times* border map showed Sikkim hardly a hairbreadth away from the clashes in Nefa. Here, except on the road, where there is considerable evidence of the military, nothing seems to stir. Almost every day we go out for a picnic, Maharaj Kumar and his friends playing Mah-Jongg, the boys flying the model airplanes they've gotten for the New Year.

Back in New York, I write that I still believe she's been there. "I didn't lie," he replies. "She wasn't here. She came to Kalimpong. Due to the new regulations since the October Indo-Chinese border clashes, no foreigners are allowed to get inner-line crossing permits. You've been the only exception. She simply came to Kalimpong to do a painting for our wedding. I'd hoped to invite her to finish it before the wedding—in view of your feelings, I won't. I love you! Don't forget you're my woman and soon will be my wife."

He writes me of the money being spent for the tent they're making for the folk dances and the banquets, that, although Sikkim will gain from the publicity, it's in my honor. Things are going on independent of me. It all seems absurd. The Dewan is sending me postcards to remind me about bringing the car he wants. Some Calcutta businessman is pleading with me to bring a jukebox—"It will be easy to fit it in among your other things." The kids are writing me dear letters in pencil asking me when I'm "coming home." Aunt Mary is calling me from the Virgin Islands to say she had heard that Cocoola has ordered that none of the guests should wear gold. She has some gold in the dress she's bought—will that be all right? What does Cocoola have in mind, and are bed jackets acceptable as the gifts she hears she must give to relations in return for theirs to guests? "Yes, bed jackets are fine." There is too much difference in cultures. I don't add that they will be giving her valuable things they can't afford—carpets, silver. I know Aunt Mary is valiantly trying to cope, and even will have to officiate at the wedding on her own. As the altitude in Sikkim is too high for his heart, Uncle Selden can't come to give me away.

Trying to patch together some sort of genealogy necessary for the ceremonies, I've just learned about my father's Irishness and "lowly" origins in the same letter from my mother's friend which went on to describe her character and her marriages and speculate about her death. I discover I'm not "totally upper drawer," as one of Aunt Mary's friends puts it. More awkward than the shock to my self-esteem is the new social vulnerability I'm aware of. Maharaj Kumar doesn't care, but Cocoola is increasingly haughty to me, going on about the unsuitability, the rawness of people who have no roots, no background. I am resentful of my father for letting me down in this new, unexpected way. The press meanwhile continue to write about me as a debutante. In fact, nothing they write—Cinderella orphan or New York debutante—fits; both are wrong.

My professors are upset that my abilities as a student haven't been mentioned. I've a stubborn sense of who I am, which has grown sharper recently, partly in resistance to Maharaj Kumar and going to Sikkim. But it is small and creaturelike—walking on top of leaves, crackling no twigs—and I would rather live in the underbrush free than stand up and fight these images that are supposed to define me. A journalist friend of Uncle Selden's is giving advice about the press, but he is too preoccupied to follow through, and in any case, neither people in Sikkim nor I are up to carrying out what he suggests—making pools, checking credentials and intended story lines.

One day *Paris Match* rings me up and insists that I meet them to be photographed. I'm no good at saying no. All I can do is not answer the phone. Weakly I agree to meet them on some street corner and then fall back asleep. I am really feeling sick. For several days I haven't eaten anything but have just drunk ginger ale. The empty bottles roll around in my bed. The *Paris Match* people ring and ring and don't believe me when I say I'm feeling too sick to get up.

People at my graduation ceremony say I've got hepatitis, and suggest that I move to a room at the Colony Club because I'm too ill to stay alone. Leaving my own bed with its unwashed and twisted sheets, my belongings strewn about, half in, half out of Manhattan Storage packing cases, I move to a pretty room at the Colony Club, where I lie shrouded in stiff linen sheets. Chintz curtains drawn, traffic noises outside. My illness makes me feel frail and childlike. Lying above the ballroom where I used to suffer in dancing class, only a wall away from the building where I grew up, I am once more a child. At mealtimes, old Irish maids I look at now with new eyes struggle up the stairs to bring me meals served with sparkling bone china and silver.

Maharaj Kumar flies over to see me "because I am sick." I'm beginning to notice we always translate our feelings or anxieties into externals instead of dealing with the emotional pain or the problems we're facing. I get up, insisting I'm better, and timidly say I'm still upset, however, about Grace's having been in Kalimpong this winter, and that that, really more than the hepatitis, is what's bothering me. In response he has a physical attack similar to malaria—drenching sweat, constant tremors, fever and chills by turns. Underneath I am angry at him for using this device to deflect my demand that he put an end to seeing Grace, angry at him for becoming a victim needing care, sympathy, forgiveness, and angry too at myself for not having the courage to tell him what I think—even more for being almost grateful for the respite his sickness brings from direct conflict. In the shade-drawn hotel room I run about getting quinine pills, nursing him, and hearing him tell me what a real, caring woman I am—a treasure. "It's me that's sick, not you," I rage inside.

Jane M.'s old boyfriend takes me out to the Palisades to get rid of stuff I can't give away and won't need in Sikkim—hundreds of unopened bank notices scooped up from the floor, bags of old laundry, odd clothes, and college notebooks. The stuff is in paper bags in the trunk of the car. We drive up and down looking for a place to burn it. Wherever we stop, there is someone looking at us suspiciously. It's like trying to get rid of a body.

I've given away to Jane and Clover the things I love best—my folk dresses and weaving from around the world, my furry Iranian jacket and leggings. It hurts, but it helps me feel less attached, more purposeful. I keep the more ladylike things given to me by friends' mothers on various

Christmases—suède gloves, slips, cashmere sweaters, chiffon scarves—that never seemed to have much to do with me.

Manhattan Storage has already shipped my furniture. Some of the things—the Sheraton piecrust table, the four-poster bed, and the bureau—I've been using in my apartment, but some (the ship paintings, the little rocker, the Newburyport candlestand, the mahogany highboy) I haven't seen since childhood, when they were packed off to storage from our Long Island house. It will be strange to meet them so far away after so long.

Strange too to meet in Gangtok some of the people who are coming out, people from all times of my life—even my grandmother's best friend, who must now be over eighty. Aside from my close friends and relations who are coming, a group of Aunt Mary's friends from Washington and New York plan to attend, which makes me feel ambivalent. In one way it's good, as some are quite distinguished: a) They will see Sikkim. b) My side will look more dignified in the eyes of Cocoola et al. On the other hand, it's false: a) They have nothing to do with me. I'm being falsely defined at a time that should be central to me. b) They'll take up much-needed space in the chapel which should go to Sikkimese who have a stake in the matter. Several of my real friends, including Clover and Robin, can't come.

I go for the first time in my life to the hairdresser's, where my hair is coated with lacquer, and drive to the airport, where crowds of photographers take pictures and exclaim over the amount of luggage I'm taking, until Aunt Mary embarrasses me by saying (although I try to explain to her Sikkim isn't part of India nor is my fiancé a maharaja), "What do you expect if you're going to India to marry a maharaja?"

On the plane I feel vaguely cheerful, rather blank. In Karachi, conscious of the moment but detached, I change in the Pan Am airport stewardess room from my Western dress, in which Clover advised me to leave the country, into a long Sikkimese robe.

6

MAHARAJ KUMAR has detailed Tseten Tashi, photographer, orchid grower, and old friend of the royal family, along with some government ministers—dressed in silk, marking the official level of the occasion—to meet us at the Calcutta airport. Tseten Tashi is a lovable man, eccentric and enterprising. He boasts with some justification that because of his fame in plant journals around the world, he has done more than any other Sikkimese to make the country well known. Over the past few years I've gotten to know him pretty well, visiting his photography shop in town to buy pink-and-green-tinted postcards of sunsets over Kanchendzeugna, yaks, and monasteries, watching him fish about (usually in vain) in the shoe boxes where he keeps the negatives of pictures that he says are particularly rare. According to him, he is famous for discovering and losing things. Aside from several plants he's discovered, he once found some esoteric bark, which he thought might be useful for treating cancer, mailed it off to a pharmaceutical firm in Switzerland that expressed interest in it, and then never could remember what he'd sent or where to find the original samples among his piles of storage boxes.

I'm delighted and reassured to meet him now—he is genuinely glad to see me, bubbling with enthusiasm about a new hybrid rose he has named in my honor. Even so, I choose undiplomatically to drive back into Calcutta with Maharaj Kumar's cousin Jigmie Dorji, Prime Minister of Bhutan. I'm fond of Tseten Tashi, but I love Jigmie, warm-hearted, ebullient, protective. I still feel a rush of gratitude to him for making me feel at home in Calcutta during my stays there in our engagement period. He's very close to Maharaj Kumar, looks up to him a lot, claiming him as his "guru" in the development work he's doing in Bhutan. Jigmie is half Sikkimese, as his mother is the sister of Maharaj Kumar's father, but when the two men are together, they spar, teasing about each other's country. Now Jigmie says, laughing, he's glad to take us as long as it doesn't mean a diplomatic rift with a friendly neighbor.

The police commissioner in Sikkim, an Indian trained in the States, on deputation in Sikkim, has come down to meet us at Bagdogra, the small subfoothill airport to which we fly from Calcutta. Like Tseten Tashi and Jigmie, he's another friend, courtly, pro-American, and full of comfortably puerile jokes, which he rattles off nonstop, inviting response in a genial, hopeful way. His relative familiarity makes Aunt Mary feel more at ease. She is a little nettled at the attention I've been getting; from "my niece," as she used to introduce me, she's switched, in a rather acid voice, to introducing herself, "I'm just Hope's aunt." Still, she's coping gallantly with the strangeness of the situation. At one point I overhear her telling a long story about a majordomo to a Nepalese politician, who stares at her uncomprehendingly, with equal fortitude.

Now we are all exhausted, and the police commissioner's jokes from the front of the car wash over us, blandly soothing. On the hills in the distance a glow of fires sparks the twilight. I interrupt the commissioner's flow to ask if these have any significance. (I've heard there's been a small vocal demonstration against the marriage, led by Kazini in Kalimpong, and am concerned that the lights, which I've never seen before, have something to do with it.) "They're in your honor," the commissioner replies, which I know is false. Later I find out the fires are the results of spring field-burning, a practice the government is still trying to control among several tribal groups in Sikkim.

At the border town on the Sikkim side of the river across from India, the police bagpipe band is playing "Over the Sea from Skye." From a group of people, a couple of little girls, one Nepali, one Marwari, their faces shining in torchlight, come forward with garlands. Blackness envelops. Only the rough swerve of the car indicates the jaggedness of the road we're on. I'm blinded and shocked when, turning off into the palace guesthouse road, there's a sudden dead-white flare of arc lights, and right on the roadside is a bank of reporters and TV cameramen yelling "Kiss her" to Maharaj Kumar.

Sherzad, who has been here a day or so, comes in the evening to tell me that Grace has been here for a week, staying at the palace. She's now moved down to the same bungalow Sherzad's housed in, where, according to Sherzad, you can't sit down, because the paint is still wet on all the new furniture, even the thunder box. "I'll keep an eye on her movements," Sherzad says conspiratorily. I'm torn between wanting to choke Sherzad and in a morbid, curious way wanting to know everything. In room number two, the little room in the guesthouse which Clover used to have last summer, I cry until early morning and finally sleep as the light comes up over the hills.

There is no privacy; the guesthouse, like every other house in Gangtok, is full to bursting. The morning of the wedding, as I'm in the bathroom getting my hair lacquered into a boxlike shape by a Polish hairdresser who's been brought up from Calcutta, photographers straddle the doorway taking pictures. Cocoola and the ayahs are fussing with the wraparound Lepcha dress it's been decided I should wear as a gesture to the Lepchas, the earliest inhabitants of Sikkim. Cocoola, a talented jewelry designer, has designed the silver belt hung with a scythe—the customary symbol of a girl's coming into adulthood in Sikkim. She herself wears a dagger, which I rather envy.

I don't know what to make of my sister-in-law. Sometimes she is overwhelmingly kind and generous. Sometimes, as well as being obviously cruel (she introduced Grace to Maharaj Kumar), I think she is practicing downright voodoo on me, or at least on my relationship with her brother. Last night, having just remarked how inauspicious it was for something to break on a wedding eve, she purposely smashed her millet-beer saucer, scattering the millet seeds (also inauspicious). Worse still, the more I look at the brocade pattern of my wedding dress, the more it seems that it has been stitched with the wrong side exposed. In Sikkim a sign of death.

Push, pull—I feel inanimate. The half Valium some nervous guest in my party has given me is beginning to work. I've never had one before and feel like a stone. The only thing that touches me is the children. They've been running around since breakfast, wearing new silk dresses, showing me the toys people have given them. In the purse I'm carrying to the ceremony is a crumpled letter Yangchen sent me in New York, telling me to hurry home. It's my luck piece.

The groom's party, including Nepali and Bhutia Lepcha ministers, have come down to the guesthouse to escort me up to the chapel. In the old days, and even now in some rural parts, the bride's family is supposed to fight off the groom's party with stinging nettles in a mock show of reluctance to have the girl leave the house. Both sides of the wedding families sing long rehearsed and extemporized songs insulting each other. Unlike India, there is no custom of dowry among most groups in Sikkim. In fact, the groom-to-be often has to pay a bride price or devote a certain amount of time working for his prospective father-in-law.

Today everyone mills about in polite embarrassment—the escort party wearing national dress, either Bhutia long silk robes, Lepcha striped handloomed tunics, or Nepali jackets and jodhpurs. On my side, the women wear long dresses, the men tails and high hats which somehow they've managed to carry here.

The Tibetan astrologer has marked my fingertips with auspicious invisible marks and tucked an arrow in the long ceremonial scarf around my neck. (He is not the man who advised us to postpone our marriage last year—the famous "black year" prediction that the press have picked up and keep writing about, as he has died during the past year—ironically, the only dramatically bad thing to have happened here during these past twelve months.) We move off in cars, past throngs of villagers, a sorry comedown from the bridal cavalcades that used to arrive on horse from Lhasa only a decade ago.

The service is simple—an exchange of scarves symbolizing a social contract between the two families, and a prayer for auspiciousness. In the old days, marriages were purely secular. Monks would not attend weddings, since it would sanction an occasion presumably leading to birth and rebirth, the thing most to be avoided in the Buddhist world view. Now monks, even though they don't preside, attend weddings, and today the lamas from Pemayangste, Sikkim's national monastery, have come.

With an aide-de-camp from the palace shepherding me, I glide along the polished floor of the Tsuk Lhakhang, or royal chapel, to light the butter lamps in front of the images of Buddha and Guru Padma-sambhava, the teacher who brought Buddhism to Tibet and Sikkim in the eighth century. Lighting the lamps, I'm grateful for the moment of pause, of concentration. As each wick catches, it seems a spark of my will, my determination to make this marriage happy. I offer a silent prayer of thanks and promise to the image of Buddha, feeling awed, as I always do, by the generous unparochial nature of Buddhism. Although I'm marrying a senior incarnation, a man who will one day be head of the Church of Sikkim, no one has yet mentioned to me the possibility of some form of initiation, let alone conversion.

Before going to sit down on the gilded, carved throne next to my husband, I reach up to the high throne where my father-in-law, looking rather frail and isolated, sits, to give him a silk scarf, the ceremonial form of greeting here. He bows his head and gives me a kindly smile, as he does to Aunt Mary, who is next to offer a scarf. There's been no rehearsal—at least I haven't rehearsed—and I appreciate dimly the smooth way the ceremony is moving.

Having lighted the lamps and offered the long white scarf, my active participation is over and I can sit quietly at my husband's side, feeling his presence, glad to be still, wishing only this moment didn't have to be shared with so many people. Halfway through the ceremony he smiles at me mischievously and tosses me a wedding ring—made, as I'd asked, from the small vein of gold in Sikkim, roughly hammered and plain. It has no part in the service, and the intimacy of his gesture clearly pleases him as much as me. Also giving me confidence is the closeness of the children. They sit next to me on somewhat lower daises, fidgeting, tired from sitting cross-legged, trying out different seated positions. Yangchen is pulling the cord of a stuffed animal, a green sea monster, that speaks in a gravelly voice when the cord is pulled. She is experimenting, letting the cord rewind slower and faster. Through the chanting of the lamas comes a drawn-out bass drawl: "You sher gotta purty dress."

Across from us on rows of benches sit my party, Sikkimese and Indian dignitaries, and the twelve ambassadors, including John Kenneth Galbraith, who, at my uncle's request, is acting as witness to our marriage. My husband is palpably happy that many notables have come. It is breakthrough recognition for Sikkim, a chance to show the country's achievement and prospects. Nehru himself had planned to come, but to Maharaj Kumar's disappointment, he later couldn't for some reason. Another disappointment: Jigmie isn't here. He has had to rush home because the King of Bhutan suffered a heart attack a few days ago. I've heard there has been trouble seating the ambassadors, since some were charged particularly to represent their heads of state, thereby upsetting the ordinary notions of seniority. Nevertheless they look glad to be here, intrigued by the ceremonies. Ambassador Galbraith is eating the offering of sweet rice from the cup before him; every guest has one. It's too early in the service—it's supposed to be symbolically offered first to the Buddha—but he looks relaxed and contented.

All the guests in the chapel have filed by to give their scarves and in some cases their love, my face cracking from the strain of concentrating on each well-wisher. Now the crowds of people outside the chapel surge through the doors to bring their presents and scarves. Tibetan refugees with skins and trays of cheese, Nepalis with baskets of orchids, North

Sikkimese carrying rolls of bright handwoven blankets, uniformed school-children carrying autograph books. Watching them squeeze into the chapel, their enthusiasm and interest so great, I feel another pang of sadness and guilt that this big crowd of people, including the press from the States, Europe, and India—some of whom are only idly curious about the service and Sikkim—should have taken up so much space. This feeling is strengthened after the ceremony, when I see the masses of people who pack the chapel lawn.

Everyone is in his or her best. Many of the women are wearing jewelry much more elaborate and showier than mine—huge turquoise-studded charms and ropes of coral and seed pearls. I admire them, but I'm glad I have the delicate cluster of little charm boxes designed by Cocoola. I'm glad too to have left the heavy purple and gold cape embroidered with dragons behind in the chapel, where it stands on the throne propped up by its own stiffness. The TV and magazine photographers running through the crowd are bowled over by all the color and beauty. They look like distracted chickens chasing after scattered feed. It's almost impossible to focus on any one thing. There are groups of Nepali men in bright red tunics and jodhpurs, playing wildly curled horns, Sikkim guards in scarlet jackets and striped kilts, Sikkimese nobles in jewel-colored antique silks, North Sikkimese in fur-lined robes leading a caparisoned horse (a present for me that, embarrassingly, dies before I've written a thank-you note), and bevies of beautiful young Nepali and Sikkimese women wearing different national dress, who move around together, conscious of their impact on the photographers. Sound as well as sight overwhelms one, and the movie crews with audio equipment rush from the Sikkim Police Bagpipe Band to the Indian Army Band, which has been lent for the occasion to the various villagers performing on drums and horns. Like a medieval revel, everything, however disparate, happens at once.

At least the press are somewhat happy. My husband tells me in a worried aside as we move down through the throngs to the luncheon tent that all the press arrangements seem to have gone haywire, that they are resisting the suggested pool arrangement, that background releases on Sikkim have been rejected as too long, and finally that someone, probably Kazini, has circulated a libelous poem about the marriage and the royal family, leaving a copy under every door in the hotel in which the press are housed.

Aside from the press problems, Sherzad reports that Indian guests are making off with cases of liquor and putting through extravagant trunk calls on the phones installed in the guesthouses. In the banquet tent, because of an influx of local gate-crashers, there is pushing and shoving to be at the head of the buffet line.

It's dismaying. I know from the months of reports I'd received in New York that all the arrangements have been worked out with pains-taking care. I want people to stop, to be still, to appreciate and be grate-ful for nuances. I feel responsible for the U.S. contingent and want to will them into giving a good impression of America to the Sikkimese. My own friends, except for Sherzad, who looks increasingly morose, seem fine—independent and cheerful. It's the older, more cynical crew from the U.S. I worry about. I want them to be impressed by Sikkim, as much as I want them to impress Sikkimese with Americans.

Just as the palace has taken care of the arrangements for the presents the bride's party, according to tradition, has offered in the chapel (tiger skins, sacks of grain, yak tails), my husband and his sisters also have taken care of the arrangements for the party that my side is to give—even to hurriedly printing new invitations, because the cards we'd had printed at Tiffany's had used the Indian title "Maharaj Kumar and Kumarani" instead of "Crown Prince and Princess," which the Sikki-mese prefer. At our lunch, in contrast to the delicious Sikkimese food served at the preceding groom's banquet, all the food is what is eu-phemistically known in Sikkim as "English," and the band brought up from Goa underscores the Western motif by playing, somewhat inap-propriately, Stephen Foster medleys and "Dixie."

The festivities are scheduled to last for a week—not a great length of time in Sikkimese and Tibetan customs; people often travel great dis-tances for a celebration. (In Lhasa, Cocoola says, some picnic gambling parties used to last for a month.) By the first night, because of emo-tional strain and remaining traces of hepatitis, I'm exhausted—too tired to notice or appreciate what is happening. In a blur I see my friends' faces, the notables, and occasionally, like a branch floating in water to be snatched at, my husband, pensive and beautiful. Mostly I stay with the children, who are still up, full of energy. Tenzing, newly barbered, his curly hair plastered down, dances with me, laughing cheerfully at my clumsiness.

I come up very late at night to my husband, who's talking with the Maharaja of Jaipur, who, true to legend, has brought with him his own cases of champagne, and beg him to please come back to the house. He motions to me impatiently. "Can't you see I've got an obligation to our guests." Tears trickle down my face, and, feeling immense loneliness and self-pity, I walk alone through the big tent to the palace, where I'm caught up by my husband, who, still impatient, says he's been urged to follow by the maharaja.

The next morning, waking up in his room, which has been cleared of its piles of belongings, the sun shining in through the bathroom window, the only window we have, I feel my cells have somehow changed. All my life unconsciously I've been led to believe that being married is a finite transfiguration, an altered plane of existence.

That afternoon, as we walk around the outside of the house together, he looks at me and says, "Just now, before the wedding, she said she wanted to have a baby by me. I told her it was a ridiculous idea, not to be silly." I don't know if he is reassuring me.

I've seen her face, white, laughing, among the mass of guests. At one party she dances with him. The man who is making an official movie for the Government of Sikkim films them in close-up—my husband's face alive, sparkling, tender—cuts the shot (I can still see her arm), and juxtaposes it with a close-up of me. When the frames are flashed one after the other, it will look as if he and I are together.

In the midst of parties, four days after the wedding, a cable informs us that Uncle Selden has died of a heart attack on his way up to the States from the Virgin Islands. Cocoola, who receives the cable, as it's addressed to the "Princess of Sikkim" ("If you'd use 'Crown Princess,'" she says, "this kind of thing wouldn't happen"), sits on the cable for a day, knowing her brother's sense of duty will make him insist on accompanying me back to Washington for the funeral, spiking some of the celebrations paid for and still continuing. As she anticipated, we do travel back to Washington together, my husband's Sikkimese sense of filial-by-marriage courtesy for Aunt Mary overriding the importance of the public-relations festivities in Gangtok.

In Calcutta, in the rush to get off and without time to think, my husband calls in an officer of the American Consulate so that I may formally renounce my U.S. citizenship in order to qualify for an Indian Protected Person passport on which Sikkimese travel. Under Sikkimese law, to protect the integrity of the small country, dual citizenship is impossible. My citizenship will be watched closely—a political test case, my husband says—particularly since Kazini, the Belgian-born wife of his political enemy Kazi Lhendup Dorji, has refused to change her British papers for Sikkimese nationality and has not been allowed to live in Sikkim. She has had to stay in Kalimpong, an Indian border town. Although her only son, a tea planter in Assam, had been killed in an accident a few days earlier, she'd been at the wedding parties, wearing her dramatic black mourning dress, talking down Sikkim to reporters. Still, although I knew I had to give up my citizenship so that the Sikkimese would respect me for conforming to their laws, I didn't want to do it this way. The words of the official renunciation read almost like a declaration of treason.

We reach Washington exhausted, in time for the service and the burial at Arlington. My feelings are in conflict. I'm proud to see how much Aunt Mary values my husband's coming, irritated with him for performing this family duty so gracefully at the same time that he is curt and thoughtless to me. When we get back to Gangtok, Grace and some of the guests are still there.

7

I'M GLAD to be home, back in the house I'm growing attached to. The journalists who'd come for the wedding described it variously as a doll's house or a New England summer house. (It was built in 1910 in English bungalow style, with a red corrugated iron roof and verandahs that run along the front.) Going from one room to another, I try to find, assimilate, the special qualities of each room before I begin redecorating. I don't feel I'm interfering or assuming Cocoola's prerogative; the house has been left like an old garden. All I'll be doing is reclaiming it.

My husband's little living room, lit by the glowing rose carpet, is almost perfect—I just need to change the salmon-pink covers of the banquettes that have been put on in haste before the wedding. Also, later I will find another solution for the windows lining the room, which at present are hung with limp, skimpy curtains that droop from enormous valances. In the round corner bay I want to get rid of the eddy of little tables and put the new tree-trunk table from the Indian representative and his wife. They'd been sweet about the sofa set and the table they'd given us, determined that the house needed new furniture, but rather shy, concerned that their present might be construed as patronizing. The set they chose isn't bad either, if we cover it.

The room I really love, at present used for nothing in particular except ironing, stands on the ground floor between Cocoola's room and the verandah, its windows looking out over the lawn and chapel. Some day I want to put together all the many books lying around the house with the books I've brought and make it a library.

The big sitting room across from the room that I visualize as the library is all right at present. The Thankas—religious scroll paintings —lining the walls, a walnut-dyed carpet, and a copper cutout Chinese motif on the ceiling give it character. Some day, though, when we can,

I'd like to get rid of the bulky English sofas that line the walls and have low Sikkimese-style seating. Most important, I'd like to repaint the dreary dun-colored walls and the dark-painted wood that fills the room. All the rooms, in fact, need repainting.

The dining room officially known as the dark dining room, which the children dread going through, is pitch black and smells of mold. Even the dining room proper, which has been added onto this one, is so dark and uninviting, except during the noon sun, that we rarely use it.

Upstairs every room is dark brown and beige. The guest room, although like our room a windowless interior room, could, because of its shape, fireplace, and carpet woven with the Sikkim coat of arms, be cozy. At present it looks ghostly. The bright piece of embroidery that covers one bed emphasizes the shabbiness of everything else—the dark open-mouthed cupboard and the two cracked leather armchairs, springs spiraling out the bottom. This is the room that is said to house the woman ghost my father-in-law used to hear. I don't disbelieve it, but I think a coat of paint might control it. The most cheerful bedroom—small, with windows opening out over the garden and the road leading from the palace gate to the Dewan's house—is the children's room, jammed with their iron bedsteads.

These are the rooms I go into. There are several more I don't enter except on rare occasions: my father-in-law's bedroom and painting studio, which lead off the upstairs verandah, two chapels, an upstairs room stacked shoulder-high with old belongings and papers, known as the clutter room, the kitchen and pantries adjoining the house, and, as a rule, Cocoola's room downstairs.

Cocoola's room has just a bed, a desk, a cupboard, piles of files on Tibetan refugee work, and tin trunks lining the walls which contain her clothes and belongings. On the occasions I'm invited in I'm always startled to see that my sister-in-law, with her love of beauty, her almost vain passion for detail in the texture, color, and design of her clothes and jewelry, can live in this unfocused room, bare of any loveliness. As she's fed up with people looking at it, even her Thanka over the fireplace is sewn shut. It seems to me possible that the transient look of her room, the piles of trunks, may be a statement of anger about the loss of her belongings and life in Tibet, her anomalous state as a sister who had married and gone out of the family back into her childhood home—unusual in Sikkimese custom.

Although she never says anything directly, she is full of anger, hard and shining as a diamond. Sometimes she pauses and allows me to be charmed, wistful for the moment to continue. Sometimes we have tea together in the cold spring afternoons by the fire in her room. I feel bad for her—I, an outsider, usurping what she has left after the loss of Tibet—her childhood home, even her title of Princess, and her precedence. When we're alone, in almost an exaggeration of politeness, I defer to her, trying to let her know I empathize, feel guilt at my intrusion.

At her brother's request, she's agreed to stay on for a year to see that there's a smooth household transition. Feeling it's presumptuous—another raid on her territory—I've not been going to the kitchen, which, black with smoke from wood- and coal-burning ovens, is in any case inhospitable. Much of the house remains a mystery to me. Sometimes I even think there's a secret room in the house I don't know of. From our bedroom to the guest room you have to go down a very long, winding corridor. Some room must be between the two rooms. I keep looking out our bathroom window, trying to figure it out from the outside.

In May, a month or so after our wedding, we take Tenzing and Wongchuk to England to enroll them in a preparatory school my husband has selected. I regret they'll be so far away, both from home and their culture. Also, they're going before I've really got to know them and feel easy with them. Despite their respectfulness and Tenzing's gregariousness, developing rapport with them has taken time, and I still feel an awkward twinge of dancing-class shyness. My husband, however, despite my mild remonstrance, feels there is no other solution, that they are not studying enough in Darjeeling, that, unlike himself, they must receive a proper academic education fitting them for any work. Like his brothers and sisters, when he was growing up, he too had been discouraged by the Sikkimese landlords from getting a full formal schooling. Defensive and frustrated by the patchiness of his own formal education, he is determined his children will not be deprived.

Before driving the boys to their school through blossom-filled Kent, we stay at an economy hotel in London. The days are spent indoors watching television, marking clothes, and looking over the room-service menu. Maharaj Kumar's second sister, Coola, and her husband are here too with their children, who are also about to enter schools. I've never traveled in a group like this and feel constrained. Above and beyond our big family group, we are also generally with English friends, some of them rather starchy, some of them accepting, and most of whom we seem to be dependent on in one way or another.

The newspapers are full of our visit. We've received so much publicity, I don't know how we're ever going to get away on our own. I want so much to be alone with my husband, or, if this is not possible, at least to push myself to the front of his consciousness, so that he will allow other duties and relationships to fall into place after he's recognized the primacy of our relationship. Aside from the frustrating lack of privacy and intimacy, which I can articulate more clearly here than in Gangtok, I'm jealous. All the time on the plane he wrote postcards, teasing, saying they were to his girlfriends in Gangtok, and then in the same breath saying, "Don't worry, they've all given me up." Now there is a letter from a girl, torn into shreds, the ink spreading but still readable, swirling in the bowl of the toilet.

We do have a honeymoon, a few days to ourselves, but he is restless, impatient. No romance. It is almost a relief to get back to the structure and context of Gangtok, where the sunny routine peace, the dull entrapment, diffuses my urgency, blunts my ambitions to have a direct emotional connection with him.

Although I feel powerless to effect any change, I am obsessed with his infidelities. Chiefly I still think of him and Grace, but in Sikkim also, now I'm here long enough for my eyes to focus, I feel all kinds of threats. Worse still, in worrying so much about his flirtations, I've begun to identify with him, act like a silent pimp, picking out in my mind the girl I fear he will next go after. One day as I'm jeeping along a rutted road through the jungle in North Sikkim to join my husband, who's preceded me by a few days, I see a very pretty girl through a fringe of trees, walking down the valley from the spot where his camp is. She is carrying a spray of white orchids and wears one in her hair. I know he's given them to her, or if he hasn't already, he will.

The police commissioner and the Dewan, even when I'm present, are always teasing him, as if I were just one of the boys, praising him in a schoolboyish way about his conquests. I have no way of distinguishing boast from reality. Ironically, this is the same bawdiness, camaraderie, I enjoyed when we were first engaged and I was the object of comment, the sexual prize he'd won and shown off to his cronies. Now the prize is someone else and I have become neuter.

In June, to make some kind of statement of femaleness, of wifeliness, I become pregnant. My husband is pleased about the coming child. And by my condition. In Sikkim a woman is chiefly connected to her husband as mother of his children. Often, instead of the word for wife, she is called, as an honorific, "So-and-so ki Am" ("Mother of so-and-so").

Much of the summer my husband is away on trips to different parts of the country and to India, where he is looking for a suitable man to serve as Dewan, or Prime Minister, of Sikkim. It's the first time that he is getting to choose whom he wants; up to now the Dewans (all Indians) have been sent here by the government of India. The new man too will be Indian but presumably more answerable to Sikkim.

When he's gone, the only people around other than His Highness my father-in-law, who stays all day in his suite of rooms, are the servants, his secretary—an efficient sharp-tongued woman—and the aide-de-camp. Copying Aunt Mary, I've invited all the government officers' wives up to the palace for a series of tea parties, on the theory that we could get to know each other better than at the official parties, where they are overshadowed by the rather dominating Indian ladies from the Residency. Although everything goes smoothly, and I'm proud of the spanking new organdy-covered tea tables, the ladies sit in glum silence and make no effort to return.

My loneliness is sharpened by having nothing to do now that my only task—often ludicrous, as most of the presents we got were so odd (miniature silver-plated tanks, for example)—writing thank-you letters, is finished. Sing and smoke and cry. Eat little at meals and live mostly on orange juice, gingersnaps, and the mounds of chocolate, some of it already gone wormy, I've brought back from our trip to England.

Upstairs in my room I listen to Joan Baez records all day and cry. I know how the Sikkimese got their eyes—little damn Mongolian eyes; they damn well cried all the time. '

When Yangchen, on my plea, is allowed to come back from school in Darjeeling, I sit with her on her bed singing all the songs I know. Hush little baby, don't you cry—gushes of tears here—you know your mammy was born to die. She watches with six-year-old puzzled eyes.

The convent she'd been attending in Darjeeling had hoaxed us; she'd never learned how to read or write a word. Her letters from school, always beginning "Please send me a parcel," had been copied off the blackboard from a model written by a nun Yangchen calls Mother Gnatius Egg. Since her return home I've begun teaching her in a piece-meal manner, three to four hours a day. The day she learns how to read my head hums. Yangchen picks along the line of words. There's no apparent reason for it—suddenly she just can. Rain pattering down on the tin roof, we sit on the bed in her room drinking Darjeeling tea—mine black, Yangchen's thick with milk. Although her present education is patchy and excludes arithmetic, I'm nevertheless determined to keep her home. Aside from the lack of successful education in Darjeeling, and her emotional need, teaching her is the only thing I have to do—and further, she is my only friend.

In late summer there is consternation over my father-in-law's health. Many doctors arguing. Eventually he is flown out, wrapped in blankets, to a clinic in England. At the motherly insistence of the Indian Representative's wife, who senses my isolation, I accompany my husband, thrilled to be returning to the West, frightened, however, of his being back near Grace. I beg him not to go to Brussels to see her, or, if he must, to promise, at least, not to sleep with her. He comes back several days afterward and during the night talks in his sleep about the fine wife he's got, that he should be grateful, and that, God help him, he'd promised not to.

On our return to Sikkim we find an NBC team that has finally arrived to do a "scenic beauty cum social development" film on the country. For months the Indian External Affairs Ministry has been putting off NBC with all sorts of excuses—publicity is part of external affairs, my husband is busy weeding Communists out of his retinue, it might cause a breach of defense and security, and other such reasons. At the same time the same ministry has had the nerve to sponsor a CBS team to go all over the country filming Indian defense efforts, the one thing NBC isn't interested in. It is the first time I've had personal experience of how circumscribed Sikkim is by India, and, despite the fact that it's only people from the Indian Representative's staff who have been even mildly friendly to me here, the injustice makes me furious. Only after NBC and I tackle the Indian Representative, threatening to expose the excuses the team has been given, do they capitulate and withdraw their objection to making the film.

At the time filming finally begins I'm seven months pregnant, my stomach coming out to meet their zoom shots of me walking through our small, shabby house à la Jackie Kennedy, who has recently been featured in a White House tour. I plead that there is nothing to show, but they insist on the format, promising that the film will be 90 percent about the country of Sikkim but needs a "news peg" to hang on. To comply, I place every beautiful object we own within camera range. "And here," I say, looking at a bowl and goblet crafted well over two thousand miles away in Tibet, "is a typically Sikkimese bowl and a typically Sikkimese goblet on a typically Sikkimese table."

The most difficult typically Sikkimese sequence is the typically Sikkimese meal. Every time I get beyond the rice I get hysterical. My mind goes blank and I begin to giggle. I and all the crew except the director crack up laughing. We repeat the take four times, the director getting sourer and sourer, until someone finally brings the *McCall's* article on the wedding, in which there's my alleged favorite typically Sikkimese menu. "Nettle soup!" the director hisses. "We start off with nettle soup!" At least in the palace sequence my feet are on the ground; outside, when I'm not expected to be doing walking shots, for some technical reason I'm asked to stand on a crate. Drawing my brocade wedding cape around me, I speak of the peacefulness of Sikkim. They've asked me to wear the cape for color, and I've agreed as it somewhat hides my stomach, which they've refused to explain in the film for fear of making it topical. BOOM go the enormous artillerylike dynamite charges that are used by the Indians in building border roads around here—BOOM, BOOM, BOOM. The orange crate vibrates beneath me.

In the midst of the filming His Highness dies. During the weeks he's been in the Calcutta hospital, a frail moth pinned down with needles and tubes, I've grown to admire him more and more. No matter how tired or how much in pain he might be, whenever visitors came, he'd reach out to them and, with real concern, ask how they were.

When he is dying, Cocoola, composed, waits at the head of his bed to make sure no one touches him, interfering with his last breath, impeding his onward journey. My mother-in-law, from whom he's been separated for many, many years, and her daughter Lhanzin come, shaking with tears.

His coffin, tiny, triangular, as he is embalmed in the lotus position, is kept on the throne in the royal chapel for some time, as prescribed by astrologers, and then taken by palanquin up to the royal cremation ground above Gangtok. Thousands of villagers pour up the winding road to follow the procession and help bear the coffin. Monks have come from all over Sikkim. Rhythmic bass chanting of prayers, not only for the late King but for the enlightenment of all sentient beings. We sit for hours on the hillside in bright sunshine, watching the flames, peaceful. I feel that the ceremony, unlike Western funerals, is an integrate of man and nature, death and life.

We can't play the record player for forty-nine days of mourning. I play it softly, my ear against the machine. My husband is being a bastard—in great part, I think, because of all the pressure India is putting on him, saying, "Poor Sikkim! What will happen now?" as if everything will collapse. They're using His Highness' death as an excuse to decry Sikkim's situation. Unfair, particularly as it's been for many years —twenty years—really my husband who's been piloting all the development, doing all the work.

The home front also imposes an enormous burden. The day all the relations come to bow to him and me I'm sickened by the insidiousness of the occasion—the insistence on ossifying us into an institution, a contract that denies both of us, but more him, the right of individuality. I can see why he's acting this way, but I can't stand it. He picks Christmas Eve, which he knows I've been looking forward to for many months, to erupt. Cocoola and I and the kids cower in her room like early Christians, trying to wrap presents for the children, folding tissue paper carefully so it won't rustle, when he stomps in, furious because he's just learned that Cocoola has sent a Christmas tree down to the NBC crew. "It is a time for mourning," he shouts. "You want everyone to know during a time like this that you are making a Christmas party for a bunch of foreigners?" He rants at her the whole evening, and she sits there saying little. The children have long ago put themselves to bed, weeping.

One thing I'm going to do despite his anger is get a room ready for the baby. It will be born in a month and nothing has been prepared. When Chogyal (the old Sikkimese title my husband has reverted to instead of Maharaja) goes to Calcutta, I get the aide-de-camp to take all the furniture out of our room (except the altar, which I don't dare touch) and put it in an unused room, with a window facing the mountains, across from the guest room. It's the room, I hear, in which my husband's uncle and previous incarnate, Chogyal Sidkyong, was killed —either by gross ineptitude or deliberately—by a Bengali physician employed by the British because Sidkyong had proved too wise and strong an obstacle to British paramountcy in Sikkim. Although the details of Chogyal Sidkyong's death are grisly, nevertheless, unlike the haunted guest room, this room seems neutral, free of spirits, and is sun-filled, even though a sparrow-nested eave hangs over the window. It connects with a big square room facing onto the verandah—one of my late father-in-law's rooms—paint on layer of paint peeling off the walls, floors cluttered with boxes of medical supplies, strong, sour odors of medicine stenching the air. I want this room for the baby. Every day, preparatory to painting them, we scrape the walls, and burn fresh juniper to get rid of the smell. The old carpenter who works for the palace is copying my small rocker from Newburyport, now in Yangchen's room, for a nursing chair, copying it faithfully even to the false-start gashes made by some seventeenth-century Massachusetts furniture maker.

Waking up every morning to the chirp of birds, I'm grateful for the window and the outdoors. When Chogyal returns from Calcutta and reprimands me for making house changes during the mourning period, I cry in self-pity but am secretly proud and self-justified. It can't be a crime to get one of the outlying storage rooms ready for this new baby. The hell with it.

The room is painted—pink—but still stinks. The rocker is perfect, except that the runners are out of scale and grind back and forth awkwardly. Still, there, perfect, keeping me awake with anticipation, the room pulses expectantly.

Chogyal's business partner, fat Mr. Gandhi, takes us around to look at apartments in Calcutta, as Chogyal feels that the Grand Hotel is too uncomfortable and expensive for a long confinement and we can't continue to stay at the governor's palace. One day Mr. Gandhi takes us to an airy Anglo-Indian Victorian apartment over a nightclub on Park Street that scares me by its closeness to cabaret stars. Another day he takes us to a new penthouse apartment in a high building. We speed up in a chandelier-lit teakwood elevator and are disgorged onto a wall-less floor, open to the sky, divided only by bamboo uprights. "Under completion," Mr. Gandhi murmurs.

We finally rent an apartment near the Geological Survey Headquarters in what is considered a fashionable part of town. Crumbling mansions once polished white with conch shells. I am happy here, the most private (despite the aide-de-camp and servant) we've been since our marriage, grateful to my husband for providing this nest before our baby is born.

Our dining room looks out over a low rooftop covered with potted plants. Every morning a gardener who fusses over the plants spreads a carpet westward on the roof and takes time off to say his prayers. At midday a woman comes up to grind spices. In the evening a boy, maybe his son, joins the man and they fly paper kites.

Each day I wake up to the sound of hawkers selling curd, a street entertainer who plays the hurdy-gurdy, and the cawing of crows and vultures that wheel by in the red Calcutta sky.

As there is little ready-made furniture in the city, I look for bargains, for anything, in secondhand stores. Alarming the proprietors, who look apprehensively at my pregnant belly, my skirts pulled above my ankles, I climb ladders in urine-fumed storage lofts. The Muslim tailors who have promised to sew curtains can't come, as communal riots in the city make it impossible for them to move about. The air-conditioning units are still not installed. For a week each wall has a gaping hole. "It's Indian air conditioning," Sherzad says.

Sherzad, glad to be away from Delhi and the lines of suitors who she claims are all four feet tall, has come to stay until the baby is born. Going to bargain in the secondhand stores, we hold our breath, run in, talking very fast, run out to the street, breathe, and run in again to close the deal.

Chogyal, despite my plea, has left for Brussels. When he's gone, the erratic swinging of the overhead fans in our bedroom scares me. I'm sure the blades will fly off and behead me. I start sleeping on the terazzo floor, my head behind the freestanding cupboard.

Some days we are so busy getting the apartment organized that we don't eat anything until evening. One night I realize it is six and I'm only now taking Yangchen, dressed in her sundress and sun hat, out for lunch. "Never mind, Mummy," she says, tapping her straw brim, "this is my moon hat." Some days I take Yangchen out to Firpo's, an elegant mirror-lined Art Deco restaurant of the thirties, and we sit eating prawns gratiné and drinking sweet iced coffee, the heavy air conditioning making us prickle with goose bumps. Midway at almost every meal Yangchen screws up her face, sighs apologetically, and says, "Mummy, I've got to throw up," and we file by the leering pianist in dark glasses, whom Yangchen calls Mr. Jackal, on our way to the bathroom.

My water bursts early one morning. I've read just enough of the baby books to know I must go to the hospital. I'm so scared. I feel such a martyr, pretend-grown-up. My first duty is to get Yangchen to eat breakfast and then take her to her cousin's to spend the day. The aide-de-camp, who has been left with me, is anxious, doesn't know what to do. By awful coincidence, Sherzad, who's been here all along, has gone off to a tryst with her old Indian beau from New York at some railway junction. My anger at being alone, and the need to take sole charge of myself, give me strength. Officiously I insist that Yangchen eat a more substantial breakfast than usual, and then, dropping her off, drive, scared to death, to the hospital.

Chogyal arrives a few hours before the baby is born and stares at me worried, loving. Mr. Gandhi and the people who've now collected cite an old proverb that says a baby always waits for his father. He's a little cracker of a baby, yellow dewlapped face—a melting candle—black furry forehead and sideburns. In oversized Calcutta-made baby, clothes, laundry-marked X, smug, oblivious, he chews away at my breast.

Flowers, baby clothes, silver baby sets pour in. My husband brings me chocolate cakes from Fleury's, the Swiss restaurant, and sits on the bed stroking my ankles. Slightly sweaty, Gauguin-handsome face, sad, loving gaze—strong, smooth hands dark on my white sheets.

Sweet-talcum, sour-breath-smelling, curled-up baby! Red spiny fingers on my huge, inflated, pretend-grown-up bosom. I lie in bed drowsing, happy in the five-o'clock hospital mornings.

On our return, the length of the road from the Indo-Sikkim border to Gangtok is lined with crowds of villagers pressing forward to see the baby and wish him long life. His father holds him aloft, bundled up in the layers of clothes in which I've wrapped him, limp and white as an old towel. "Maharaj ko jai. Kumar ko jai." "Long live Maharaj. Long live son." Much as I'm worried by the halts, the dust, the heat, the baby's pallor, I'm touched by the commotion. This baby is going to belong, really belong to these people, and through him I will belong too.

It's so hard. Chogyal is in the guesthouse playing Mah-Jongg with his cronies. They all tell him—and me too (although I'm pretty certain it's not the custom of the country)—that men need to have as many women as they want. I lie in the little sitting room drinking wine, a new habit, and reading soft rice-paper letters from Grace that I've found stacked in the clutter room. Sometimes she writes to him on crisp rustling paper that I can feel tucked in his robe when he hugs me. At night I wait for him to untie his sash. If a letter drops to the floor, I read it while he is saying his prayers. Outside, the Sikkim guard is making his rounds, and for the first time the crunch of his boots on the gravel frightens me. What would happen if they, our supporters, suddenly turned against us?

Chogyal returns from the guesthouse; I cry and rail at him until the phone rings. Jigmie, of Bhutan, has been shot dead, killed as he sat playing cards in the Phuntsoling guesthouse on the Indo-Bhutan border. "They got me," he had said. The night before, he'd apparently slept on the floor, as if he knew someone was after him. Jigmie, who'd wanted to quit work, live the good life. Just recently, in Calcutta, he'd told my husband he felt he'd done enough for his country, that he was burning out, that if the king, his boss, would let him go, he really wanted to get out of harness. Glad to be able to put aside my anger and hurt, which now seem insignificant, I hold my husband all night as he lies awake, shaking.

My husband flies to Bhutan, where everyone is taking sides in what seems like a positioning for a civil war. Chogyal feels the Sikkimese presence there diffuses things, helps avert more trouble. There is talk that the gun that killed Jigmie was a gift from the king to his mistress, a Tibetan with ties to the king's family.

We fly back again for the cremation. Jigmie in a tall rectangular standing coffin; the quick rigor mortis from the gunshot has made it impossible to embalm him in the lotus position. All the visiting Indian officials push to be among the first to put their scarves on the pyre. The queen, Chogyal's cousin and Jigmie's sister, who, Chogyal tells me, doesn't know the rumor about the gun, holds onto the king's arm for support, looking up at him, saying again and again, "Oh, Jigmie."

None of the lists of names we've been given by the Dalai Lama or the other high lamas for the baby includes Jigmie. I'm going to use Palden, Jigmie's second name.

According to Sikkimese custom, when Palden is six months old, we take him back to "his mother's home." When Tenzing was little he'd been taken on horseback across the mountain passes on the one-month trek to Lhasa; now Palden, along with his big brothers and sister, comes with us to New York. The portable bassinet is filled with duty-free liquor and perfume we've bought for presents. As we stand in the glare of photographers' lights at the top of the ramp holding the bassinet, we realize that Palden has been left curled up on the Pan Am seat.

Everyone we have entertained at the wedding is entertaining us. We progress from North Carolina through New York ("What a lot of queens there are here," Tenzing marvels, leafing through the Queens Borough telephone book) to Maine, Tenzing and Wongchuk dressed still in their thick school flannels, Yangchen in her Calcutta sundresses, myself embarrassed in long silk robes.

Wherever we go, there is publicity, journalists tracking every move. I feel myself a doppelgänger—both inside my skin and outside of it, recorded, defined in ways that have nothing to do with me. Strangers lie about us, consume us. One day, shabby in a borrowed raincoat, I go into a liquor store to buy supplies for a cocktail party. "Yes," the proprietor is saying to a customer, "I used to date her when she was at Sarah Lawrence. It's very sad. She's had a very sad life. Her mother was killed in a flying accident when she was a baby." Cringing over a low shelf, I wonder whether or not I dare complete the purchase.

Articles on us, as one friend says teasingly, have run the gamut from "Princess Hope's Dilemma: Should I Raise My Children by Astrology or Doctor Spock?" to "My Thirty Favorite Ways of Preparing Yak" to "How Will I Tell My Children About the Communist Chinese in Tibet?" Thank God, in Sikkim I just get the *Herald Tribune*, which Clover has subscribed to for us, and don't have to read or be around when others read the things written about us. The stuff written is not vicious, simply banal, but its effect on me here is paralyzing. We are owned by strangers.

Publicity, dinners, lunches, the public-relations work for Sikkim at Asia House, the International Press Club, the children, the dentist. I'm oppressed even by my friends, my best friends, and feel stone-heavy with guilt and regret. I'm so exhausted, all I want to do is rest, withdraw from any encounter. I'm never coming back. I feel eaten alive, no scrap left to myself. At the same time I can't, I don't want to go back to Sikkim. I can't stand the continuing pain of Chogyal and Grace, whom even now he intends to see on his way back through Europe. "You must act at the strength, the level where you are. No one else can tell you what to do," says the psychiatrist I go to see, looking at me quizically. "No one can tell you."

8

CHOGYAL discounts his personal conduct to himself as well as to me. In his view his wife is an institution, not diminished or even affected by his play. In a sense it's true. Although Grace and I are fixed points in his sphere, it seems to me that we, and, more important, he, are peripheral to his identification with Sikkim. His commitment to Sikkim is so nearly total that in many ways he sees himself and *is* purely an instrument of the country—a self-perception reinforced by the Buddhist disapproval of and ultimate disbelief in ego. Critics see an arrogance in his identification with Sikkim, but in fact it is the reverse— a humility, a surrender. There are two ways to read "L'état, c'est moi."

Even when he sleeps he dreams about Sikkim, often waking abrim with worry or enthusiasm—depending on the dream—for some current project. His childhood monastic training, which was at least as important as the intermittent English education he got in India, gave him a special feeling for traditional Sikkimese values, and his "harnessing" as a young man into government gave him the opportunity and obligation to work for Sikkim. At the time of his coronation in 1965 my husband, who was then forty-two, had already worked for the government for twenty-two years—a long time since, yanked suddenly out of school, he had stood, shyly, stoically by the palace verandah waiting to receive his elder brother's coffin.

Keeping Sikkim free from a merger with India after India's independence in 1947 had been the hardest part of his career. Sikkim's relations with Britain, the preceding power on the Indian subcontinent, had been formalized in 1817 by a treaty with the East India Company. The agreement confirmed the sovereignty of the Sikkimese dynasty (which had ruled Sikkim since early 1600) over all its present territory plus a good deal of land, including the Darjeeling area, the Chumbi valley in Tibet, and chunks of eastern Nepal that were later lost through warfare or diplomacy. Subsequently, in 1861, after the East India Company had given place to the British crown in India, Sikkim and the British government entered into a treaty of "friendship and alliance," which continued up to 1947.

When India became independent in 1947, its new government tried to treat Sikkim like the Indian princely states, which were either voluntarily or forcibly being merged into the new union of India. Maharaj Kumar, on behalf of his father, refused to sign the instrument of accession on the grounds that Sikkim had never owed allegiance to the British crown but had been a separate state tied to Britain by specific rights and obligations specified in the Anglo-Sikkimese treaty. A good deal of pressure from factions in the new Indian government that wanted to merge not only Sikkim but Nepal and Bhutan, Sikkim's larger Himalayan neighbors, was put on the young prince, who, without benefit of advisers (who were disallowed by the Indian Foreign Office), argued Sikkim's case in Delhi in 1950. "And every day," Chogyal was fond of repeating, "I'd go alone and face an army of ministers and their lawyers. The only good thing was that half of them didn't know I could speak English and would rattle on, giving away their legal arguments as if I was a real jungli."

Possibly partly because of Pandit Nehru's fondness for Sikkim (the one place he'd like to retire, he told friends) and his avuncular feelings toward the young prince, and also perhaps because of the advantages of a row of buffer states between India and China, the government of India, after an abortive last attempt at fostering a demand in the country for merger with India, honored Sikkim's historically separate status and signed a new treaty with her in 1950. It was a harsh treaty for Sikkim, as she had to agree that the government of India would be responsible for matters relating to Sikkim's defense, external affairs, and communications, along with other galling areas of control. Still, the treaty was a prize because it specifically stated that India would guarantee the territorial integrity of her new protectorate and also because the very fact of signing it reaffirmed Sikkim's identity and a degree of "international personality."

After that struggle my husband had had to contend with the landlords at home. Like his Uncle Sidkyong, the young ruler who'd been seemingly murdered for his resistance to both British encroachment and local landlord power, the young prince on his return from Delhi fought to further reduce the authority of the landlords, which in 1950 was still considerable. Much of the arable land was in the hands of a few families that exercised almost feudal powers over the tenants who worked for them. "Not easy," Chogyal would say, "not easy—especially when there was the Indian Representative to run to, and he too ready to turn things to India's account."

Chogyal's determination that landlordism be severely reduced in Sikkim stemmed only in small part, I felt, from the traditional alliance between king and commoner against the aristocracy. In my view, Chogyal's motivation seemed to flow from a strong empathy for the Sikkimese "masses"—if you can use that word for comparatively few people. Unlike his relations, who seemed more comfortable with the landlord group (Kazis), he seemed most at home with the non-Kazis, as they were called. Particularly the very simplest class—the drivers, some of the guards, the carpet-weaving women—were his real friends.

The landlord problem resolved by legislation (leaving a residue of sour feelings on both sides), Chogyal's next priority had been to throw himself into Sikkim's development, seeding it both within the country and from India. The Indian government, upon repeated demands and threats from Chogyal to bypass them, finally agreed to give Sikkim financial aid. From the mid-fifties to the mid-sixties the country's revenues and per capita income had multiplied, mostly from development generated within. However, as much as Chogyal fought for aid, he also fought against taking too much, lest the country become economically dependent. "And I don't want them to give us money for things we will get used to, and then have them turn on the screws, cut off aid, and leave us unable to look after them. Everything we set up with aid we must plan to be able to support by ourselves."

One of the results of the higher standard of living in Sikkim, posing another problem, had been the continued immigration there from neighboring countries, particularly from eastern Nepal, where the tribes cut off from the development in the Kathmandu valley, still lived a rather scratch life. The three-party system set up in 1953 was now working fairly smoothly, and Sikkim, the only Himalayan kingdom to have an essentially democratic framework, had had three elections. But the Nepalese majority in the country worried Chogyal and the minority Bhutia Lepcha founders of the country, who feared that some of the Nepalese politicians were not committed to Sikkim but worked instead for a greater Nepal (a concern reflected in the voting system which, under a parity arrangement, gave equal weight to the Bhutia Lepchas and the Sikkimese Nepalis).

Chogyal's present priority, now that economic development had gathered its own momentum, was to work toward ending parity voting, to work for an end of communalism, and to encourage all groups in the country to view themselves as Sikkimese above all, a unity essential for the survival of a small country caught between powerful neighbors. In the early sixties, as both India and China were flexing their nationalism, Sikkim increasingly felt the pinch. Ironically, at the same time that India wanted increased control over Sikkim (and indeed Nepal and Bhutan), Chogyal and the Sikkimese intelligentsia wanted a looser relationship with India, one that, while providing India with any areas, particularly defense, she felt were essential, would reensure Sikkim's separate identity and also return to her some areas over which she felt able to assume authority.

Throughout the twenty-two years of Chogyal's apprenticeship an increasing number of Sikkimese men and a few women had graduated from college in India; a further handful had received degrees abroad. This core of young people, ranging from their early twenties to forty, partly from lack of private opportunity and partly from a strong sense of nationalism firing them with belief that Sikkim could be transformed into a perfect state, had joined government service. They were an impressive group of young men, each passionate about his own skill, whatever it was—agriculture, engineering, forestry—passionate also that this skill should in some way transform Sikkim.

Finally, in 1965 preparations for the coronation bring them together. From high to low, everyone is doing some kind of work for the upcoming festivities. Carpentering, tenting, music rehearsing—everyone is contributing. In the middle of it all the Development Commissioner, who is in charge of events, rackets around in the jeep now known as the "bacon jeep." "There's no room, Princess, so I sit on top of the bacon for the guest bungalows," he says as he rushes in one day to inform my sister-in-law that no more thunder boxes need be made. "It's going to be fantastic," he says. "If we can't get a bloody cannon to fire off twenty-one shots for the Chogyal, the boys are going to use the old Sikkimese way of exploding bamboo. This is it for them. They're so full of spirit, they're about to burst."

All the tailors are busy making Chogyal's and the family's regalia. No one brings up the subject of my dress until the afternoon before the coronation, when Cocoola gives me a beautiful piece of red and gold Chinese brocade. As the master tailors are still busy, a tailor I haven't met before agrees to come and fit me. The piece is too small, and we get the giggles as he turns me from side to side, figuring out where patches can be sewn so they won't be seen. My headdress too hasn't been made, and in the evening Gyalyum, my mother-in-law, who is coming back to the house and taking part in ceremonies for the first time since her separation from the late Chogyal, comes to ask me what jewelry I've got that could be strung for a headpiece. I show her my "coming-out" pearls and my grandfather's watch fobs, and she sighs and laughs. It will be the only crown in the East that ticks.

Early in the morning the tailor comes with my dress wrapped up in newspaper. All day long at events I see him in the crowd, beaming, loving, proud of his dress, and maybe of me too.

Everything is improvised, impromptu. Even the new tiles around the library fireplace, made to impress Mrs. Gandhi, who's staying with us, have been finished by the potter at the last minute and hurriedly jammed in, half upside down, just before she comes. One skinny little tile only two inches wide we make on the spot to chink a gap.

Chogyal is fine in his spectacular gold dragon robes. It is not just the dress but something in his face—a radiance and purpose. We shall make, he says in his speech from the throne, a paradise in Sikkim. We shall not rest until every last bit of want and ignorance is swept from the land. In his voice there is no trace of his occasional stammer, and he speaks out vibrant with feeling. During the ceremony he himself puts the Siberian fur crown on his head. His face has the happiness and sadness of a Madonna's. He is holding Sikkim in trust, an inheritor. The lamas give him the signs of kingship and their blessings for an auspicious rule. "It's not a coronation in the Western sense," he says sweetly to visitors later, "but rather an occasion for lamas to pray for Sikkim's future. In that sense it can and perhaps should be repeated at any time."

At night in the huge tent that has been put up, as at the wedding, on the front lawn, a Goanese dance band in spangled tuxedos sways and croons, backing up a fat Anglo-Indian woman, Delila, who is poured into a tight mermaid-scaled dress. Soon, however, the energies of the Sikkimese guests can't be contained, and sweeping the Indian and European guests along with them, they start forming circles for folk dancing. Hwak, clak, hwak, clak. I've never heard anything like it. It seems everyone in the world is there stamping feet, singing out praise to the new Chogyal and to Sikkim. There is so much connection between the circles of dancers that, even though we're swinging our arms, not holding hands or touching, it's as if an electric current passes through us.

Mr. Thapa is my first friend and has asked me to do my first job. Soon after the coronation was over he came up to the palace for an appointment with me. I'd only seen him before, not spoken to him, shy partly because he is a Sikkimese Nepali, one of "the others." In the two years I'd been here, although I'd hardly had any contacts except for perfunctory ones with the palace staff—mostly Bhutias—I'd sensed the strong differences that exist: not only the class struggle between the "common" and aristocratic Bhutias (the tribe from which my husband was descended, which entered Sikkim from eastern Tibet in the twelfth century) but between the Bhutias and the Lepchas, the aboriginal Mongolian tribe they supplanted.

Still more tense was the relationship between the Bhutias and the vastly more numerous Sikkimese Nepali tribes, which had settled in Sikkim mostly since the beginning of this century. The Bhutia Lepchas were fearful of what they saw as rising Nepali dominance in language, politics, and landholding. The Sikkimese Nepalis were aggrieved by what they viewed as a manufactured system, both political and economic, designed to curb their ascendance. Social and religious differences (the Bhutia Lepchas are Buddhist and the majority of the Nepali Sikkimese Hindu) had been further exacerbated by the essentially communal system of voting.

Mr. Thapa, although categorized as a Sikkimese Nepali, was Magar, coming from a Mongolian tribe speaking a Tibeto-Burman language, early inhabitants of Sikkim. Now these people were listed in the Sikkim census and voting rolls as Nepali because the part of Sikkim they had originally occupied had since been annexed by Nepal. Mr. Thapa, an ardent Sikkimese patriot, was angered by his tribe's categorization as Nepalis. Further, he was troubled by all the census categories—devised by the Indian government—as he felt the labels were not merely inaccurate but added to the country's polarization.

Eighty percent of the so-called Sikkimese Nepalis here were, like Mr. Thapa, of Mongolian stock, probably originally from Tibet, and had a Tibeto-Burman mother tongue. Mr. Thapa believed that if only they would rediscover their original roots and develop enough pride in them to declare themselves Mongolians (instead of neo-Aryans, which, for historical reasons, many of even the most Mongolian-featured tribes aspired to be), they would learn that they were virtually the same people as the Bhutia Lepchas and would be accepted as such.

Mr. Thapa was undaunted by difficulties. His belief in the basic kinship of the tribes in Sikkim fired his hope that once this was accepted, the country would be one, socially and politically. Already, by the time of the coronation the term "Tibeto-Burman" had become popular around Gangtok, although most people weren't quite certain of what it meant. Generally it was understood to be a vague supratribal category that more or less embraced all the tribes in Sikkim, and also meant "Not Indian."

Mr. Thapa's face wrinkles into a beatific grin when he talks of what he wants to do: make a commemorative coronation book for the schools. "We must capture this moment, Gyalmo" (Sikkimese for "queen"). "The coronation enthusiasm is an important base on which to build. I think now we really can begin to forge a united Sikkim." His request for help with the book is like water for a dry plant. I'm thrilled to be needed and included. I appreciate his evident kindness as much as his charge to me, and know I will be grateful to him, in fact to all Nepalese forever. Intuitively I know they will take me in quicker than will the Bhutia Lepchas, who, at least among the upper classes, were offended because Chogyal hadn't kept the tradition of marrying someone from Tibet, the traditional source of brides and panache for the aristocracy and royalty in Sikkim.

That year, on Phanglhapsol, National Day, after the ceremonial dances in honor of Kanchendzeugna, the protecting deity of Sikkim, we celebrate with an evening gambling and dancing party at the palace, to which the entire roster of government officers and their wives are invited. To make more room, the children and I have spent the afternoon taking out all the furniture, laying down carpets and sofa pillows all over the house, later putting cards, dice, and ashtrays in the center of each area, and making corners for Mah-Jongg and roulette. The kids paste up shakily lettered posters to let the guests know where the different games are. Our big sitting room is set up for bingo, which many of the women like, and also for dancing if rain makes us dance indoors. A visiting English journalist compares the "expecting welcoming emptiness" of the "homey" palace to a wedding party in London's East End, "where the small over-furnished houses are stripped almost bare to accommodate all relations and friends."

Outside on the lawn we've got a wooden Ferris wheel and a tall bam-

boo swing that the Nepali Sikkimese use during Deshera, and the bagpipe band begins to play "John Peel." It's incredible, but all three hundred government workers and their wives come, squeezing into our small
house. The journalist writes, "No lion-hunting hostesses, no filthy rich,
no clever talk, but fine festivity, a running feast." Most stay all night.
The rooms are thick with smoke, and the pillows, which the children and
I tried to group according to color, are scattered helter-skelter. All the
people not still gambling, including the servants, sit in knots around the
players, placing bets, cheering on their choices. "Sho, sho, sho" ("Come,
come, come"), the dice players implore. "Pong, pong," the Mah-Jongg
players cry as they shuffle the rattling counters. High from my night of
dancing the Nepali folk dances a young engineer has been teaching me,
I'm too restless to go to bed, and move from circle to circle, the gamblers
asking me to stay with them for a moment to bring them luck. I sit with
Chogyal in the corner bay window of the little living room, my hand
resting on his leg, feeling my connection to him, our whole connection
to the people here.

Still much as I've begun to feel at home in Gangtok, Chogyal feels his
real base of love and rapport is with the villagers—"villagers" being used
loosely, as, in fact, owing to the mountainous terrain, we have in a true
sense so few villages. Most of the people who greet the Chogyal on our
tours of the countryside travel for the occasion from quite far-flung
homesteads. Today, on this visit, because of a road breach that held us
up, they must have been waiting for a long time. I feel bad, as I know we
don't intend to stop long, just long enough to inspect the school before
going on to the dak bungalow in western Sikkim, hardly leaving time
to absorb and appreciate the efforts that have been made for our arrival.
"That's the worst part of jeep travel," Chogyal says, "the zipping
through." In the old days, before the wide network of roads was made,
he used to travel on foot, visiting each major settled area at least once a
year, and every settlement, no matter how small, every three years. "And
we used to really stay. Then the food and drink people offered wasn't
just a ceremony but something to light into." Now, though he still
travels extensively throughout the country, he regrets that it is less often
on foot than when he was young. He misses the contact. The young
government officers, he says, are worse. (I think part of what he says is
the usual generational feeling that the next generation is in some way
softer.) "The first question I always ask them when they come back from
a tour is, 'How much walking did you do?' Some of them won't go a foot

off the road. We must see to it that that's a key factor in their promotions. Do you know, one village leader came to me and said there had to be a pukka road right through their bazaar, and when I pointed out all the hardships and noise it would bring, suggesting instead that the road run just around the village, he said, 'Oh, sir, then none of the school or health inspectors will come.' Disgusting."

Today, as usual, as if we'd made a long trek, all the traditional refreshments had been put out on tables by the roadside. Bamboo jugs of beer, a teapot of steaming, milky tea, piles of biscuits both traditional and tinned, oranges, and sugarcane. Mounds of juniper burned to clear the air, and firewood put politely to one side—the firewood a traditional gift to a distinguished visitor who intends to spend the night. And the delicacy of keeping it aside a recognition that this time we will not stay. Still, it's all right. Chogyal had a good chat with the headman, who seemed to have made several strong points in his long address—mostly about water supply—a village spring, I gather—and about teachers for the new school. Chogyal listens not only to the headmen, usually village elders, but to anyone petitioning—always careful, if the problem touches a subject not under his direction, to refer it to the officer whose department should be dealing with it. Much as he loves these encounters, he is particular not to let himself as an individual overstep his governmental powers, a point I doubt that many of the villagers understand. They seem to look at him so completely for comfort and action.

As poignant as the hearty refreshments given the travelers, and the elder villagers' entrusting their care to the constitutionally circumscribed Chogyal, is the difference, which causes me a frisson, between the old and new signs of nationalism we see on these trips. The villagers touch his feet, calling him by title or circumlocution "King," and because of his investment with kingship, it follows there must be a country. The local government officers and teachers invert the process: because there is a kingdom, there is a king. They deck the place out with Sikkim national flags, march up a little muster of police to be reviewed, and give the schoolchildren signs to hold when they sing the national anthem, "Long Live Sikkim, Long Live His Majesty."

"Majesty" is the new catchword these days among the young "educated," as it bolsters Sikkim's sovereignty vis-à-vis India. I wonder how the two concepts of nationalism will mesh. They seem to coexist easily enough in Chogyal. Relieved at being away from the bureaucracy in Gangtok, refreshed from his contact with the people, not bothered in any case by symbols, concerned about more practical things, my husband enjoys himself. After the folk dance presentation at the school, he's made a thorough inquiry into the building's plumbing and found that the pipes used were only two and a half inches in diameter. Angered at the wastefulness of the tiny pipes, considering their cost of installation, he turns the conversation to a larger discussion about the Public Works Department (or P.W.D.—"Plunder Without Detection," he calls it) and its general involvement with the village. How long had it taken to finish the footbridge? At what price? Where exactly did they intend to put the new chain bridge? The afternoon continues, with the villagers, encouraged, asking increasingly tough questions of the Chogyal and the officers of various government departments accompanying him. The Chogyal in turn acknowledges the government's slowness and ineffi- ciency or, drawing from memory and from the statistics given by the officers, defends specific areas of progress, cautioning the villagers not to dump responsibility solely in the lap of government, to shoulder their part.

As time goes on, the aides-de-camp shift restlessly. There are four or five more receptions scheduled before we get to the dak bungalow, and we clamber up the hillside under the red arch—one side picked out in white cotton wool saying "Welcome," one side saying "Farewell"—jump in the jeep, and as soon as we're out of sight behind a curve, tear off mounds of wet garlands enveloping us from shoulder to mouth, so our clothes can dry a little before the next reception and the next load of flowers.

Just before dark, leaving the road, we slide along a path to the dak bungalow, slipping on mud and wet ferns. Here and there someone has put a purple hibiscus flower to mark the way. The high keen of the curved Shenai horns and the bass rumble of a drum trill and boom through the air ahead of us. A group of Nepali Sikkimese villagers who've come to meet the Chogyal have brought the horn players, and the drum is played by an old Lepcha man in a faded tunic, a peacock feather wag- gling in his cane hat as he bends forward to beat the kettle drum sus- pended on the back of a younger man walking in front.

After we've been greeted by all the townsmen, who've gathered at the dak bungalow to offer presents (eggs, milk, a whole pig carcass, cheese, for all of which we return the cost plus 10 percent), and the Chogyal has heard still more petitions, we have supper in the gaslit dining room. With the eggs we've been given, the Chogyal makes cheese-and-brandy

133

omelettes for everyone, including the government officers who've come with us from Gangtok and some district officers who've come up to the bungalow. After dinner the talk, as always, is of Sikkim—ranging from assessment of today's meetings to long-term development plans.

The amount of worry and work Chogyal puts into overseeing the internal development of Sikkim is equaled by that he puts into Sikkim's complex relationship with India. Sometimes, in view of the changing expectations of the two countries toward each other, the connection is strained. Until the death in 1964 of Nehru, whom Chogyal had known and loved since he first entered government, he had been confident that things would work out, that India would continue to respect the rights of even a very small neighbor. The Prime Minister had always extended himself and, despite his busy schedule, had always taken time to see my husband unofficially as well as officially when he was in Delhi.

Soon after we were married we'd been honored by having dinner alone with Nehru and his daughter, Mrs. Gandhi, who was then acting as his housekeeper. At dinner she had been impatient with her father, chiding him for the conditions in Delhi's Palam Airport, overriding his defenses: "It's terrible. What would you know, Papa—everything's always cleared up before you go anyplace." I was surprised at her readiness to disagree with him. I myself was transfixed, so awestruck to be in the presence of my hero since adolescence that I sat in stupefied bliss until finally, at the end of the verandah supper, I got up courage enough to say inaudibly, "There's such a strong scent [the word "smell" did not seem refined enough to use in front of the great man] from your gardens." Whereupon Mrs. Gandhi jumped up and, in an excess of courteous agreement, buried her head in the long silk drapes of the living room, saying, "Yes, you're right. Funny, I never noticed it." "No, no, not curtains, *gardens*," I whispered in my head, "gardens." Nehru was beautiful —everything about him—graceful hands that made definite but poetic inflex, expressions that turned from sad concentration to mischievous grin. When he talked to my husband about Sikkim his face was alight with affection and interest. Finally, Nehru, disregarding the ill health that increasingly beset him, escorted us out of the long corridors of the Prime Minister's house, throwing his arms around Chogyal as they walked in front of me still talking.

"It was good of the old man to walk all that way," my husband said when we got back to the hotel. "Sikkim's got a true friend in him."

He died the day Chogyal was due to begin talks with him on Sikkim's future relations with India. The army plane sent to bring us from Calcutta to Delhi was circling over Palam when the pilot, receiving the news by radio, came down the aisle to inform us. My husband, after a moment's stunned silence, broke into tears. Minutes later we landed.

The Prime Minister's home, to which we went directly upon landing, was already full of relations and friends milling through the upstairs. Mrs. Gandhi and her sons, Sanjay and Rajiv, all three dressed in white, the Hindu color of mourning, received condolences. One of the weeping mourners my husband pointed out was Sheikh Abdullah, the leader of Kashmir's independence movement, the Prime Minister's old friend and political foe whom Nehru had jailed for much of his lifetime. Despite the emotion of the group, Nehru's bedroom—sparsely furnished, with only one painting, the mountains of Sikkim, done by the late Chogyal—was peaceful. Someone had put a rose in the hands of the old man laid out on the bed.

The next day an estimated two million mourners gathered between the Prime Minister's house and the ghat on the bank of the Jumna River, where he was to be cremated, according to Hindu custom, before sundown. The limousines we had been assigned inched along, bumper to bumper through the crowds, often nudging one another. Several times we bumped into Foreign Minister Bhutto's car in front of us, once provoking an angry scowl through the rear window from the future Pakistani leader. Throngs of youngsters, avoiding the army men who tried to keep the road open, broke through the cordons and dashed up to peer into the windows of the limousines and guess who the occupants were. "Chou En-lai," they howled delightedly when they saw my Mongolian-faced husband, "Chou En-lai." Despite the sadness, the occasion was becoming rather manic. I began to enjoy the discomfiture of the Indian Representative's aide who was escorting us when the people cheered "Hindi-Chini Bhai-Bhai" ("India-China brother-brother") at our car, and his equal discomfiture when they recognized us and gave a cheerful yell, "Long life to the King and Queen of Sikkim."

A good many limousines boiled over in the heat. Branches overloaded with clinging bodies broke, crashing onto the heads of the crowd below. "Remember the late Prime Minister's impatience with unruliness," my husband said, "how he'd get out of his car and admonish them as if they were children acting up. I wonder what he'd make of this."

At the ghat were heads as far as one could see—unimaginable. I was staggered, a little afraid. Two women, in-laws of the late Prime Minister, took my hands to hurry me off to sit with the Nehru family near the cremation site. I was flattered that they both should befriend me, particularly as I'd heard the Nehru women didn't get on very well, and touched that they were inviting me to approach the inner sanctum. However, in the dust and confusion I saw my husband being pushed toward the diplomats' seating area, and I broke away to follow.

Like many Hindu ceremonies (the late Prime Minister, despite his expressed wish as an agnostic to have a secular funeral, was being cremated with orthodox rites), the activity entailed mostly squatting on the ground, so there was little to see until Rajiv, the elder grandson, rose to light the pyre, and afterward the flame shimmering through dust-filled air.

At night when we returned to Raj Bhavan, the President's Residence, where we'd been staying, a storm broke out. Huddled in the thirty-foot-ceilinged guest room, which in British days had been the viceregal bedroom, we talked with Sherzad and her mother, who'd come to see us. Strains of dirges played by the presidential band filtered through the windows opening on the garden. Sherzad and Mrs. Sayyid were worried for the Moslems in India. "Late Panditji loved the Muslims and was fair. Now already Hindus are going around Delhi sneering that we've lost our MaBap [mother-father]." The Sayyids were sad in a personal way too. The late Prime Minister had been a friend since Partition, when a Sayyid uncle had been an important Cabinet minister. "When we were children," Sherzad said, eyes shining, "he used to let us swing on the gate of Tin Murti. He used to push us and tease us."

"I don't know," Chogyal said, "what's for Sikkim now."

9

A YEAR AND A HALF after Nehru's death, in the autumn of the Sikki-mese coronation year, 1965, Ayub Khan, the President of Pakistan, demanded a plebiscite for the state of Kashmir, and an undeclared Indo-Pakistani war broke out. As both India and Pakistan crossed the old cease-fire line and made salients into each other's countries (the armies con-servatively always holding back, going more slowly than the political counterparts in both countries wanted), rumors flew that parachutists were being dropped in the large cities and that soon bombings would begin.

At home people are concerned that, as India is considerably stronger militarily than Pakistan, China might make a show of strength along the borders—possibly in the Sikkim-China sector—to tie down the Indian divisions deployed here so they can't be moved against Pakistan. Ten-zing, Wongchuk, and Yangchen help the servants put Scotch tape crosses on all the windows to prevent shattering. Palden toddles after them tapping his chubby hands together with a fierce one-and-a-half-year-old's concentration. For the few nights left before the big children are due to go off with me to their schools in England (Chogyal and the baby will remain at home), the Chogyal decides that for safety's sake they should sleep in the bathtubs downstairs, which thrills them—particularly Yangchen, who sleeps curled up in a tub with Palden.

In Siliguri, on our way down to make connection with a plane that will take us to Calcutta, and from there to Bombay and the West, we have another odd sleeping arrangement—we stay in a guesthouse lent us by the rector of North Bengal University. The strategic importance of the train and airport center in the narrow neck of land that joins Bengal to North Bengal, and the main body of India to Assam and the frontier states, otherwise largely surrounded by East Pakistan, makes an attack here seem more probable than at Gangtok, where the possibility of trouble seems rather dreamlike. Chogyal, who's come to see us off, Tenzing, Wongchuk, Yangchen, and I crowd together on a single big mosquito-net-hung charpoy, giving each other security, enjoying the feeling of tension outside and the coziness inside our nest. It reminds me of my recurring childhood bedtime fantasy. Red Indians circling outside, I nestling and reassuring a gangly brood of children in the snug safety of our covered wagon. Through the windows we hear periodic rocket bursts and sirens. Searchlights stroke our bed.

When the children and I reach Bombay on the evening of the next day, the war has again taken on a dreamlike aspect. The pool of the beachside hotel where we stay, waiting for our westward connections, is full of Bombay movie stars who, in between exhibitionistic dives, stand on the board, silhouetted against the sky, and pledge their lives for the country.

On the plane the sleeping tablet I've taken has begun to work when a stewardess comes down the aisle to the economy-class section, where we always travel, to tell me that the Secretary-General of the United Nations, U Thant, whom I had known through the Sayyids when his son used to come to Sherzad's parties, had invited me to come up front to have a chat. Mr. Thant is returning from trips to India and Pakistan, where he has been trying to get Prime Minister Shastri, who has replaced Nehru, and General Ayub Khan, the President of Pakistan, to agree to a cease-fire and begin peace talks. He is affectionate, solicitous. Now is the chance to express to him our anxieties that Sikkim might get caught in the power plays going on. Being himself from a small country, he is sympathetic. What a piece of luck that he's on the plane! He himself is saying it—I think. He is saying that now Sikkim might be in danger from her protectors—I hear him foggily, I can't focus, my tongue is thick and won't form any words. He looks at me kindly and says I need to rest. I've messed up this chance; we could never approach him officially if we needed to explain any predicament. At London airport the children have trouble waking me.

Tenzing and Wongchuk soon go off to Harrow, where my husband, to my mute dismay, as it seems a very stuffy place, has decided they should go, now that they've finished their junior school in Kent. Only Yangchen and I are left at the Hilton, our room awash in tissue paper from the last-minute things we've bought in Harrods. Her trunk with the purple-and-white-striped uniforms, straw hat, games, and holiday clothes is already at the school, just outside of London. It will be her first term abroad. I will miss her dreadfully, but she is refusing to study with the accredited teacher who has replaced me in all but reading lessons, and the Gangtok schools, I know, aren't a viable alternative. It hasn't occurred to me to oppose the decision to send her away. The school she will attend—if you can accept the idea in the first place of nine-year-olds living away—is a cozy child-scaled place, better than most in England. Yangchen seems reconciled to the idea of going, and, although she is a bit quieter, more clinging than usual, she doesn't express her anxieties.

Coming back from Knightsbridge in a taxi one day just before she is to go off, we pass newsstands with evening papers that say in large headlines, "CHINA SET TO INVADE SIKKIM." When we reach our bedroom in the Hilton, two newsmen are sitting on our beds waiting for us. China has sent an ultimatum giving India seventy-two hours to remove the fortifications the Chinese claim have been built on their side of the border or they will invade. I'm not sure how many hours have already passed. I'm so shocked by the news and the intrusion that, although the reporters turn out to be quite nice, if too resourceful, I can't stop shaking. The hotel's public-relations woman rings up to apologize for the incident, offering the services of a bellboy until the crisis is over, and also to say that she can arrange a press conference for that evening, as at least one hundred press calls or newsmen in person have come to the Hilton trying to track me down. To collect ourselves, Yangchen, the bellboy, and I go off on a walk to the Serpentine in the park in front of the hotel, where in the fall sunshine people are sailing little boats, poking them free from the reeds lining the banks.

Cocoola, having dashed over from Ireland, where she had been vacationing, is at the hotel when we return. Even when there's no occasion, Cocoola always uses the word "dash." Today I'm profoundly glad the term applies and she was able to get here so fast. She's very cool, very managing. I'm awed, intimidated by her sophistication, hardheadedness, and courage. Although over the past years in Gangtok I've repressed the feeling, emotionally, viscerally, I'm scared of the Chinese. In fact, in 1962 in an undiplomatic move, as Sikkim was sitting tight in the Indo-Chinese border conflicts, I'd mailed off, out of fright aroused by looking at The New York Times maps, a sizable check to the Indian Prime Minister's defense fund. I couldn't help it. I'd been brought up that way. Now that Palden, whose dark, strong gaze peers at me from the photograph on the hotel desk, is subject to this threat, all the fears I've pushed down are surfacing. "Don't worry, Mummy," Yangchen says, watching me look at the photograph, "Palden is a good hider." Cocoola, who not many years ago had come down from Tibet a refugee, her husband's lands seized and many relations killed, who had more gut reason to fear the Chinese than I, remains rational, adamant in her response. "We've got to stop the Indians from taking advantage of this. Already in their official reports about the situation they're calling Sikkim an area of India and talking about our border being the Indo-China border. The nerve. We've got to remind people of Sikkim's identity before it gets lost. They're doing it deliberately—they know this is a perfect chance."

Cocoola's friend David Astor, editor of *The Observer*, which for years has championed the hill peoples' rights in India, is coming over to the hotel to give us advice about what to do before I go down to meet the press. We've ordered tea and cream cakes in advance, but as the hour grows later and later and he's still not come, Cocoola decides we'd better hide the tea things and order drinks and salty snacks instead. When he arrives, I'm disarmed. He's handsome, shy, and frank at the same time, and has good ideas to boot, which he and Cocoola animatedly debate. I feel privy to a formative, important occasion and am somewhat self-congratulatory until, concluding, he opens the wrong closet door to get his hat and, to Cocoola's and my open-mouthed horror, the tray of cream cakes, which we had stashed on the closet shelf, slowly slides out, showering his shoulders with pastry. Worse still, he doesn't say anything, but blushes, smiles a funny little apologetic smile, and goes off promising to keep in touch. We're mortified, he is of all people the one we would have wanted to impress. We laugh and laugh, partly because of the incident, partly as a release from the tension of the day. I've never felt so close to my sister-in-law.

Downstairs in the big conference room the public-relations woman has made ready, I'm still feeling light-headed, which sustains me when the batteries of press and TV newsmen begin to fire questions about the situation. "Make light of it," Cocoola has instructed. "Tell them it's been much overinflated." I have nothing ready to say. My legs are trembling both from thinking about Palden at home and from fear of the press itself. Even to me my words sound vacuous and tinny, particularly as I have no reassurances or in fact any direct news. Falteringly I say that, in general, reports about the borders are usually dramatized and things on the whole are calm in Sikkim.

In our own room again, we watch pictures with an ominous sound track on the late evening news—mule trains carrying army supplies up the winding road to the Nathu Pass and schoolchildren digging trenches at the Gangtok girls' school. My fears for Palden are deep and contradictory. One part of me is so afraid for his safety that, forgetting the hour and our resolve to keep neutral, I ring up a relative in the State Department to find out what the U.S. is doing. (The relative replies, grumpy with sleep, that "the situation is being watched.") Another part of me (remembering the scorn the Sikkimese had conferred on the Indian shopkeepers who'd run away down to the plains in the '62 conflict) is equally afraid for his and thereby Sikkim's honor. For Sikkimese morale, I'm anxious that Chogyal shouldn't hastily remove my son to a safer place. Crying as I give the message, I ask a BBC man to telex my husband in Gangtok to please keep the baby with him.

The next day the Indian High Commissioner in London, who has never bothered before, sends several officers to call on me—one brings Yangchen a big doll—to tell me that the deadline for the ultimatum has been extended. Some people say it is a diversionary tactic on China's part to disrupt the upcoming Ayub-Shastri peace talks in Tashkent, as they're jealous of the Russians for the role they're playing in hosting it. Some say it is to give Pakistan a breather and show of support, since (despite the fact that Britain and the U.S. are considering sanctions against both Pakistan and India to induce them to end the fighting) China is convinced that the U.S. is backing India.

Although the ultimatum is withdrawn a few days later, almost coincidentally with the end of the Indo-Pakistani war, the dispute over the Nathu Pass fortifications is not officially settled, and Cocoola suggests that after I've taken Yangchen to school, I should fly to the States and try to get on TV to reinforce Sikkim's identity. Having finally received cables from the Chogyal that Palden is fine and the situation is settling down, I feel I can afford to be away a few more days and fly over to New York to stay with Hamilton Armstrong, the editor in chief of *Foreign Affairs*, in his house on West Tenth Street.

Ham had first visited Gangtok as a guest of the Indian Representative, and ever since his stay there he had been a loving and gallant champion of Sikkim's identity, introducing my husband to his influential friends who might help, and following Sikkim's progress with concern. Now, although in his mid seventies, he was ready to assist in any way, great or small, running up the steep stairs of the old townhouse with my heavy bag to the top-floor guest room, dusting the unused room with his handkerchief, and, crucially, barraging TV stations with requests to get me an interview spot. The last was a hard job, although finally I got on the Walter Cronkite broadcast. My news that tension in Sikkim had abated was really non-news, made still less important because the upcoming Tashkent peace talks and the U.N. efforts to keep India and Pakistan observant of the cease-fire line were deservedly dominating reporting on Asia.

Back in Sikkim, I'm depressed by the children's absence, particularly Yangchen's. Her room, the blackout curtains drawn shut during the day to keep the rug from fading, her rows of left-behind dolls propped up against the mirror, is still and dead. Although I'm happy to be with Palden again, he's not yet real company. Still, I feel good and mature for my twenty-five years about the way I've acted or think I've acted during the crisis. "Chogyal is proud of me," I write a friend. "He knew I wouldn't get panicky."

In 1962, when India and China had fought over border areas in Ladakh (northwestern India) and Nefa (northeastern India), Sikkim, whose border with China had been demarcated at the turn of the century, had not been involved. Even so, masses of Indian troops, which under the Indo-Sikkim treaty were allowed to be posted in Sikkim for the mutual defense of the two countries, had been introduced into the country to supplement the small deposition of Indian Army already stationed there. Soon after, and continuing through the rest of the sixties, mutual accusations of border troop concentrations and violations between India and China began, each recrimination played up, it seemed to people in Sikkim, somewhat disproportionately in the U.S. papers, as if the U.S. sought to bear out its views of China as warmonger.

Although sympathetic to the Indian Army and dismayed by the earlier Chinese take-over of Tibet, a kindred Buddhist country, Chogyal was concerned about the heightening of tensions on the border—some of which seemed manufactured—and the alarmist reportage. In the groundswell of sympathy for the world's largest democracy, threatened by Communists (and Chinese!), lay the danger that the hawks in India might get away with "hardening" her borders by gobbling up the little countries on the frontier. In view of the tense reportage both in India and the United States, it was hard to convey to the world that life in Sikkim went on according to daily routines and that the main concern was with Sikkim's internal development; if you weren't frightened by 'em (the Chinese), presumably you must be for 'em. In '64 at the Overseas Press Club in New York, when reporters asked what ravages Sikkim might expect from China and my husband, trying to lessen hysteria, blandly replied he had confidence in relations, The New York Times synopsis recorded: "Sikkim Ruler Hails Red Chinese Ties." China, reaffirming its support for Sikkim's separate status, also piqued the situation by sending two direct cables to the Chogyal: the first a message of condolence on the death of the late Chogyal, and the second a message of congratulations at the coronation time, which India charged breached protocol and had "deep implications." A third communication, received some years afterward, a Christmas card with a photograph of their hydrogen-bomb explosion, never became a point of issue.

Contrary to occasional unattributed allegations in several Indian and Western magazines, China, as far as I know, did not meddle in Sikkim's internal affairs, nor did they defame the royal family or promise to "liberate" Sikkim. Except for the formal messages mentioned, they kept their historical hands-off approach, verging on disinterest, to the small kingdom south of the Himalaya watershed. Also, contrary to occasional allegations, with the exception of one North Sikkim village headsman, who apparently had some dealings for monetary gains with the Chinese and was subsequently caught and jailed by the Sikkim police, there was no pro-Chinese faction in Sikkim.

In sympathy with India's defense needs and despite China's purported neutrality toward Sikkim, the Sikkim government, from 1962 onward, joined India in imposing a state of emergency, primarily so that the country might more efficiently cooperate with India in a mutual defense effort. As border incident followed border incident, however, the Sikkimese became bored or even mildly skeptical ("Scuffle at Pass," the local paper noted if there was trouble). The indifference resulted partly because, despite the existence of the ambitious National Civil Defense preparations, they weren't encouraged to participate in any defense measures, nor in fact were they permitted near the Sikkim-China border—a constraint in their own country which people found particularly galling.

As well as loss of self respect, Sikkimese also suffered an economic loss from the Indo-Chinese friction. The sealing of the Sikkim-Tibet border, which had been effected by Sikkim in the late fifties, to cooperate with India's expressed security needs, led to loss of trade, especially in livestock and wool-based industry, for the country. In addition, the owners of good paddy and forest land handed over to the Indian Army in Sikkim were often underpaid or not paid for years. And such losses were not compensated by the spending power of the army, which was channeled in almost every instance to Indian contractors from outside Sikkim. Furthermore, although the Indian Army, considering its numbers in relation to the Sikkimese population—in 1968 an estimated 25,000 troops, a ratio of one to nine—behaved admirably, the civil population had to

143

bear occasional rapes, rowdyism, spoiling of the countryside, and murderous convoy driving.

Notwithstanding all these points of irritation, the Sikkimese didn't blame the army for being such a presence in the country. In general, there was even affection for it and respect for the hardships it endured. Particularly touching to local people was the change in the army from what it had been when it first entered the country in strength in '62—ill-equipped and ill-clothed for the snow levels and unacclimated from the plains—to its present professional readiness. And, by and large, Sikkimese goodwill was returned by the military, who saw in Sikkim a small but loyal ally sometimes offhandedly treated by their country. Because of the regard and trust most army officers invested in Sikkim, the Sikkimese government prided itself on cooperating, and was proud to note that in Sikkim any army request for land brought results in a fraction of the time it took the army in the neighboring Indian state of Bengal to command a similar piece of land.

Much of the rapport between the army and Sikkim during the sixties hinged on the rapport between Chogyal and the senior commanding officers. (Of the two divisions stationed in Sikkim, one had a major general stationed in the country, while the other was commanded from outside.) The local general, or "our general," as we called him to distinguish him from the generals in neighboring Bengal, usually divided his time between Gangtok and his headquarters "up the hill," nearer the border. A phone call announcing "I'm coming down the hill" was always a source of happiness. As Sikkim was a nonfamily station, the officers looked to people locally for companionship, and close ties were forged.

Chogyal's armed-forces connection had always been strong. Aside from being an honorary major general in the Indian Army, he was, like his friend General Manekshaw, the brilliant, outspoken Commander in Chief of the Indian Army, an honorary colonel of a Gurkha brigade (many of which served in Sikkim) and also had had a brother killed in the Indian Air Force, a hero. The brotherhood, the bonding that exists in any army situation, particularly in nonfamily stations, was extended to me. Again, as when I first met my husband traveling with the band of army officers in Darjeeling, I often felt, and enjoyed the feeling, that I was Wendy with the lost boys.

It was our connection with General X that got me home from Delhi to Gangtok when it seemed Palden was dying. My husband had wept on the phone, "Palden is very ill with convulsions, he might be dying, the lady doctor has pronounced him dead." Numbed, I hadn't known what to do, but in a stupor called up one of the general's brigadiers who'd been recently stationed in Delhi. Within an hour the brigadier had commandeered an army plane and I was off to Siliguri, alone on the big transport, heart in mouth, repeating Chogyal's message over and over again. It had sounded, the way Chogyal said it, as if he might already be dead. What had he said? "I'm afraid," he'd kept saying, "I'm afraid." I tried to will the plane to fly faster. At the Siliguri airport the young air force pilot whom the army had requested to helicopter me to Gangtok saluted, saying nothing. I was too scared to ask him anything, and, in silence, much later than helicopters were authorized to travel, we flew through the blackening sky, low over the Tista, the river gleaming as we sluiced through the dark.

Landing at the army helipad, I could see Chogyal's big black car rolling out to meet me. There was no car flag flying from the hood. Palden was dead. Chogyal and Mary, the Indian Representative's wife, and General X were all crying. I was crying. They embraced me. "He's all right," Mary finally thought to tell me. "He's all right." And there on our bed, sitting up, fine in his yellow pajamas, was Palden. "Nye Amala," he said proudly. Nye Amala—"my mother." There were army belts and liquor glasses all over the house. They must have spent the whole day in vigil. Several hours later, when the pediatrician finally got to the palace from Calcutta, the general and some of his officers were still with us. Holding Palden, we sat before the record player listening over and over again to Bach's "A Mighty Fortress Is Our God."

The next general I vowed not to like so much, partly because the Sikkimese were beginning to complain that we spent too much time with the army and partly because the pain of loss when one left was so great. I couldn't help it. While General X had had courtly manners and a charming, slight deviousness of heart, General Z had disarmingly rugged manners and a shining, openly loving heart. Half Scottish, half Sikh, his straight no-nonsense personality enjoyed the directness of the Sikkimese, and he made friends on all levels. Chogyal found him a delight to work with; in small matters he was quick to redress any army-civil wrong, and in big matters, such as the question of Sikkim's right to identity, he was a strong believer in our national and human rights. "I just can't believe those people on the other hill," he'd say sometimes, motioning his head toward the hill where the Indian Representative lived. "I can't believe them."

One day when I'd told the general that the Representative's office, having gotten it into its head that it was a security breach, had taken down the little *Gangtok O Mile, Nathu-la 12 Mile* signpost that had been a tourist attraction for decades on the turning near the cottage industries, he looked at me amazed. "They did that, did they?" The next morning when I walked down the Ridge Road leading from the palace, there at the intersection where the road forked down to town on the left and up to the Representative's house on the right, the most conspicuous intersection in town, in bright yellow and black paint, was the most startling signpost I'd ever seen. *Palace,* one board pointed; *India House, Nathu-la, Jelep-la, Army HQ, Tathangchen, Deoraili Bazaar*—practically everything but heaven and hell. Every time I passed that sign on my evening walks I had to smile and salute General Z someplace up the mountain.

Although outside interest in Sikkim stemmed from her situation between India and China, it was neither with her military vulnerability nor the military that defended her that Sikkim's real problems seemed to lie. The real problems seemed to be with the Foreign Office in Delhi, and more particularly its representatives in Gangtok, whose "parish" had included Tibet until the Chinese take-over and Bhutan until its entry into the U.N. in 1971.

Friction between Sikkimese and the Representatives from Sikkim's huge southern neighbor had a long history that had survived the transition of power from Britain to India. Just as British justice to Sikkim had seemed to get fairer the farther away it was deliberated (some of the voices in the British governor general's Cabinet, in their disagreement over the British decision to annex Darjeeling, were truly astonishing in their liberal championship of small countries' rights), so did Indian justice. There was always a feeling in Sikkim, held particularly strongly by the Chogyal, that the local Indian Representative in Sikkim was not presenting Sikkim fairly to Delhi, and that if lines to Delhi were clearer, the Indian government would be more understanding and Sikkim's problems would be solved.

The first Representative (then known as the Political Officer), John Claude White, an engineer persuaded into government service, who came to Sikkim in 1901 (where, as it had the mixed blessing of being more "civilized" than the other two countries under his charge, the P.O. stayed), tried, and briefly succeeded in supplanting the Chogyal, then Thutob Namgyal, and his wife. Having jailed the royal couple in India (where my husband's father, the late Chogyal Tashi, was born near the turn of the century), the P.O. flexed his new power by changing around the Sikkim Council, the social system (by creating new landlords), and —as he opened up massive Nepalese immigration—the demography. The aim, which he described in a contemporary Sikkim gazetteer, was to replace the Tibetan prayer wheel with the Hindu fire, or, more prosaically, to replace a proud, independent Bhutia Lepcha yeomanry with a more malleable, rootless constituency.

Although White's rule was reversed and power restored to the Sikkimese, subsequent P.O.s retained an exaggerated sense of authority and paternalism, generally to Sikkim's detriment, although occasionally to its advantage, as in the case of Sir Basil Gould, who came as P.O. to Sikkim in 1935. Almost immediately on his arrival, Gould, a recent widower, undertook a good deal of responsibility for the royal children, who, he felt, owing to their parents' separation and other reasons, were not receiving a well-rounded upbringing. Among many things, he taught my husband and his brothers and sisters English table manners—which was no mean feat, as in those days the table was set with a bafflement of forks and knives, not to mention, for the grown-ups, two wineglasses, one liquor glass, a water tumbler, and a whiskey tumbler. He also gave them lessons in riding, swimming (on holiday trips to the Indian seaside resort in Puri), and punctuality. The last he taught by example, riding his horse around and around the palace until the exact minute of his appointment, when he dismounted. Finally, he tried to expose my husband and the other children to different kinds of music, which so affected my husband that he and his sisters stole one of the P.O.'s records, which afterward, in a fit of guilt, they melted down.

The Indian Representative's residence, later known as India House, had supreme presence. Sitting up on a higher hill than the palace, surrounded by gardens that each successive generation of flower-loving English Political Officers had worked on, the Residency, built in English Bungalow style at the beginning of the century, exuded authority. Living there, one might easily have imagined one was inheriting an imperial mantle. The illusion would make it more galling for its occupant to face the Sikkimese insistence on independence and the Hertz–Avis No. 1–No. 2 polarity that was the current political and social reality in Sikkim. Everything in Sikkim—the seating arrangements, even the telephone numbers and the license plates—was designed (reasonably, as, after all, the Representative essentially was just an ambassador, albeit the only

147

one) to underscore that relationship. Even the existence of a Sikkimese Dewan and the local general, over both of whom the Representative took precedence, didn't take the fundamental sting out of being number two. Neither did varying degrees of personal friendship with the royal family. (Gangtok was a small town and we met each other several times weekly.)

Often personal factors influenced the Representative's behavior. One was rumored to have been too pro-Chinese while serving in Peking and now had to prove his adherence to hard-line Indian policy. Another had to take a firm position because, as a minority Goanese Christian, he himself was suspect. Some had family problems that embittered them. One had a wife who, pining for a post in Europe, scorned Sikkim and her husband's career in a diplomatic-social backwater. Another had a son who was about to go underground in the radical Naxalite movement of neighboring Bengal. For whatever reasons, and despite some strong areas of cooperation and regard between the two countries, there remained much contention in the decade I was in Sikkim.

To begin with, there were economic rubs. Despite the much-vaunted Indian aid to Sikkim, Sikkim had paid India more money in excise tax over the years than had been received in aid. (Ironically, the return of the money to Sikkim through the later intervention of Morarji Desai nearly coincided with the 36 percent devaluation by India of its rupee, which severely afflicted Sikkim, Nepal, and Bhutan without giving them recompense.)

Moreover, Sikkim was denied many rights:

To directly export products, such as cardamom, an important foreign-exchange earner of which Sikkim was the world's largest producer. (Most of the profit reverted to Indian middlemen and was of no benefit to Sikkim.)

To enlist the aid of expert help in discovering and developing resources (such as hydroelectric power and mineral wealth), which the Sikkimese felt the Indian government impeded.

To procure foreign and Indian participation in developing industries. (Even Indian businessmen were discouraged by the Indian government from investing in Sikkim, and virtually all foreign investment was eschewed.)

To invite U.N. or other specialist technicians or teachers (such as silage experts) that India herself wasn't able to provide.

To encourage tourism. Although vast numbers of international tourists who came through India wanted to go to Sikkim, only a few dozen permits to exit from India and thereby enter Sikkim were issued annually by the Foreign Ministry, and these were obtainable only after extreme delays and inconveniences.

To share in at least some of the benefits of trade and transit rights that (with Nepal's determination) the Unctad Conference on the Rights of Landlocked Nations was hammering out during the sixties.

To receive punctually the rather meager rice quota from India (for which Sikkim had already paid), or to buy rice directly from Nepal or Burma if the Indian government continued, as she was doing, to delay the rice shipments until the supply in Sikkim was virtually finished.

To receive the money that the U.N. had earmarked specifically for Sikkim and twenty-four other underdeveloped countries.

Allied with many of Sikkim's economic grievances was resentment over Sikkim's inability to belong to international organizations, such as:

The Colombo Plan. (In fact, the money India gave Sikkim as aid was listed as an Indian contribution to the plan.)

The Asian Bank. (The bank accepted even such colonies as Hong Kong as well as protectorates such as Brunei.)

The International Postal Union. (The Sikkimese felt they could make considerable money by issuing their own stamps.)

The Red Cross. (Even during disasters such as the floods of 1969, despite the fact that international relief organizations had brought relief goods for Sikkim, they were not permitted entry.)

Even the few international organizations, such as the World Craft Council, which Sikkim did belong to, were often inaccessible. Despite the Indian constitutional guarantee of a passport to its citizens, including its protected persons, passports as well as foreign exchange were sometimes withheld.

A forum of youngish Sikkimese officers had formed to study some of these problems. They felt that the Dewan, head of the government administration, as an Indian was unable or unwilling to stick up for Sikkim's rights and that the Chogyal, handicapped by the need to be circumspect with the Indians, could take issues only so far.

The Sikkimese representations to India were erratic. Often when redress for a particular grievance was asked, the protester was branded by the Indian Representative's office as anti-Indian. Therefore, in order to remove the sting from the complaint, much praise of India (ironically, mostly sincere) was advanced with every demand. There was much propitiation (a peculiarly Sikkimese characteristic, religious and psychosocial; even the alternate English name of Phanglhapsol, National Day, was Day of Appeasement). We played up the smallness, the fragility of our nation-building effort while clinging to a truculent notion that we would prevail because of our righteousness. The problems were not being dealt with. We tried to develop by going around and around the obstacles, and any new success, no matter how small, brought elation, even a feeling of victory. The issues were cycled and recycled. Among the educated Gangtok intelligentsia there was little talk of anything else but the relations with India. In the palace it was a constant undercurrent.

PART TWO

10

CHOGYAL WORKS in a cluttered little room added onto the side of the house, next to the ADC's office. Toward noon, trailing files, he generally comes back either to the living room if it is during the summer rains, his loafers squelching water from the short walk, or, if it is good weather, to the garden at the back of the house. Often he brings with him whomever he's been meeting with for a drink that turns into lunch. Since we eat off trays on little tables, and there's always a bit of extra food ("My God, woman, why don't you control what goes on in the kitchen? You don't even know what's going on"), it's no trouble to ask someone to stay. The office conversation continues. I eavesdrop in an unconcentrated way, enjoying the concreteness of the problems that the men discuss and the male concreteness of their vocabulary—catchment area, cusecs, grids, gradients, diesel power, silage. . . . Palden bangs his spoon and points his stubby finger at his mug. "Dih?" he says enquiringly, looking at Memeh. "Dih?" At two he has been exposed to so many languages—English, Nepali, Tibetan, Sikkimese, and Lepcha—that he hardly speaks, but simply records words, constantly asking, "This?" "This?" Memeh, the Apache-faced Tibetan ayah, answers patiently, "Sheyka, Pempo ki sheyka," "Cup, little master's cup," at the same time dabbing his face free of stray noodles.

I'm happy that Chogyal works at home, that we are all together—work spilling over into home life, home life into work. After lunch I'll go back to the library, newly carpentered with floor-to-ceiling bookshelves and hung with my grandfather's ship paintings, to work with my new secretary on mail until it's time for Tibetan lessons and Palden's tea at four. "Seucha jayshaybo?" ("Won't you have some tea?") I repeat falteringly after the Tibetan teacher, an unprepossessing man who

153

teaches me boring conversation-stopping phrases by rote. "The axe is in the kitchen."

It's slow going: Palden knows more than me. The lama teacher and I both stop gratefully to drink, the teacher noisily stirring his sugar. Memeh, bending over, buttering Palden's thick slabs of gray bread from the bazaar, averts her eyes, pretending not to notice my stupidity. She and I are getting on better and better and, even though we have a language block, feel quite cozy together. Memeh palpably wants me to succeed and is embarrassed when I don't. It's been so long since there was, in Sikkimese parlance, "a mother of the house" that the servants, particularly the women—in part because I'm so attached to the big children, whom they've brought up—are extremely responsive. My favorite time, just before going down to have supper with my husband, is the hour spent in Palden's room playing on the floor with him as Memeh or Aiyee, the Sikkimese nanny, whoever is on duty, putters around putting things away for the next day. Clover has sent me a print of one of Hicks's "Peaceable Kingdom"'s which the carpenter has framed, and it is now over the fireplace in Palden's room. I feel we in the room are part of that harmony, that peace.

Downstairs, often the same man who was there at lunch, looking a bit weary and making excuses about needing to call his wife, is still there, going through files and quoting figures. Two or three other men have joined them and are sitting quietly on the banquette, only occasionally whispering among themselves.

"Well, here's my wife. Wherever have you been? On strike?" My husband pats my fanny as I come in. "We're all dying of hunger."

"Sir, I really must go. If I can just borrow the palace jeep," the lunchtime official says rather desperately, looking at me. "I'll wait in the ADC room."

"Whew," says the Chogyal when he's gone, dropping from the banquette to the carpeted floor. "That sure took long enough. Now we can play a bit." And the betel-chewing man who's been waiting brings out a leather pouch of shells from his robe for Sho, a favorite game. "Woman, ring the bell for some snacks before supper and then come sit by me. Some music wouldn't hurt either—Beethoven, if you can do without that Joan Baez."

When the ADC on duty comes to say good night and take his leave, the Chogyal says, "And next time when old [so-and-so] comes, ask him exactly what it is he wants to talk about. No more of this 'just to pay respects' business. I want to know exactly what it is he's got to discuss."

We go up the side stairs to our bedroom, where a fire has been lit and the single servant who remains on duty in the house at nighttime is waiting to bring in the offerings for my husband's evening prayers.

My birth sign is Cancer the crab, which is right. I need a shell. I love my shell. When I've finished some new project with the carpenter or painter, after the workmen have left, I sit in the room we've been working on in long, gloating thought. I'm so happy with our house. It really is beginning to take shape—or rather, I'm finding its original shape. In the big sitting room, which is used mainly by the children for rough-housing when there are no receptions, we've replaced the overstuffed Western sofas with carved and painted banquettes, and the walls have been painted orange, setting off the Thankas. My husband tells me that fifty years ago the room had English rose-patterned wallpaper, which his father's elder half brother stripped off and took with him, along with palace furniture, when he went to settle in Tibet. I often wonder about the rolled-up paper carried on the long mule trip and what happened to it in Lhasa.

The dining rooms are also rooms we hardly use except for parties, since we eat off trays in the sitting room. (Palden, finding it a most admirable house, has taken to having his tea served under the table.) The walls have been painted creamy yellow and the brown chairs lacquered a burnt orange. The little sitting room—with Chogyal's consent, as he was a bit anxious—is a dull gold that complements the rose and gold carpet. Also, we've done away with the lank curtains drooping from the huge valances and have put up traditional hangings edged in Bhutanese weave. Upstairs, Yangchen's room is splendid with the blue and yellow Chinese carpet from Calcutta and a Thurburesque princess bed I've made, using mosquito netting for the canopy, which flows from a Gorgonzola cheese box painted and cut to look like a crown.

The boys' room, our old bedroom (they're both in it until I can plot to get Tenzing a room for himself), is, considering its windowless plight, as cheerful and airy as can be, with bamboo furniture made by our carpenter and bright Tibetan carpets. Our upstairs guest room is delphinium blue and white, full of the guest-room furniture from our house in Long Island, and the downstairs one (Cocoola's old room before she moved back to her own house) is Chinese red, accented by red, white, and black Lepcha handloomed material. Both, I think, are nearly perfect.

Palden's room, although it has some nice things—the rocker, a sheepskin rug, a big carved cupboard—is still rather haphazard—as is ours, full of cupboards and doors. I've made only a small start on the pantries and kitchen—the smoke stains from the charcoal make it an almost unthinkable task—and haven't touched the upstairs clutter room, the two chapels, and the late Chogyal's rooms, where his belongings are still neatly laid out.

Including the Tibetan and "English style" Indian cook, fifteen servants work in shifts at the palace during the day. (Some just come for the prestige it conveys. Our head butler, who gets 150 rupees a month from us, owns a fleet of taxi jeeps and pays his drivers 250 rupees a month.) They do a fairly efficient job, although I think things would probably work better if we had fewer servants and more precisely allocated duties. Except for the kitchen, which because of its wood- and coal-burning stoves is hopeless, the cleanliness of the house is reasonable, and the polishing and the floor-waxing is dazzling. It's mostly small things that remain a problem, like getting rid of dead flowers or having dry towels for guests, and—a constant battle—keeping the furniture where it should be, not pushed back, military fashion, against the walls.

Even the nuances of housekeeping, however, are beginning to be observed since the arrival of the new housekeeper, Mr. Manuel, an Anglo-Indian from Calcutta. Mr. Manuel's job is to oversee the servants, work as liaison between the staff and myself, do the marketing, keep the books, control the foreign stores (we order a supply of foreign liquor and foodstuffs by mail from Denmark each year), and look after the palace outbuildings, including the guesthouse. When my tea is brought in the morning, Mr. Manuel, bearing *The New York Times Cookbook*, is always two minutes behind. Dressed in his age-shined jacket and trousers, a tarnished tie clip holding down a skinny tie, nervously clicking his dentures in and out, he has such a reduced but defiant dignity that I feel both vulnerable for him and a little mean. It is the same ambivalence I feel when watching an old, not very good magician—praying the cruel children in the audience will not see the object disappearing up his frayed tuxedo cuff, but a little thrilled as well as embarrassed when they call out that they have. Mr. Manuel, standing over the flowered teapot that Clover has sent—the pot, despite my constant protest, three inches deep with Darjeeling tea leaves that later, the servants will use to brew their own day's tea—turns the pages of the cookbook using the backs of his hands (the cold in Gangtok has aggravated his arthritis) waiting for me to plan the day's menus. He's made out a suggested one in the elegant, old-fashioned script in which he keeps the accounts and inscribes the occasional poetry and spellbinding ghost stories he writes.

We have all kinds of food—Sikkimese, Tibetan, Indian, English. Sometimes I say, "Let's have anything," which expression Dahden, a smart-aleck young servant, repeats one day to an English-speaking guest who gushingly asks what it is he's being served. "Enny ol ting," says Dahden, smirking, inflecting his voice to sound as much as possible like mine. "Gyalmo say, 'Hellennyolting.' "

As it is awkward for me to go to the fresh-food bazaar, the one exception I make to my rambles around Gangtok, I trust Mr. Manuel to tell me what is currently in or out of season. Although our cook is getting better and better, and our party cuisine is beginning to outshine the food served at India House, my offhandedness about what is available sometimes leads to trouble. One day, as it is near Thanksgiving, I remember that at the dairy farm there should still be some turkeys that the American Consulate in Calcutta had given us—the only aid we ever received from America—and I think it would be nice for a change to have one carried in, American style, for Chogyal to carve at the evening party. The rather sober affair, for a Buddhist society, in contrast to our usual buffets, is a seated dinner, as the party is small and the guests elderly. I have been around the table—I can never get the count right— half a dozen times and finally am convinced that the place settings are right. At dinner I am pleased with the way the flowers and bright-colored gourds look, scattered down the center of the gold-embroidered damask tablecloth, and am anticipating with pleasure the surprise to come. For some reason there is a long delay, and our guests, who in any case don't have much fund of idle chat, begin to fall silent. Then suddenly, out in the pantry there is an enormous clatter, scuffle, groaning noise, and I can hear Mr. Manuel's angry voice.

The dining room door bursts open and in stagger two servants bent over under an enormous platter they are carrying on their shoulders, one in front, one behind. On top of the platter is the largest carcass I have ever seen—as big as a buffalo. I'd forgotten that turkeys don't stop growing, and this one must by now have been some years old. The two servants veer into the table between a startled Mahabodhi Society member and my husband and lower the platter with a crash. All quasi-vegetarian heads down the table turn as one, and my husband, when he's recovered, his face pinched with annoyance, tells the servants to take it away and bring it back cut up. Thereupon, with some difficulty, they reshoulder the bird and, shuffling under the weight, make their way back to the pantry.

We entertain often, at least once or twice a week. Thanks to my embassy upbringing, I don't find it daunting but fun, and, if there is a purpose, such as gaining the ear of a visiting V.I.P., either Indian or foreign, even exhilarating. If there is a visiting guest of honor, we always have a buffet. In this way cordons of young Sikkimese officers can outflank him and talk to him about Sikkim while another detachment pins down the Indian Representative and his aides so they can't intervene. If we are seated, the dinner is a loss, as the guest of honor is always placed next to me, and I'm not supposed to say anything. Also, the flux of a buffet gives the illusion to us locals of new faces—divertissement—important because the same people from the gazetted officers' list are always on hand.

India House and the palace are in unspoken competition with their parties, for as much as we talk up the country, at their parties the Representative's staff usually gives the visitors a rather sour briefing. The understanding between us is that the palace gets first choice of entertaining visiting firemen with a meal or with drinks, and they fill in the other slot. One day when a group of military aides from different countries is visiting, the Representative, breaking custom, insists he wants to give the dinner, and we're stuck with giving the less charismatic "drink party," as a cocktail party is called here. A friend who's staying with us gets her dander up. "Drink party, indeed," she snorts. "We're going to give them dinner on a toothpick. Anything that has a toothpick in it counts as an hors d'oeuvre." That evening the V.I.P.s, surfeited with the battery of toothpick-stuck courses they've been served, stagger out from our reception groaning at the thought of the upcoming dinner.

As often as we entertain, we also eat out—at India House, in the wainscotted living room with the big wooden thrones intended for but never delivered to the Dalai Lama, at our Dewan's house, where Chogyal spent several cloistered years as a monk during childhood, and at the army mess, where we wait for dinner until midnight, drinking sour beer, eating cashew nuts out of regimental silver dishes, making excruciating small talk with the young officers. Occasionally we go down to the Scottish headmistress of the girls' school, the only Westerner in Sikkim other than myself, for a teetotal evening of charades. The headmistress, an elegant, strong-minded woman with an Elizabethan capacity for swearing, has decided, as a semimissionary, that she will not drink east of

Suez. I find her dry parties a relief after the almost sickening drinking that goes on in Gangtok. My husband, however, is always saying he wants to meet her in London, west of Suez.

Often, on a night when we least expect it, we will have a party. Some evenings we screen movies; some evenings suddenly the general will arrive with a jeep full of officers and we'll play board games, or he will coax everyone after supper into parajumping, a game that delights Palden, as the adults clamber onto tables, crouch low, and on the command "Green light, action—station" throw themselves onto the floor in a slow roll. Often there is music. Perhaps a Lhasaan music teacher from the high school will come to sing Tibetan opera, taking several parts himself and enjoining Chogyal to sing the chorus, halfway through breaking into a Tibetan tap dance, his long robes scattering plates and whiskey glasses. From time to time people send up food—a special treat of some kind—and this too becomes cause for a celebration. Cheese that a friend's cowherd has just brought in, the big mushrooms that our ADCs know the Chogyal loves, fish if someone is just back from Calcutta, yak meat from North Sikkim, and occasionally, sent down by the army from the high altitudes where it grows, giant six-foot rhubarb, it's stalks so tough we keep it simmering on the stove for days.

When the children are home during the summer, especially when Chogyal's brother's children are staying with us because their father's had a breakdown again, every meal is festive. Listening to the rains pour down drumming on our tin roof, I feel like Mrs. Noah, cozy in the ark, or, as I write to Jane M., like a strong, provident tree full of shade and fruit and branches for nesting. I'm beginning to grow up, to be responsible—more than responsible—strong. Furthermore, I'm going to be strong for these children; the cycle stops here. These children will be happy. The wheel of unhappiness that both my husband and I grew up on will not go to this generation. A fierce resolution is in me.

I've stopped being floaty, boundless, nonattached. Perhaps it's because I've borne a child that I feel attached, rooted, earthbound—and I love it. Also I don't, I won't see things as illusory—maybe impermanent but not illusory. I don't care if Buddha's insights were meant to save us from the sadness of all things perishing. I will accept the tragedy of things ending because it gives a human dimension, tenderness to their present reality. Two world views. Christ *gave* his life—in Western thought the biggest sacrifice one can make for mankind; the bodhisattvas, who could, if they chose, pass into nirvana, *continue* their lives for the sake of less enlightened beings—in Eastern thought the biggest sacrifice one can make for mankind. I'm coming closer and closer to the first view. Despite the gore and grief, life's a prize.

Ironically, much as my new respect for life comes from having had a child, it comes also from living here, from Sikkim itself, and from my husband. Although the spoken message is one thing (in any case, we don't exist, my husband will sometimes tell me icily in closing an argument), there is, underneath Buddhism and Hinduism, a strong animism full of life impulse. (In the old days Buddhist monks wouldn't attend weddings because the union presumably would lead to more children born into the unhappy chain of this world; now, as at my wedding, they attend, although they don't actually sanction the union. Rather it is the animist shaman who officiates, and, contrary to the Buddhist ideal, all the prayers said are prayers for life—a house full of children and a shed full of animals.) Sometimes I find this strong clutching at life unnerving, as in the way the clothes and slippers of the late Chogyal are still kept out in his bedroom. Sometimes I think that the conflict between the Buddhist ideal of cessation and the animist life principle is a factor in some of the alcoholism and psychological troubles here. (Despite the bucolic appearance of the country, there is much alcoholism, and numerous mental problems exist both in the villages and Gangtok. Nevertheless, in general there is a healthy sense of being alive, more palpable here than in many places.)

The monks too share this vitality. It's funny. I've virtually stopped reading all the books on Buddhist and Hindu philosophy I used to be overwhelmed by in America, and when I'm with lamas here I'm only mildly interested in the abstract points they sometimes discuss with my husband. What I enjoy most about them, and this surely must be an un-Buddhist perception, is the strong, loving sense of being they radiate.

Often taking a picnic over the weekend, we go down to Chogyal's late guru's shrine at the big chorten on the outskirts of Gangtok. Joining the sizable group of worshipers, the majority of whom are fairly elderly women who've walked down from the bazaar, we circle the smaller chortens, stopping finally in front of the main edifice to bow to the Buddha. Afterward, lighting butter lamps in a small altar room, the children, heedless of admonitions to concentrate and say an internal prayer, jostling with each other, vying to light the most, picking the outer ones where the heat is less intense, we greet the consort of the late guru, an unkempt, raffish-looking old lady, absentminded but enormously amiable, who oohs and aahs over our visit, always delighted to see us. Prayers over, we sit in her little room eating the hard-boiled eggs and cream "cracker biscuits" she invariably produces. If we've come for the day, we all go down to the jungle clearing behind the chorten, where a tent is pitched for sessions of cards or talk that lasts into the night—more and more gas lanterns called for as it grows dark. The kids, bored with sitting, demanding to go home, swing on creepers, giving Tarzan yells, or play tag around the chortens, always careful to circle them clockwise, the good, auspicious way.

As the heavy rains in Sikkim are destructive—the oldest surviving monastery in Sikkim in fact dates only from the sixteenth century—many of the monasteries are being refurbished, largely with community-raised money. When we visit them on trips, it is gratifying, after finishing butter tea and prayers—blessings for Sikkim and the royal family—to look around at what new carvings or paintings have been done. The master painter of Sikkim, whom I know through his daughters (they borrow his fine brushes for their eye liners—he accuses them of taking longer to paint their eyes than it takes him to paint the eye of the Buddha), is repainting the whole of Pemayangtse Monastery, Sikkim's foremost monastery, in a vast undertaking in which he has already spent several years just drawing the cartoons on the walls. Several monasteries are being rebuilt from scratch, and the Chogyal and I have participated in some complex cornerstone ceremonies, walking round and round the foundations of the buildings, laying down varieties of offerings at desig-nated spots as the monks chant.

The main Buddhist ceremonies during the year, aside from those on Phanglhapsol, when, after the service in the chapel, warrior dances are performed outside in honor of Sikkim's presiding guardian mountain deity, Kanchendzeugna, are the sacred dances marking the end of the year, the Sikkimese New Year, and the Tibetan New Year, which is also celebrated here. The sacred dances at the end of the year, which, like the dances on Phanglhapsol, are held outside the chapel on the palace lawn, must be performed in order to dispel the evil spirits lingering from the old year before the new one begins, whether or not anyone is there to see them. Indeed, the dancers, although spectacular in their brocade costumes and grotesque masks, are not engaging. (Some of the masks are made deliberately appalling to acquaint a spectator with the horrible apparitions that will be seen in the forty-nine days' journey between death and rebirth, so that the deceased, recognizing the masquerade of evil as his or her soul journey, will not be ensnared.)

The dancers circle round and round, self-contained in sober, almost slow-motion celebration of the victory of a good Buddhist king over his pagan would-be assassin. Only a few dramatic moments break the gravity. At one point a stag-masked dancer, in a solo, cuts up a small dough effigy. ("No, no. That's not supposed to be good conquering evil," the scholarly ecclesiastical secretary keeps worriedly telling over-simplifying guests, "that's transience, ephemerality.") At another point a drawing of a savage-looking demon is held by attached strings over flame and dispatched with war cries. (The crowd, including Palden, who hovers near the dancers holding a gas balloon someone's given him, draws back quickly so the unlucky ashes will not fall on them.)

During the dances—which, despite their Buddhist construction, seem to be a harmonious compromise of Buddhist and pre-Buddhist animist tradition—an animist priest, in the true spirit of Himalayan religious tolerance, is busy performing cathartic rituals on the fringes of the dance area. Afterward he will come back to the little chapel in our house for a longish prayer service enjoining the royal family's prosperity, which he half chants, half sings in Lepcha, the aboriginal language of the country.

I am curious to find out more of the cross influences between the two religions, as I think this would explain a good deal of what still remains mysterious about Sikkim to me, but have found it one area better left unexplored; there is a defensiveness, a denial of the connection between the two. In fact, there are quite a few questions about religion it doesn't seem right to ask here, veiled areas revealed only to the initiate, such as the deity room of the monasteries, where only a very few can enter, or in fact the Thanka, covered with silk over our bed, of a deity so secret, so powerful, I have never dared lift the hanging to look.

Aside from these celebrations there are frequent Hindu holy days observed by many of the Nepali Sikkimese when we go to the Hindu temples—always in town, in contrast to the hilltop Buddhist monasteries —to take part in prayers. The services, even the ones in honor of Durga, the goddess of destruction, always startle me by their domesticity, their hearth origins. We squat on the ground, and the Brahmin priest, like an Indian housewife at her inner-sanctum fire, sacred even in an ordinary household, offers vegetables, fruits, and spices to the lamp-surrounded shrine. During the Durga worship observance, when the Hindu Nepalis begin a week of blood sacrifice, starting with crushing an insect and working up to beheading a buffalo in a single stroke, the town is electric with colored lights, marigolds, and door-to-door troupes of drummers and dancers. Group after group come to our big living room, refusing to leave until Chogyal and I, swathed for the occasion in Nepali skirt and velvet tunics (although the elder Bhutia Lepcha aristocrats frown on it, I've now begun to wear Nepali dress for their holidays), have joined in a drink and many Cossack-style kicking dances.

Their music and good humor is infectious. I feel increasingly at home with the Nepali Sikkimese, bearing out my early intuition that, as an American by birth, I am considered to be in some way more theirs, or at least more neutral, than if I was of Tibetan or Bhutia Lepcha origin.

Every holiday of every religion represented here and countless secular holidays are celebrated. They are red-letter days, literally printed in red on the government calendar. Half the days of the year, it seems, are holidays. Sometimes the holidays are not good times for me. I feel alien, irritated because I have to make an effort, fix myself up, extend myself to rows of relations who have the right to be at the palace, even if I would like to be alone. With the exception of Cocoola, I get on quite well with my family-in-law, but it seems they are always feuding with one another, and the strain of being equable to all of the different factions when they've collected is horrible. I resent the fact that Mr. Manuel isn't here, that Monmaya, my secretary, isn't here. There is no one to give instructions to, no one to follow up on projects. These holidays, some of which go on for days at a time, can be so dull, underscoring the fact that much leisure time here is dull.

When I'm working, however, it's okay—I feel alive, even exhilarated. Although the projects are generated by me, or have devolved on me through friends, they nevertheless are beginning to acquire their own momentum, find their own course. When I work on a project, I find I'm not only happy in doing it, being able to lose myself in it, but happy too to feel part of the general excitement of Sikkim's development. Everyone here is working for a single end, and the scale of Sikkim is small enough for us to see the results, feel the camaraderie. Mainly I'm busy with the foreign orders that, thanks to Clover and Alice, a recent friend from Sarah Lawrence, are beginning to come to the cottage industries.

For weeks I've been in an artistic spin, creeping about on hands and knees looking at skeins of wool and carpet designs. We've also started metalwork, even sending some of the uglier wedding-present tea sets to Calcutta to be melted down for our pilot silver designs. Every month brings a long letter from Alice mainly containing information on how the New York stores want things made: "Leave the cotton fringe on the carpets, reinforce the sides with extra wool. When they're finished, damp and block them. Get some decent backs made for the jewelry (can be sent from the USA if need be). Don't let them use green lining on the jacket pockets. Try to see that the Lepcha bags are woven in more summery colors."

We've stopped the airport art we'd been making and are getting back to traditional Sikkimese design. The only touristy item we're continuing is dolls—and this is my fault as Alice got a big order from the Brooklyn Museum gift shop. At least they're now in Sikkimese costumes and not in Punjabi-Japanese dress, as before. At this moment several hundred of them cover every inch of the palace dining table, where they have lain for the last month. Monmaya, my new secretary, and I have been packing and unpacking them endlessly as we have forgotten one thing after another—to remove the price tags, to remove their wooden bases, to keep samples for reorder.

Although still not streamlined in production (I call the cottage industries the Penelope Weaving Company, after Ulysses' wife), our carpet section, under the turquoise-earringed weaving master, who's married to Memeh, one of the palace nurses, in particular has done well. Our spectrum of vegetable dyes we've been reviving increases rapidly, and the few vegetable-dyed carpets we were able to export were a huge success, selling out in a few days. The Lord & Taylor rug buyer was so impressed that when some Tibetans tried to go to him with their carpets and steal our market, he loyally told them (to their annoyance, as they were Tibetan chauvinists), "No, thank you, we've got the *real* thing." Now it's just a matter of continuing to look for good wool, and also of finding ways to export the carpets which India can't thwart.

Most of my correspondence with friends, particularly with Alice, is full of detailed work assignments and advice. "Quick write up a batch of letters to the Pope, Nixon, de Gaulle. Keep the carbons, burn the originals," Alice suggests when I write her that Boston University has asked for my letters. "Best policy not mention amount in thanking Mrs. X Stop Express gratitude her interest in Tibetology, Buddhism, and perhaps casually mention floods," she cables when she finds a philanthropist interested in duplicating the book collection down at the Tibetology Institute to keep it safe from fire or disaster.

Sometimes Monmaya giggles when opening her letters, and my heart sinks. "Send flower photos fast. We've got a Sikkim garden in the National Flower Show. What happened to the children's pictures? We need them to decorate the Sikkim evening at Asia House—our standard's so high now we can't slip—even J.D.R. III had to jostle his way in at the last meeting. What's the point of the meetings—can we use them to support a hospital? A school? Try for a supplement in the Sunday *Times?*" "Have checked out Designer X—Big Ego. Don't let Sikkim's mystique get blown up in a way that will just help the designer, not the country." "No word from the record people—what you need is not a big commercial label but an ethno-musicologist who would go in and record the people with sensitivity—"

Clover suggests collections for the American Museum of Natural History in New York; Jane M. corresponds about an interest the Levi's jeans-manufacturing company has shown in putting up a factory in Sikkim, and fund raising for a rhododendron sanctuary we're trying to start; Simon writes about the seeds and flower specimens we are sending to Kew Gardens; the O'Briens report on my music-festival fantasy ("There is some interest among music critics in England—we seem to be in the position of sorcerer's apprentice"); Ellen gives an account of her photocopying of the rare material in the new Simmons College bibliography on Sikkim; a geographer friend outlines a film, book, and map project that will entail our researching all the original names of local sites; and a cousin discusses a World Wildlife plan to make a pan-altitudinal animal reserve. Finally, there is even correspondence with a distant relation about making the country better known through his racehorse named Sikkim. "Send me a short history of Sikkim to be included in news releases on the horse." We do, and for some seasons (until the horse breaks a leg) are regaled with the clippings he sends in return—"Sikkim Captures Hialeah," "Sikkim Takes Aqueduct."

So many people want to know about Sikkim. Quite a few of the letters are from crazies and obscure monarchist groups—"We have voted Your Majesty the best Queen of the World." But there are impressive letters too, written by intelligent and sincerely interested people from all over, which Monmaya and I always try to answer—in the third person, the way people say it's done. "The Gyalmo has asked me to thank you for your interest in Sikkim and your kind encouragement, and wishes you success with your project" (a paper on Tibetan refugees, a book on herbs, or whatever). The project is the catch; we can never respond with just a polite letter. There is always something to do, something to get—Sikkimese license plates, dye samples, national flags, health statistics, postcards, Tibetology bulletins, education surveys—

and no use sending it on, as Mrs. Kennedy does, according to Washington friends, to "the relevant department." The relevant department either doesn't exist or would sit on it.

Monmaya, a good-hearted, perpetually pregnant woman, who writes English as it sounds regardless of sense ("The Gyalmo doesn't want it known she rotates," she once typed after I'd dictated a letter to a children's book company that "I'd do the foreword but didn't want it known that I wrote it"), spends long hours chasing information and objects. Sometimes we grow silly, making up explosive recipes for people who want to include Sikkim in an "international cuisine night," but more often we're respectful, particularly to the children who write, postal orders earnestly enclosed, wanting to know more of the country.

Despite the farfetched efforts of the Indian Foreign Office (some Indian lobbyists in New York even protest that a Sikkim Council at Asia House might jeopardize Mrs. Gandhi's majority in Parliament by provoking "unnecessary controversy over Sikkim's international status at a time of tension between India and China"), Sikkim is becoming known. "Congratulations," Alice writes. "You've just made it as a question—Where is Sikkim located?—on the New York third-grade public school social-studies exam. It's saturation Sikkim."

When I stop working, however, boredom wraps me in a sad net. There are no new ideas, no new faces. Everything is spent. Outside there is no place to go, or rather, only two roads to choose from, as the third is too steep for Palden's pram. In the evenings when Palden, Memeh, the security officer, and I walk along one road or the other, I inhale the diesel smells of the army trucks' exhaust and try to imagine New York. The green countryside has no plot, no drama. The leaves stay all year, just getting dusty. I miss the greening of New York, where every spring leaf and forsythia bud has to struggle to break through a concrete shell. Here things just are green. Worse still, because of the leeches, you can't step off the macadamed road.

When I reach home—darkness and army traffic making it unsafe to walk outside any longer—my frustration is still unrelieved. I want to go someplace, do something. I'm not yet ready to sleep. There is only the sitting room, and that is still full of people, or the library, and I have been there all day. I'm sick of my records, sick of being responsible for what I hear. In any case, I rarely play classical music anymore—it requires too much emotional energy to listen to. Only the banal lyrics of my folk-rock records talk to me, make me feel less alone. I haven't read a book of substance for years, and I'm sick of mysteries. I must

have read every single Agatha Christie, because more and more frequently, after a couple of chapters into a "new" one it turns out to be
familiar.

Too often there isn't anything good to eat, never any way of getting
something on the spur of the moment if you feel like it. The leftovers,
even if one wanted them, are always eaten up right away by the servants.
The few goodies—cheeses and treats we bring back from Europe—are
usually quickly finished, even the wrappings of the boursin licked. The
thought of getting something like a chicken sandwich is an undertaking
so arduous—someone's gone home with the bread-box key; there's no
chicken anyway—the electric current's been low; is the mayonnaise still
good?—that the impulse dies aborning. I want to be passive, bombarded
by stimuli, by choices, delicacies, music, inventions that I don't have
to seek to build, to generate, that take me by surprise.

Only the weather here—by turn lashing rains, mountain-shaking
thunder, crescendo hail, gentle mists, rainbowed sunbursts, and cold,
dazzling days that make the snowy ranges loom almost overhead—is
diverting and unsolicited. I love being acted upon by it, soaked to the
skin as we run home from our evening walks, lulled by heavy pattering
on our tin gabled roof, bone-chilled by cold that defeats even a blazing
fire. All my other pleasures I have to create. As Palden says one day
when we've been sitting for a long, boring afternoon in the garden
doing nothing but watch a Himalayan panda, which looks like a raccoon,
his tail hanging down off the ledge, sleep in his wooden box, "This is
Sikkimese television."

The long letters I write and write are unsatisfying. Often things I'm
doing, experiencing, feeling, don't seem real because I have no one to
tell about them. I am the tree that has fallen in the forest and no one
has heard the sound. I can only discuss projects through the mail. I
can't write what is really on my mind; all the letters are opened (as if
by police dogs—the flaps jaggedly torn, reglued with heavy paste that
sticks the letter to the envelope) by the Indians. "So kind of you to
rewrap my letter," Alice writes in a postscript to the censors. "Hi,
Vivek," I add, also in a postscript, to my old friend from adolescence,
the Indian diplomat in Teheran who years ago was going to make me a
village-level worker and who, I've been told, is now assigned to reading
my mail. (I've also learned that he is not greatly interested in poor
people anymore but is building a lavish house in Delhi and is asking
300,00 rupees dowry for himself.) "Salutations to your lotus feet!" I
can write only in ellipses. Not being able to express myself makes my

thoughts less clear, the urgency of my emotion warped, mocked in the twisted codes. "There is a rumor the painter is coming for several months to restore my father-in-law's painting. Mon dos est en haut." Grace is coming—my back is up, merely? That's a joke. In truth my gut is pulled into a tight skein of jealousy and anger. I can't write this. I can't write that Cocoola tells people she will drive me from the palace, that I'm so scared of her I take Valium before I see her. "Ma belle-soeur," I write, "continues to be a little bit difficult."

My friends in America are more and more tied down with responsibilities—children, jobs—so they travel less. There are few exceptions. One is Robin, and her husband, Bill, who reach Sikkim on the dot of their announced time of arrival, having left Kathmandu in the only available plane, a little Piper—naked lady painted on the nose cone—flown by a free-lance kamikaze-style Filipino pilot, who took off from a hayfield, landed in a wet patch of rice in submontane Nepal, and subsequently flew off, leaving them to figure out how to get to the Indian border with their new honeymoon matched luggage.

"And then," Robin said, "we met this farmer who, with much bowing and pleasantries in sign language, agreed to take us, so we put all our luggage in his bullock cart and got in and climbed on top and sat there, and the farmer very slowly unhitched his bullocks and walked away. Then, on the distant horizon we saw an elephant with a mahout, so Bill and I were running through the field with our matched luggage like a war movie, but the elephant outdistanced us, then, some time later after we had forded a river, we came to a border post, where this Indian guard accused us of being"—and here Robin gathers her Minnesotan R's together—"rumrunners. Ha! And I said to them, 'Would I be wearing [she is now back to wearing clothes her mother approves of] patent leather pumps and a houndstooth skirt if I was a rumrunner?' " We laugh all the time, and Chogyal takes us driving in his convertible, loud with tapes of the Supremes, or Bill and Chogyal sing Gilbert and Sullivan as we whizz through the green-fronded countryside, which, now that I see it with my friend's eyes, seems pleasant, even beautiful. The siren screeches, and as passersby on the road look back to stare at us, I turn around and point at Robin, her black hair just-married coiffed, and yell, "Lucy Baines Johnson."

Only Marilyn, the *Life* photographer who first took pictures of me when I was engaged—the one before whom Kesang advised me, "Preserve your dignity, be aloof"—and Alice come regularly, just about every year, although Marilyn's visits, cozy as they are, spent polishing up our Peter Sellers Indian accent, eating up the old food we have saved from Europe—olives, canned Kraft cheese, canned steak-and-kidney pie, don't quite count, as she comes from Delhi, not from "Phorrin." It is Alice, with her luggage loads of artifacts ("Can I bring anything for your narcissism? Altruism?"), who represents another reality. The outside world doesn't seem real once I'm back here. Everything seems suspended, frozen in time—only when Alice comes can I imagine the outer world moving, existing, independent of me.

Night has fallen and she still hasn't come—held up by the Indian border guard, who is turning her passport and permit over and over in the little pool of light from his kerosene lamp, or stuck on one of the road breaches, the mountain falling away in clots above and below. "The jeep's passed ninth mile, the jeep's passed Ranipul," the ADC reports, and, as he's speaking, the servants, hearing a spray of gravel in the drive, are gathering at the door to carry in the many bags they know she will have brought.

"Whew, and thank God, Mr. Gandhi, fourteen ground crew chasing after him, met me. Otherwise I'd have been sunk!" Alice nods toward the suitcase full of Christmas-wrapped presents. "I had walkie-talkies for the boys, which I knew would make customs berserk, and four pounds of moisturizer for you." Alice always talks in terms of weights and measures (she once sent twenty cubic feet of Sara Lee cheesecake, which rotted in a Calcutta deep-freeze power failure). I love her New York exactitude combined with her Rabelaisian prodigality. Already the perfect guest room—towels folded just so, little table aligned exactly with llama-skin rug, fresh flowers in vase over chimney—is beginning to billow in a sea of tissue paper as she searches through the bags for the Batman suit she's brought Palden.

My pajamaed son has got Memeh to bring his prebedtime milk here and sits curled up in my lap watching. Memeh is folding things as, one by one, she takes them from a suitcase. Around us are the noises familiar to this room—the scamper-clatter of the cats chasing each other overhead in the attic and the constant gurgle of the urinal no one can shut off in the bathroom. The fire we had lighted to dry out the room before Alice came is beginning to die, and I ask for more logs to be brought. Tonight, although I know Alice is tired, I must talk and talk and talk and listen about my friends. Hearing Alice, I feel both the immediacy of America and, at the same time, the pain of distance as things are made more real. Rather like the weird night we listened to the staticky Voice of America transmission of the moon landing—the moon and America both so close and so far from us in Gangtok.

I envy Alice her freedom, her access to the world. She is a souvenir, a reminder of a place, a way of life I can't rejoin. I sit telling her of my unhappiness, aware there is nothing I can do to change my situation, relieved, still, to talk to someone who is free. At the same time I'm talking to her, I know, even though she sympathizes with me, that after the journey from her lonely single life in New York through the decay of Calcutta and the long dark jungle trip here, she is envying the voluptuous coziness of this house. "Coming here," one guest wrote, "is like coming home to a place one had been longing for for years."

11

A COUPLE OF TIMES a year Chogyal and I, leaving Palden behind with the palace nurses, make a trip to Delhi and then on to Europe. All the trips revolve around some Sikkim project or seeing the older children in England during their long holidays. For days before we leave Gangtok my heart is in my mouth. I'm thrilled about going, while at the same time the thought of going makes me love my surroundings more dearly. I'm full of energy to finish projects that have been languishing for weeks, months. Lists. Lists of lists. The deliciousness of crossing things out. Injunctions. Orders. I'm in a tizzy. Mr. Manuel and Monmaya eye me warily.

If the day we're leaving is a bad day astrologically for any one of us traveling—the logistics of trying to find a day that suits everyone is Byzantine—we make a false start a day earlier. Throwing our semi-packed Samsonite suitcases (the only kind of luggage that will withstand the rough ride) into the trunk, we jump into the car (if the roads are clear, the jeep if they're not), drive up to the chapel to leave a scarf at the altar of the family deity, roll down the road to the outskirts of Gangtok—and then come back to the house, feeling a little silly.

When we leave, people bring us scarves to say farewell, and if we're going to Europe, they bring us last-minute presents—ropes of hard cheeses strung together, chili pickles—for the four Sikkimese nurses studying there and for Karma, a young man studying at Manchester University. The Sikkim distillery man brings his heavy collection of sample liquors and giveaway key chains, penknives, and calendars, half of which we abandon at Sherzad's in Delhi. Her house looks like a Sikkim liquor showroom. "Please, Your Majesty, just so more people there will know us," he says, looking at Chogyal out of the corner of his eye. Some people ask us to bring back specific things—the tailor has brought a note asking me to get a certain sewing-machine bobbin, "for which act of kindness [he'll] always pray my long life."

In Bagdogra, the little airport in the foothills, a knot of American tourists on their way up to Darjeeling start in surprise when they see me getting out of our flagged cavalcade. "That's her. That's the American girl." They point and stare. I'm embarrassed but pleased too, proud to be part of our band from behind the hills, feeling some scorn for these visitors' peripheralness, their role as viewers, not participants.

In Delhi, if we stay at a hotel, not at the President's Residence, it's the same thing—tourist couples watch and accost me. "Pardon me, but aren't you . . .?" "You know my sister in Milwaukee." "I know you're from Philadelphia." In Sikkim, at least, I feel invulnerable to this kind of depersonalization. There I've got a certain kind of self-consciousness from being Gyalmo, but I don't have to cope with this. This is a double displacement. In Sikkim no one has read the rather lurid misleading magazine articles about me that my friends send me with notes: " 'Graciousness and shy gentility'—groan," writes one. "I never noticed those characteristics." "Saw your recipe for nettle soup. What a star you are." These people have read everything. They're intrusive, proprietary, as if I'm a park bench, public property. They insist they're right—that some friend of a friend of theirs was my roommate at school—even when they're wrong. I'm scared too that, since they believe they know everything, they're going to tell me something about my father, that they have met him. This year friends have written me that, his ranch investment in Wyoming apparently having failed, he's become a rafting guide down the Snake River. I'm angry that at a time when I've just begun to feel familiar with, even proud of his Irishness, and mine, particularly my inheritance of an Irish talent for words, poetry (although I still don't know if I'm descended from poetic Celts or prosaic Anglo-Saxon occupiers), he has let me down again. I'm ashamed, and ashamed of my shame. My damn grandmother's shame. Half these people must know him. I know they're going to tell me something. Coming from Sikkim to this neon lobby is like being ripped out of a womb into an operating-theater glare.

Chogyal's day is mapped out: talks with Prime Minister, Government of India; lunch with H.E. the Deputy Prime Minister; return call on H.E. Home Minister; call by H.E. Foreign Secretary. Mine is free until the evening, when we go to the army commander's for drinks before our goodwill dinner. I spend the morning in sybaritic torture at the hotel beauty parlor, my semiannual hairdo piled higher and higher, conceit upon conceit, curl upon braid upon "modified" teased beehive, everything topped off with a cocky little shepherdess-curl hairpiece made by the Chinese beauty parlor in Calcutta. The entirety is lacquered thick with spray and studded with huge hairpins that afterward fall out, clattering, as my hair, which had congealed in the Delhi heat, stiffens and contracts in the freezing hotel air conditioning.

Before I go to Sherzad's I want to explore a bit, go to the Delhi cottage industries. Nehru's old driver, who now works in the Foreign Ministry motor pool, has asked to be assigned to us again and brings the late Prime Minister's old green car. I feel honored both to be in Panditji's car and to be liked by the driver. I think the Sikkimese in general are liked in Delhi—at least by the junior people—because they're so informal and free of caste. This informality doesn't work as well with the higher-ups, who tend to abuse it; every time we're self-effacing with the Delhi bigwigs, it seems we get effaced. I was telling the Chogyal that Sikkim's policy vis-à-vis the government of India is like the Piantem folktale in Sikkim. The Piantem is a legendary creature that looks rather like a coffeepot with a beaker nose. Piantems make an odd whistling noise, and whenever you hear it, you should run, as they carry off prey, particularly children. However, if you can't run, you should stand your ground, look at the creature, and say, "I'm smaller than you." Out of a spirit of competition the Piantem shrinks, and then again you say, "I'm smaller than you," and so on until he disappears. I think we're trying to do that with Delhi, but they don't play by Sikkimese rules and keep getting bigger every time we appeal to them on grounds of magnanimity. "You've got to stand up to them, at the same time keep their confidence," our Indian friends in Delhi counsel Chogyal. "Make them realize your interests are theirs." The question is how.

Sherzad has been living at home with her family since her divorce. They live now in a concrete-bungalow colony for middle-level government workers set back behind the villa-lined streets where Chogyal is seeing ministers. Their apartment is simple, almost bare. I feel greedy, crass, my handbag full of cloth swatches, samples for Sikkim House, which is being built in Delhi, luxuries I've picked up on the way to their apartment. They've brought virtually nothing from New York. All the furniture they were so proud of has been sold; even their mattresses, including the one dented by Mr. Sayyid's constant naps, are up with me in Gangtok. The living room contains nothing but trunks covered with towels and embroidered cloths, wooden Public Works Department chairs and table, and along a wall, a bookcase containing what Sherzad calls her New York collection—sociology books from the public library. In one corner is a noisy, humming refrigerator emblazoned with the brand name "Rosebud." "We Indians are so proud of our refrigerators, we have to keep them out front. Won't you have some ice?" she asks dramatically. "Damn it to hell, have some ice, Hopie."

Mrs. Sayyid's stopped dyeing her hair and it's virtually white. When Sherzad goes out, she sits holding my hand, rocking back and forth, crying. "Oh, Hopie, what's happened? We were so happy in New York."

"You won't believe it," Sherzad's sister Mimi says fiercely, "he got her pregnant on purpose so he could divorce her when the baby was born. He sent the cable the same day—and she was trying, trying so hard to adapt. It wasn't fair, Hopie—she gave up all her old friends. She gave up records, wearing makeup, smoking—really tried to be a South Indian wife. And he was planning this all along. The man is crazy."

Sweet Sherzad, romantic Sherzad—up to the last she'd fought it. And then had surrendered. Just before the divorce Sherzad had written, "I've fought myself and won and I've won my husband too. Life seems more beautiful now. There's no longer the unbearable conflict inside—occasionally he's cruel but mostly kind—we haven't had a real fight in three months." One of the most poignant things is that stuff—the Korvette gadgets, Mrs. Sayyid's dowry for Sherzad from New York—still down in South India, mostly unopened.

In the evening before I have to return for the party, Sherzad drives us—driving is the only pleasure she has kept from America—through the mauve-skied city down the empty Raj Path, past India Gate to old Delhi. Much as she fantasizes about New York, running through our life there again and again ("Sometimes, Hopie, at night I try to remember each step of the way down Eighty-sixth Street from the subway stop to our house"), she is acquiring an increasingly heightened awareness of being Indian—talking passionately about her family's utopian village, near Lucknow, and also of being Muslim. We visit the shrines in the old city, where, standing, hands pressed together in supplication, Sherzad calls out "Amin," peace, again and again in refrain as the mullah leads the prayers. Afterward she snaps back to her old irreverent self. "Half those prayers were for some students he was mentioning by name who want to pass their exams. I thought I'd join in anyway. Actually," she says before dropping me off at the hotel, "I was praying about my son. Mustaph is threatening to take him away."

In London at Heathrow, in a healing fog after Delhi's acid sun, the boys, looking blanched, their summer tans faded, come to meet us in the V.I.P. room. The customs officer presents Her Majesty's compliments; the children and I eat from a huge plate of sandwiches—real butter, fresh English butter, no more buffalo butter. "Mummy," Tenzing says, looking at me with mild reproof as my hand reaches out to the plate again. They're getting old enough to be embarrassed.

The boys are as beautiful as their father—Tenzing the most beautiful boy I have ever seen, with heavily lashed amber eyes, feline-tilted over rugged, high-sloped cheekbones, curving, sensuous mouth, mop of curly black hair. Wongchuk also is handsome, but paler, with more delicate features, his main beauty lying in the grace of his tall, lean body, sensuous even now under the stiff flannel of his Harrow uniform. Luckily both boys have a trace of adolescent pimples bridging their foreheads, making them more human, more regular. Even so, it's hard when you haven't seen them for a long time to keep from staring at them.

Chogyal chats with them in Sikkimese, gauging how well they still speak the language, concerned about inroads the long spells of time abroad may be making on the children's Sikkimese culture and language. Both boys respond fluently, barely betraying an English accent. Their accent in English, however, is pukka—upper-class—even more so when they are in a situation in which they have to prove themselves. Sometimes they parody it, joking between themselves in a haw-haw Colonel Blimp tone. I regret the class awareness they're picking up in England. It's reminiscent of Indian caste, not relevant for Sikkimese.

At Harrow, having sherry with their housemaster, I want to ask for a martini, although I loathe gin, to break the role-playing. I'm stunned when, discussing Wongchuk's future life and studies, the housemaster writes him off as the "number two" son, saying, "I imagine twenty years ago you wouldn't have had to worry—he would have just gone into the Church." Oh, yes, sir—oh, yessirree, Mr. Housemaster.

They still have fagging at Harrow. "They get the boys to run up the hill, and prefects lash them? Where? On the ankles? Buttocks?" I'm open-mouthed. Aghast. Although they don't defend the English class system or the exaggerated hierarchy within their school, the boys somewhat tend to see life as learning to accept and use authority and are defensive about my view that life's a matter of self-responsibility. Actually, the defensiveness is not so much against my view, I think, as against my interference. For good or bad, it's their world, and they don't want anyone meddling, particularly this affectionate but gawky "American gel," as the headmaster would say—stepmum.

They're right too. I am subversive. I would like to see Wongchuk, in particular, find his center, assert himself more, even at the expense of harmony. He feels the pressure, senses its repercussions, withdraws, irritated. Chastened, I vow again not to intrude myself. Actually, their world view about authority works for me, as, automatically, just because I'm married to their father, they accord me more respect and affection than most stepmothers could deserve and win.

Chogyal's a loving parent, not vocal about emotions—sticking to talk about their reports, their games—but exuding affection and pride. Physically they are quite close. Even now, as teenagers, before they go to bed the boys and their father do U Tu, the Sikkimese forehead-to-forehead greeting, which is somehow more manly, at the same time more tender than a kiss.

In London we live cooped up in apartments people lend us, either a flat near Victoria—wood-cage elevator, Victorian dormered windows looking out on Mary Poppins chimneys—or a pied-à-terre on Shepherd Street, the red-light street of Mayfair, at night full of men from the nearby Hilton Hotel running down pavements with their collars turned up. Both places are small, and the scale, especially when we have with us Chogyal's three nephews and nieces as well as our own three children, establishes a delicious coziness.

My husband, more domestic, or rather more particular about housework, than I, tries to create some coherence, organize our numbers by dividing up chores for all of us, himself included. He really likes the details of housework, and to my mind, since I have a greater appetite to be out tearing into London, does such unnecessary things as ironing. I agree with Yangchen, who says, "Oh, body heat will get it [wrinkles] out." Her job has been to wash the large piles of dirty clothes brought back from school, which she does, her gray uniform hiked up above her knees, by putting them all in the bathtub and treading precariously back and forth.

Yangchen hates being away at school, so much so that she has blocked out much of any academic grounding she has acquired. The headmistress doesn't know what to make of her. As we usually come at Christmastime, which gives an added dimension of familyness, the contrast between her homesickness and the closeness of being with us now is heightened. Together we trudge back and forth to Harrods, our hands cut by cords of heavy Christmas parcels, waiting for a Knightsbridge bus to rescue us.

In the flat near Victoria it's impossible to light the antique stove. We try to Hansel-and-Gretel each other into seeing what's wrong with the gas burner. The gray turkey, bought at Harrods, is never going to cook. We're going to have to subsist on the Christmas cake that Karma, the Sikkimese student, has brought down from the Manchester bakery in which he works on weekends and holidays. "The icing, Your Majesty, is not very good. Cherry [his English girlfriend] made me put it on before the cake part had properly cooled." Karma comes down to be with us whenever we're here, living with us, squeezed in as part of the family, in an odd combination of formality—he always addresses us by title— and pajamaed intimacy. The student nurses from Sikkim don't stay with us but come to pick up the bottled chilis and cheeses their families have sent through us, and return often for curry lunches; and for Christmas.

There are too many people, however nice, to see, not just to see but to connect with: Ferdoz, the Sayyids' eldest daughter, whom Chogyal is trying to persuade to give up her squalid salesgirl job and return to India; the children's guardians, two families who have looked after the boys and Yangchen as if they were their own children; and a score of influential well-wishers of Sikkim.

We need a full-time banquet consultant, traffic manager, product engineer, camp director, and staff coordinator. During a single week we give a series of five dinner parties in a row. I'm enjoying it but feel tired, rattled. One evening, when David Astor and his friends who represent the "liberal brains trust" in England come for drinks and a talk with my husband, my only job is to make toast. (Chogyal has bought caviar and even cut up some lemons.) I'm so interested in the conversation I hear through the kitchen hatch that the toast burns, filling the tiny mews house with smoke. I put a new batch of bread in the oven and, so I won't be distracted by eavesdropping, go upstairs, to come down and find the new toast burned and the whole "liberal brains trust" doubled up outside in the middle of the street gagging and whacking one another on the back.

I'm ambivalent about the numbers we always travel in. One year when the Chogyal hasn't accompanied me, feeling like a madam, I stay at Brown's Hotel with five boys—Tenzing, Wongchuk, and three nephews. The desk clerk raises his eyebrows when we go in and out. Occasionally too, in this miniskirt era, I'm embarrassed by trailing around in my long Sikkimese dress, my Asian family (Sikkimese men and children often wear Western clothes—never the women) all dressed in Western clothes. I love it and sometimes hate it, wanting to rush out alone and record London for a memory bank to take back. I need stored impressions. In Gangtok I will have nothing but these to draw from. I'm not getting them; our trips here are simply extensions of our life and responsibilities in Sikkim. Only seldom, very seldom, can I even slip out to a movie. Even then, planning to see the other part another day, I see only half.

I have to buy reminders of Europe I can carry back with me, small things that will amuse us and will evoke the West—postcards from the National Gallery, embroidered handkerchiefs, tiny crafts, packets of flower seeds, daffodil bulbs, grosses of felt-tip pens, Maple Leaf Notebooks. Records, heavy piles of records, are the only exception to the size rule.

Our last few days are spent in a frenzy of buying things for ourselves and presents we are expected to bring back, and carrying out commissions (such as the bobbin) we have been asked to undertake. One must never return empty-handed. One year I buy dozens of collapsible umbrellas, another year dozens of bedroom slippers, leaving the salesclerk so dumbfounded when I place the order that he just stands there not moving. My last errand always is to go to Fortnum's and Harrods to buy pounds of Gorgonzola, boursin, boursault, and pastries. No matter what else has been happening on our trip, I've spent so much time reveling in the *matière grasse* I miss so much, dream about in Gangtok, that, approaching the cash register at Harrods with two gallon jars of mayonnaise I've bought to take back, it's almost inevitable that I'm recognized. "Aren't you," the cashier begins, and while I brace myself to shout, "No, I'm not Hope Cooke, I'm not the American girl who became queen," she looks at me piercingly and concludes "the girl who a year ago used to buy all the ice cream?"

I'd like to stay back, seeing three movies a day after Chogyal leaves. In fact, I'd like to go on to America, which Chogyal urges me to do. But this is galling. Aside from the publicity in America that plagues our visits, I'm so jealous I don't dare let him leave without me. One year, on the way back home we'd stayed at Grace's house in Brussels. She wasn't there, but she'd left out all her belongings. I can't get them out of my mind—little satin puffed slippers, negligee draped over a chair, lace wrapper hanging in the bathroom, hairbrush full of long red hairs.

As the children's vacation ends and after they've been taken, as their father says, for their last "big tuck before jail," we drive the boys to Harrow, and Yangchen, very quiet, back to her Elizabethan manor house boarding school. The headmistress pops her head out at the sound of our car to reprimand us for being half an hour late. Shortly thereafter we leave for home.

12

I'M TWENTY-SEVEN and married four years. It's an odd time. I feel a certain strength, at the same time a lack of direction. I'm scared I'm going to allow myself to flirt with General X. I know his restrained flirting with me is just a power play against Chogyal, designed to hurt, diminish my image, Sikkim's image. Still, he's the only person who has even indicated he would like to flirt, perhaps because he's the only one here with the requisite social standing. Although my work, shared causes with the young Sikkimese officers, is partly a displacement of sexual energy, as Gyalmo I couldn't possibly flirt with them. General X's attention is the only thing that keeps me from feeling myself virtually neuter. At the same time, my fantasies about him are in direct conflict with what continues to bind me to Sikkim and my husband—our work for national integrity, and self-respect free of Indian domination.

I've thought again and again that the best part of being Gyalmo is that it gives me structure, makes me carry out things—finish what I start, be responsible—which is contrary to my nature. I fear my old penchant for wriggling out of things, slipping away. It doesn't occur to me that I've changed, that for years I have been responsible, committed, that I've earned the right to do something different for myself. Part of the problem is that my adult identity is entirely connected to Sikkim, to being a wife. There is no alternative, no place outside of this to stand.

Even so, although throttled, without any clear idea of what I'd like to do, could do, I'm at a point where part of me would like to change course or, as I see it, wriggle out. Quickly I begin a baby so I can't. If it's a girl I'm going to call her Leezum, a Lepcha name meaning "home unity"—the unity of Sikkim, the unity of our family.

The waiting time in Calcutta is cozy and relaxed, so different from that before Palden was born. It's the closest to a real vacation we've ever had, Chogyal feeling near enough to Sikkim to be in touch but carefree enough to explore the city with me and Palden. We three walk in the last cool Calcutta weather before the heat, a security officer who doesn't approve of our informal outings tagging grumpily behind us. Radical Naxalite politics are at a height. Each day brings scores of killings in the city. Every wall surface is covered with exquisite Bengali-scripted political slogans. Once, through the traffic, we even see a scrawny sacred Brahmin cow walk by, a Communist hammer and sickle scrawled on her hide.

In the daytime we browse in the Oxford Book Shop, and visit the auction shops along Park Street, full of ornate malachite tables, cut-glass chandeliers, and ormolu clocks invariably described as from the "Tagore" estate. So this is what the old preacher of boundlessness and transcendentalism lived with—my old teacher of the Great All. Behind the Grand Hotel I've found a butter store where they sell smuggled Danish butter, and sometimes we shop there, the proprietor nervously eyeing our security officer from the Calcutta police as he takes down the black market order. In the evenings we go with Palden to the zoo or drive to the outskirts of town to watch the artisans making images of Sarasvati, the beautiful many-armed goddess of wisdom, which on her festival day will be carried by rickshaws through the city, immersed, swept away by the Hooghly River.

When our daughter is born, Mr. Gandhi, Chogyal's Gujarati business partner in Calcutta, who, although a self-made man, full of the work ethic, also believes very much in luck, hears she was born at midnight, the Lord Krishna's hour, and prepares to give her trays of presents that will ensure his own fortune. When the time is corrected and he discovers the birth was really at eleven, he withdraws the presents and sends only a small gold coin or, as my daughter tells the story later, a little rubber duck.

She is a beautiful baby—silky brown hair, gleaming white skin, long almond eyes. We call her Hope Leezum. Partly I want to call her Hope because I've always felt the name itself magic, giving the custodian some special power of spirit. Partly I want to call her Hope for my mother, who did not survive. As I have survived, this Hope must triumph.

At home, although I nurse the baby, I spend most of my time with Palden, just as, when Palden was born, I concentrated my attention on Yangchen. Much as I'm fascinated by Palden's recent rapacity for learn-

181

ing, I also take a new interest in him because of Joyce. Joyce, a graduate of the Bank Street College of Education who's been teaching with Clover in Harlem, has been sponsored by Clover to work for our Tathangchen Village School, and finally, after months of waiting for her permit to be issued by the Indians, has arrived. She and her daughter, Danielle, a beautiful towhead Palden's age, come up to the palace every afternoon for reading lessons. We print on cards, asking the children to choose words—"geranium," "hungry," "angry." The children, happy to learn what they themselves have initiated, race along—even Palden, whose English, I'm just realizing, is very scanty. (Up till now, because of some depressed reasoning that he belongs only to Sikkim, I've spoken to him mainly in my broken pidgin Sikkimese.)

After the lesson under the magnolia tree, when Joyce and Danielle have gone back down the hill to their quarters near the school, I sit reading with Palden in the children's bedroom, going through the Lucy Fitch Perkins Twin series and an English series on civilizations—Rome, Persia, Babylonia, China, India. "Did it really happen?" Palden keeps asking. He has an enormous reverence for what's real and a scorn—although he enjoys the fairy tales the ayahs tell him—for fiction. Enjoying the physical warmth of each other's body while the baby sleeps in the crib beside us, we read together until supper.

My son is enchanted by learning—ancient history, planting bean seeds, the equator, Sikkimese economy. He confuses everything. Having heard so much about Sikkim wanting to get in the U.N., he has a plan to put all the Sikkimese in a Trojan horse and deliver it there. Everything he does alone or with his friends he does with a fierce energy and concentration—building Lego fortresses on the verandah, digging bunkers on the back lawn, hurling his brothers' football, trying to head it as he has seen them do, begging the guards when they are off duty to show him how. Even when he draws, he crouches over in an excruciating posture, gripping the crayon, determined to make the picture perfect. He is rarely satisfied with his drawings, rarely keeps them. Instead he hangs on his bulletin board the pictures of his older friend Phurpa, who paints in dazzlingly realistic style, half comic-book, half traditional. Even though Chogyal and I sometimes tell him that it's all right not to be best, Palden won't ignore our unspoken demand for excellence.

At school he extends himself with the same energy. The only fight he's ever been in—tearing a boy's shirt, throwing a paint box at his head, being beaten in return with the boy's 007 James Bond belt—was fought on a Saturday morning over a cleaning contest. The children volunteering in a neighboring classroom had stolen (he alleged) the cleaning materials for his classroom. Both children, crying, run up the hill to tell their story; their teacher toils up sometime later.

Palden's competitiveness is all aimed at uplift, either his own or that of his surroundings. It is never social, never based on being a prince. On the contrary, he is consumed by a wish not to be different, not to be treated differently, to be one with his friends. Outside of a small bit of deference from the teachers and his brown oxfords (he longs for a pair of long black pointy "go go" shoes from the bazaar), he succeeds.

Although I have a much greater sense of Palden than I did, a new respect, partly learned from Joyce, for him as an individual, I still sometimes see him as a symbol—a tiny mascot, just as I myself am, of Sikkim. When he comes in every morning to say goodbye, dressed in his brown school uniform and knee-high gum boots for his descent down the muddy hill, I'm full of pride in him and also what he stands for— democracy in Sikkim. Tathangchen, the school he is going to, built privately as a model by the Chogyal with his own funds, is a village school, whose students mostly are the children of farmers, drivers, or palace servants—the opposite of the Academy, where all the children dress in English-style uniforms and follow a derivative Anglo-Indian education. Maybe, through the example of our son, we can get Sikkim's upper class to stop running after the "coat and tie" education they get at the Academy, or, better still, stop them from sending their children, as many do, to boarding schools in India. If it catches on, it would be a big plus for social integration in Sikkim. Already there is some movement to press the Sikkim and Indian governments to replace their present scholarship programs, whereby children are sent to study in India, with stipends to be used in Sikkim itself.

Palden's school has drawbacks. The primary one is the condition of the building. As many do here, the contractor has cheated on cement, and the upper story, built with the help of our wedding present of money from my sister Harriet, is crumbling; the ceiling beams have cracked. For a year or so, not wishing to upset Chogyal, we haven't raised the subject. Now, however, as it becomes clear that the building is unsafe, Joyce and I inform him. He is furious. He doesn't want to hear the school criticized. Also, although years ago, when we were first engaged, he'd suggested I could work at Tathangchen to make innovations, he's tired of my moving in again—meddling in something close to him. Finally engineers bear out that the top story is unsafe and must come down. Angrily agreeing, Chogyal yells at me that if I'm going to interfere I might as

well take over the whole thing. I see his point. It's galling to have someone criticize who is not actually taking responsibility. I do this quite a
lot. This time, however, I'm glad, heedless of how he'd meant it, to take
up his offer of responsibility for the school. Quickly, before it's withdrawn, I accept, and arrange to rent a new building in the village while
repairs are made. The new, temporary school, the best we can find, one
that the children endure for the long, cold winter, is unfurnished—rough
cement and no glass in the window frames.

Aside from the buildings, teaching at the school needs reform. The
staff presents problems. The teachers, even though they're rather young
and have little teacher training, are good—at least prospectively good—
but the headmistress, an older Indian woman, displaying both glaring
insecurity and rigid dogma, will not permit the children any independence of action, nor is she able to give them any guidance. The school
jerks and stumbles ahead. Joyce is in the delicate position of trying to
remain subordinate, inoffensive, while at the same time infiltrating some
good ideas; I am in the delicate position of trying to back her but not
upset the applecart and the Chogyal.

Children here have always stayed in the classroom, learned by rote.
Now Joyce gets her classes actively engaged in projects—making collections of flowers, building things, collecting minerals, going out in the
village to map clusters of the children's houses. The youngsters seem a
little confused, sometimes afraid. One day when Joyce takes them on a
nature walk, they all file by a certain tree with their eyes screwed shut.
"It's Arkya Shingh, the tree with evil powers," they say. Parents too are
reserved, watchful, suspicious, although the school is free, that their
children aren't getting a valuable education, that they will be deficient
in the ABCs and numbers, the magic formula for success. Palden as
much as anyone shares this awe of accountable formulas. He is spellbound by numbers and letters. They are his key to controlling the
world. "ABC," he chants as loud as he can, back and forth, at random,
ignoring Joyce's and my phonetics. He doesn't want to hear "aay," "aye,"
"ah"—he knows he's got the real thing, the charm to bind down and
make less dangerous and embarrassing all the things in life he doesn't
know about.

Partly because they're basically so bright and outgoing, partly because
they're growing fond of Joyce, find her helpful, unthreatening, one by
one the teachers and the children at the school begin to relax about
learning, realize it can happen in all kinds of ways. Dugyal, a little Lepcha
boy whose father works at the palace, brings in a bamboo bow and arrow

he's made, Karma Thinly brings some rabbits to school in a cage, and Rita an odd terrarium full of monstrous bugs. Occasionally even the parents begin to participate, mending the school fence so their animals don't stray in, putting up a few prayer flags to bring the school luck.

Increasingly children come over to play at Joyce and Danielle's house and are intrigued by the few unusual things they find—Danielle's Playskool toys, Liberty print dresses, a collection of glass animals. At the same time they are reassured, comforted by the familiar scale of most things in Joyce's house—tin-bucket bathtub, wood-burning stove, slat wood furniture, and her simple New England manner that makes her approachable, equal. Danielle is beginning to enter the children's make-believe games—their favorite, lamas. Sitting cross-legged in rows on Joyce's little porch, stopping often to clear their throats, pretending to drink tea, they rumble their voices as far down as they can make them go, ring bells, crash cymbals, and blow imaginary thighbone trumpets.

Eventually our house too becomes an alternative school site. Palden's friends camp here all the time—running through the upstairs playing cops and robbers, using our big freestanding cupboards for games of hide-and-seek, often joining us for a supper of rice and dahl, the quickest and cheapest thing to cook at the last minute. Mr. Manuel, looking harried, tries to get a head count.

Hope Leezum, invincibly hairbowed by now, pigtails at a defiant angle, adores the company. She follows them around the house, her red shoes, bought a size too large, making satisfying clopping noises as she runs.

In the evenings the Tathangchen children join Palden and Hope Leezum (changed by Memeh, who loves them into yet another lacy party dress that Alice's mother has sent), for our usual walk, and we start down the hill, trotting to keep up with Palden's wooden truck, which he's let coast down the gutter. Walking along the Ridge Road, we stop on the Japanese bridge, put up by the Forest Department, to poke the tadpoles in the artificial pool. The children see everything, remark on everything. Partly, perhaps because their English is so stilted, what the Tathangchen children say comes out graphic and poetic at the same time. "Oh, look, Gyalmo," Dugyal says, tugging at my arm and pointing at the moon coming through a long cloud, "the moon is the crocodile's eye."

Some nights when there is an English movie, we go to the cinema recently put up in the bazaar next to the Hotel De Sikkim. Around dusk, if the children get a hint of the trip to the movies, more and more brothers and sisters arrive. They hang around the verandah waiting to

185

jump into the car, everyone on top of everyone else, and swoop down to town singing their heads off, thrilled at being in a vehicle (pronounced "wickle") and by the prospect of the film. On these occasions we tumble out of the car like circus performers while the proprietor (a Marwari, my husband's Mah-Jongg crony) rushes out to greet us and I, secretly pleased, watch the commotion we've caused and the surprise of the Indian military moviegoers at seeing Chogyal swept along by a score of raffish village kids.

Inside, we scramble upstairs to the royal box, as yet an unfinished concrete stall draped with pieces of patterned cloth from the bazaar, and settle back, waiting for the treats. The proprietor, combining good business with an attempt to repay us for the many meals he eats at the palace, starts passing around Sikkim orange squash, Coke (bottled in Gauhati and recently come to Sikkim), and phorrin whiskey, mixed, I think, with Indian. After the lights go out, there is much rustling and whispering, occasional *ssh*'s from the people in the rows in front of us. (One day Hope Leezum knocks a glass of orange squash into the turban of a Punjabi seated below, who turns, bows, and says, "Oh, never mind, Princess.") Trays of vegetable turnovers, and hot spiced gram, from the hotel next door are circulated. "Do shut up, Hope, you're taking advantage," my husband scolds as I keep up a running dialogue with the children, trying to explain what is happening in the violent Italian (filmed in Yugoslavia) western. Two of the reels are reversed, and one seems to be missing altogether, not having been sent up from Calcutta. (At home, overcome with remorse over taking the children to such a gory, unredeemed film, I sit down with them, all of us grouped rather like a Chinese self-confession meeting, and talk about the film's shortcomings and that they shouldn't really like it or take it seriously.)

The summers explode with children. All of them are home—our own big three back from school in England, and now also the three children of Chogyal's Calcutta sister Coola and her husband, who have recently died. The house hums with rival record players. The driveway gives off a constant spray of gravel, as, despite the monsoon rains, the kids, true to teenage dictates, zoom in and out. The logistics are overwhelming. We consume twenty dozen eggs a week. Mr. Manuel runs backward and forward between the palace boilers, trying to keep up with the amount of charcoal being used. Even so, there is often not enough hot water for everyone's bath. If it is only mildly wet, Tenzing organizes football games, which we watch through the fog; if it is pouring, we play Monopoly, turning for help to one of the cousins who's been at school in Switzerland, as the set we've brought back from Europe turns out to be in French, not English. During breaks in the weather we roll up to North Sikkim with the incumbent Indian Representative's family, to whom we're very much attached, in a convoy of jeeps, ambushing each other at curves, holding moss fights, pitting bathers against nonbathers in the Yumtang hot springs while steam swirls around us and, screeching with laughter, we chase one another.

I love being in the middle, the Ma Kettle-Ethel Kennedy of this group. In a way the disasters, tragedies (the latest being the death of Coola and her husband) that beset us on the outside give a special warmth, resolve, to our inner circle. There are so many horrors, outside dangers. Beginning with late Jigmie's assassination, it seems every year has brought new misfortunes of almost epic, absurd proportions—floods, wars, travel dangers: Palden and I stuck on a train for twenty-four hours in an Assamese jungle until we were rescued by the army; Palden lost in a road breach for two days during a flood in Bengal; Chogyal's secretary's jeep gored by a rhino on the road to Bhutan.

It's almost ridiculous, unthinkable. Just recently an army truck full of munitions fell off the road, caught fire, and we sat up all night watching flares, listening to volleys of gunshot, thinking it was "the real thing" (a Chinese invasion), as the colonel of the Sikkim Guards put it. We are so taxed by insecurity that sometimes we don't take it into account, and yet the anxiety is always there, giving a special quality, a heightened value to those you love and want to protect. The night the army truck went off the road we were so scared, before we knew the artillery fire was just munitions going off in series, before we knew the flares hissing like snakes were flares shot up for reassurance, that everything became particularly precious, dear—each tree *the* tree, each child *the* child.

At the same time, although it feels good to have an embattled strength, a foxhole love that gives me the energy to go on, to be a grown-up for the people dependent on me, I'm tired, stretched, displaced. I need to talk with my husband about what's happening to us, to conceptualize our new, bigger family responsibility, make ourselves more germane to what's happening. Sometimes I feel that it's more a crowd scene than a marriage. Chogyal takes everything for granted, including relationships. He works and worries so hard he doesn't have the inclination to talk, which, after a balked bid for attention, makes me bitchy. Cocoola, who stays in the guesthouse from time to time, compounds it. In some ways, as coguardian of the cousins, she's a help, but to me personally she's unnerving, actually terrifying. Ever since Alice's *Redbook* article on me, when Cocoola called her an opportunist adventurer—she meant me but couldn't quite say it—she's been incredible. The more I feel at home, the worse she gets. I think in the beginning she thought I'd disappear fairly soon and is in a fury that I haven't. At the palace she always asks in exquisite hostility, "Won't you have a cup of coffee, Hope La?" "Er, no thank you, I mean won't you have a cup of coffee?" Chogyal's so busy, and he wouldn't want to hear it anyway. We've never even discussed the fact of the cousins and Cocoola living here.

It's odd. What I first liked about Sikkim is what troubles me now—that here there are so many concrete problems, basic needs to resolve, that we (I) can't think too much about who I am, what I am doing, where I am going.

Norbu and Joyce give me some support. I'd met Norbu, a Tathang-chen village boy and captain of the senior class at the Boys' High School, through Tenzing one day when he'd come to the palace to play on Tenzing's soccer team. Talking to me afterward, he'd noted my Sikkimese was still terrible and offered to come up to tutor me. After that he's come every day. He's not a pet, not a palace pet, as my husband grumbles. He's too strong for that. Also, in an odd way, as he can seem rather arrogant with his certainties, with his passion for improving Sikkim, he's quite selfless—not cut out to be a protégé.

We meet, often in the library, drinking cup after cup of tea as Norbu labors to improve my Sikkimese, which, although I'm able to understand a great deal, in speaking is still limited to a kitchen and social-amenity level. He's a relief after my old teacher, who taught me about the axe in the kitchen; Norbu teaches me words that open up a Sikkimese world view to me. Nuances for philosophical thought, nuances for concrete surfaces, very few for middle-level emotions, such as love. Please, Norbu, I plead, isn't there anything else to say except "lame," "good"? After some time, when the going seems too uphill (Norbu teasingly says he's not teaching me Sikkimese but I'm teaching him to understand my garbled version), we lapse into English so we can talk without hindrance about the things we still need to bring up.

It's extraordinary that although we meet every day—"lives out of your pocket," Chogyal grumbles—we still have so much to talk about, never get bored. He tells me tales of hermits, pilgrims, shaman customs, and forest lore. "We always led the British expeditions into fields of aconite. If their mules grazed, even overnight, a good many died. . . ."

Sometimes he tells me of his small plans—how to make village ovens hold more heat by adding lime, how we could make an electric crematorium in the traditional Mandala shape which would preserve Buddhist custom while saving poor people the cost of firewood, how we could make a flaming sword out of cotton and gasoline for the child playing Jambayal, the deity of learning, in our school play. Sometimes he talks to me about his big hopes: how good education can take root in Sikkim, how the ethnic groups in Sikkim can be united (as a start, adopt village names instead of tribal ones for last names), and finally, always, how Sikkim could function if returned to its old independence, free of the restrictions we endure.

What's amazing is, as much as he has an inside view of Sikkimese society, he also has an outside view, can see Sikkim as an outsider would and can make associations with my frame of reference. One day when I'm explaining Halloween, Norbu lights up and says, "It's a catharsis—like we have here. After someone dies in the village, and prayers have been said, the children are allowed to go wild—throw stones, make noise, weaken the props of the steps so when the lamas leave the house the steps collapse. Partly it's to frighten away evil spirits, but partly it's an impulse we have to act out before order is restored." Sometimes, tired by our rush of theoretical or uplifting talk, we just gossip. Norbu often tells me the problems at the boys' school—still no proper laboratory equipment, rapid turnover of teachers, delayed exams because of the university strikes in Calcutta.

We have the same banana-peel sense of humor. It's good to have someone to joke with. Lots of things strike us as funny. One day when Chogyal is away and the guards at the gate are a bit lax, an American tourist family in a camper pulls up on the lawn and settles down for the night. It has never happened before. The ADCs keep going up and talking to them in a worried sort of way, but the strangers don't leave, and the ADCs are too polite to make them. From the verandah Norbu and I watch them dig in more and more, putting out wash on a makeshift clothesline, arranging some sort of outdoor grill. "It's like Woodstock," Norbu sputters, and the two of us crack up, overwhelmed with the silliness, the outrageousness of the situation.

Sometimes we just sit listening to records—Cat Stevens, James Taylor, Judy Collins. Occasionally he plays a flute he made himself from bamboo, or sings folk songs in a deep, sad voice, a few made up by himself, one (something to do, I think, with his feelings about being recently orphaned) about Buddha's mother, who died soon after the Buddha was born. Joyce has been teaching him American folk songs, and he's been translating them into Sikkimese for the Tathangchen children—"Where Have All the Flowers Gone?" "We Shall Overcome," "Go Tell It on the Mountain." In the mornings I can hear the children singing at the top of their lungs on their way to school.

In the past I used to see myself just as my husband's wife. Now—and this has something to do with my friendships, the outside acceptance of me, but more with my own acceptance of myself—I have a feeling of my own core, and sometimes my own worth. It's ironic, sad too, that Chogyal, on the other hand, although he won't admit it, just as we never speak of anything personally significant, seems to be getting weaker, less sure of himself, drinking more, and in an odd, resentful way is becoming more dependent on me.

It's the last straw. He threw my record player out the window, and it's lying crumpled and broken in the ADC's cupboard. The ADC doesn't know what to do—too embarrassed to ask my permission to throw it away. Chogyal knew it was my lifeline. He knew that without my record player I had nothing. Ever since I gave the money for the damned floods he's been flipping out. I can't believe it. When we reached Moscow and heard about the floods in Sikkim, I flew back to Delhi and on to Gangtok a few hours later, virtually flying the length of Asia and back—Mongolia to Moscow, Moscow back to India nonstop—thirty-six hours or something. What the hell, and why? So he could have his rinky-dink goodwill talk with the Russian cultural people. Meanwhile three hundred people were killed here, there was two million dollars' worth of damage, and the Indian Representative was getting all the credit for helping, airdropping rice on people's heads.

To do something, I donated three thousand dollars and some medicines and started trekking into the stricken area towing government officers after me. It wasn't my thing. There'd been a bit of glory in it—5 percent. The rest was pure agony. First of all, I'm shy, God help me, meeting villagers I don't know without my bloody husband, and, second, I had blisters up to my kneecaps in the boots I'd been lent. Furthermore, at night I could hardly sleep because of a sunburn and mica dust that had gotten into my eye. And then, after I'd been showing the flag for him, to have Chogyal blow up, on the pretext that some self-seeking politician had been sore because I'd dished out my own money, which I'd contributed, directly to the afflicted villagers instead of through official channels! I can appreciate the politician's anger, because I unintentionally had shown him up as having done nothing to help in the floods, but to have Chogyal take his side—what kind of anger does that come from?

And he hasn't stopped there. Now that I've finally got friends, he's systematically been striking out to isolate me, telling me off and putting things out about them, hinting they'll get sacked or just making it too embarrassing for them to come. He deliberately did the record player thing in front of nice General Z. Norbu's the one who sees me cry, and I can't tell him anything, nor can he ask me. Neither can I tell Joyce. Even when I write my friends in America—and not only because of the censorship—I tell them things are okay.

I don't dare leave him. In fact, I inveigle him into coming with me and Palden to England, and leave Hope Leezum behind to ensure my return. One night before he leaves London he tells me that I must go to the Indian Embassy to sign a paper to the effect that Palden will be home within eight weeks. Next morning he has forgotten, or else he knows I have no nerve. Palden and I go to France; I pretend I'm escaping, knowing I won't, traveling to the châteaux on the Loire, trying to see something that has endured, something that, however remote the connection, evokes something of my Western history, Western being.

Palden is unflagging, wide-eyed, rapturous at seeing all this beauty, this history. After each château we go to a cake shop and choose something —"Tout petit peu de ça." "Tuppity, tuppity, tup," my linguist son sings, picking up the rhythm right away. The whole bus applauds as, in a six-year-old's high spirits, he swings aboard still babbling about crenellations. In Chartres we stand together in the stain of light from the rose window while a choir in the chancel is practicing, the echoes flying like birds around the cathedral. "It's so beautiful, Mummy, it's so beautiful." Palden is gripping my hand very tightly. I squeeze my body with every muscle, trying to induce this beauty inside me, force by magic some measure of its endurance into my being. I must endure. I will endure. I too will become stone.

As usual, it's work that saves me. For years in our school system we'd been making do with shockingly inappropriate books from the open market. Recently the Textbook and Curriculum Committee has been formed, which I chair. With the advice of Oxford University Press in India, we've started to write books for Grades 1–8 in social studies, the four mother-tongue languages, English, Sikkimese geography, and flora and fauna. Previously students had learned little or nothing that related to themselves or Sikkim. Despite initial bumbling, we now have active production. Teams of students are recording stories all over the country for the various readers, and four translators work to translate the material into each language of Sikkim so that for the first time the children, speaking different mother tongues, can study the same body of material. Aside from readers in English and various other languages, several social-studies books have come out, and more are at Oxford needing only a little editing. The books are impressive. Already one of the Indian hill states is considering copying their format, and, despite their initial apprehension, our own teachers too—in part because the government has introduced teacher-training sessions to ease the changeover—have largely approved the new child- and community-centered approach to primary education.

But Chogyal's fed up with my projects. Even though he basically appreciates them—at least when they're done—they're still a drain on him, one more thing to think about when he's already full to the brim anyway thinking and worrying about Sikkim. I've seen him react the same way when Cocoola tackles him about refugee problems. You can't help but sympathize with both of them—Cocoola wanting concrete problems solved, her brother used up, stretched to breaking, feeling he can't extend himself another inch. I know that, and sometimes when I ask his help I waver. ("Hope, you began this. You solve this. You only want to get the credit. You do it as long as things are going right for you and dump it on me as soon as things begin to go wrong.") In some ways he's right—not about the credit but about his bailing me out. I hate the hard parts. Firing people, for instance. I want to be loved so much, would do anything to be loved. He's saved me more than once. I know I'm Eleanor Roosevelting, nagging Franklin, and he too weary to coast away in his wheelchair. Still, I can't help myself. First of all, when I see glaring things, or people tell me glaring things, that need attention, and I know that through access to the Chogyal I have the possibility of getting action, I feel a moral responsibility to take up the cause—not everything, but a good deal. Another thing: the projects are the only things that keep me going. Without them I would shrivel up, have nothing to get up for, even—I hear this dimly—no reason to be here. A paradox. I involve myself in the projects because I'm unhappy here. The projects make my husband angrier, and I get into more projects.

I'm determined to keep on. Aside from the valid reason my husband has for wanting me to quit, the pressure I add to the pressure he's already bearing, I'm increasingly certain he wants me vulnerable, shorn of support, so I'll again be more subject to him and his moods. Something is really eating him up. Even if I go into another room he follows me, saying thickly and loudly, "There can only be one captain. I married you anyway to be the mother of the house, and you don't clean out the icebox or look after the bills, and people are cheating us blind." He's right on the last three counts. On the other hand, our house is beautiful, our meals good, and the children happy.

An ethnomusicologist from Brown University is here now finally trying to make the recording we've long sought to produce. But things are going badly. Chogyal is so angry he hasn't spoken to me for three weeks. Everything possible's been put in the way to circumscribe the work. Each time anything's recorded, a special board constituted by the Chogyal listens to the piece, and if it's "not pure," shreds it. The musicologist is trying so hard; he really is pure in intention and execution, with enormous respect for Sikkimese culture. Every piece has its source or inflection from someplace. It didn't spring up full-blown. The musicologist keeps trying to say that, although he will aim to get only traditional songs, any song is authentic if it is authentically attributed and presented for what it is. (If there are, for example, Western hymn influences in a Lepcha song, that must be stated.) Nevertheless all the Bhutia Lepcha material is being cut out in a frenzy of cultural purism—puree is more apt. Very strange ambivalence, because at the same time Chogyal keeps genuinely worrying about Sikkimese culture being preserved.

Every time it seems that Chogyal and I have reached an impossible impasse in our relations, some far greater disaster outside forces us to suppress or allows us to suppress whatever our own problem is. Unconsciously, when we discuss the past, we've even come to date things by awful happenings: "No, it was the year of the Chinese ultimatum. No, you're wrong, it was the flood time." We're both wrong. It was when late Jigmie was assassinated. Now Cocoola's got a blood clot in her arm. This time, however, unlike usually, my unhappiness and baffled anger stay suffocating in my breast. I can't get rid of it. Nor can I take solace in my few friends here. Norbu's gone, away studying at college in Darjeeling. General Z's gone, replaced by an arrogant political man, and Joyce has returned to New York, as she feels Danielle should get reconnected with America.

13

WITH MY FRIENDS gone, there was no one to talk to about private funny things. All the educated Sikkimese talked of was the need for recognition of Sikkim's international status and their right to work out a place in the world by themselves. People didn't want a rupture with India, but an end to what was considered New Delhi's colonialism. The more outspoken talked of "independence, with mutual defense arrangements with India"; the more conservative spoke of "thorough treaty revision"; the very careful spoke of "treaty review." Mr. Thapa's new paper, *The Sikkim* (its motto: "To die for one's country is sweet and proper), several times officially reprimanded by the Sikkim government, was the voice of independence, detailing one by one the changeover to independence of almost all the colonies and trusteeships throughout the world, reminding Sikkimese that although Sikkim's status was more sovereign than that of a colony or trusteeship, its de facto neocolonial status remained unchanged. The paper, a fortnightly, inveighed against the inability of the Sikkim Council to discuss revision of the treaty between India and Sikkim, a process that repeatedly had been ruled out by the Council's president (the Sidlon, formerly known as the Dewan, or Prime Minister—on loan to Sikkim from India).

The wish for greater autonomy had been brewing a long time. In 1967 the three executive councillors of the three main political parties, representing fourteen out of the eighteen members of the Sikkim elected council, had issued a joint statement saying it was "not a crime but their sacred duty" to demand revision of the 1950 Indo-Sikkim treaty. "Every country has its inherent right to exist and maintain its separate identity and, therefore, to review and revise its treaty obligations in the wake of changing circumstances . . . any right which has become the responsibility of the Government of India under the treaty has been entrusted to her on our behalf by Sikkim. It is therefore an obligation on the Government of India to gracefully sponsor our membership of various international organizations."

Indian newspapers, which usually followed the India government line in belittling Sikkim in order to frustrate Sikkimese aspirations, attacked the credibility of the Sikkim elected personnel, the Sikkim government administration and the Chogyal. "There's no democracy, no constitution," they alleged, to which the Sikkim government responded that the principles of a constitution had been laid out in 1953 by the late Chogyal, under whom an elected council was set up, and that all laws had been properly codified, using relevant sections of the Indian penal code as a model. "There are no fair elections," the papers alleged, to which Sikkim's elected executive councillors (two of them Sikkimese Nepalis) replied, in a manifesto supporting the move for treaty revision, that they were happy with the parity arrangement between the Sikkimese Nepalis and the Bhutia Lepchas—a formula that had come into the Sikkim political scene with an all-party agreement of 1953—and that India was raising the question of a Sikkimese Nepali voting majority to hurt Sikkim's solidarity.

The councillors had been severely censured by the Indian Representative; moreover, they had been let down by the Sikkim government. As under the existing treaty, at India's behest, the elected officials had no right to discuss Indo-Sikkim relations, Chogyal had been forced to make an apology for the statement and to discount what they had said. The councillors, having declared themselves, were naturally upset that they had not been backed up. It was Catch-22. When Chogyal himself, even gently, tried to bring up treaty revision (which was called "sitting around a table to find out and strengthen the points of affinity between the two countries"; Sikkim's wish to join the U.N. was called "our rightful place in the comity of nations"), the Indian government said that Sikkim should be more democratic and that only "the people" could bring it up.

If the Chogyal couldn't speak, people asked, and the elected representatives couldn't speak, who could? People in Sikkim were frustrated, uncoordinated, defensive—as a rule reacting rather than acting. The study forum organized by young government officers did its best to coordinate Sikkimese thoughts on how to proceed, but, having no official status, it was able only to give form, articulation, to inchoate aspirations; it was unable to represent. Even *with* a voice it was difficult to be heard. The outside world didn't care much, and India was getting so jingoistic that the good Indians were powerless.

In 1968 the Sikkim government officers had boycotted the Indian Independence Day function—an extraordinary action in a country in which politeness took precedence over everything else. The same day, there had been the first demonstration I'd ever seen in Gangtok—a hundred or so boys and girls carrying signs. One placard said, "We shall not be overcome," a true Sikkimese passive inversion. The Indian Representative was enraged. Calls flew to Delhi. The general, who came that night for drinks to the palace, said, "Oh, that lot, *that's* what they're making a fuss about? I passed them in my jeep this morning and gave them a wave."

The Indians in some ways were embarrassed by their colonial situation, wincing at the nineteenth-century word "protectorate," but they wanted to change the name, not the treaty (referred to by the Representative as "the happy document"—"of them, by them, for them," snorted *The Sikkim*) or the status. It was very weird. The main reason the Indians wanted to keep Sikkim, I thought, was to satisfy a psychological power drive—there was no other real reason, particularly as Chogyal and all the people who wanted treaty review had said again and again that even if Sikkim were to become independent, it would want to keep the same defense arrangement with India it had under the existing treaty.

In 1968 Mrs. Gandhi, now the Prime Minister of India, and Morarji Desai, the Deputy Prime Minister, made official visits to Sikkim a month apart. Mrs. Gandhi was accompanied on her visit by her Italian daughter-in-law, Sonia, who used to stay with Karma, the Sikkimese student, at the same rooming house in England. The homey connection made us feel warm and unofficial—even free enough to laugh. Moreover, Mrs. Gandhi, as always, was a delightful guest—unassuming, appreciative. The only trouble was that, although privately she seemed to respect Sikkim's otherness from India and to be pro-Sikkim, she might not, people said, have the strength to press for Sikkim's case. In fact, she advised Chogyal to wait until she was more securely in power and could help more. Her public talk on this visit about "indissoluble bonds of friendship, partners in progress" had been disappointing. Treaty revision was brushed aside.

Morarji proved to be a totally different kind of person and guest. Before he'd come we had been sent a memorandum: "The Deputy Prime Minister does not take meat, fish, eggs. Among vegetables he avoids tomatoes, potatoes, onions, leafy and fibrous vegetables. He prefers pithy and pulpy vegetables like carrots, pumpkins, peas, cucumbers, cauli-flowers. No fried foods—vegetables may be boiled or stewed. He likes unpolished, hand pounded rice, whole wheat bread, preferably brown, fresh cheeses and milk. He likes fruits but not sour varieties. He goes without lunch on Tuesday, Thursday, and Saturday, and takes milk and juices for dinner on Monday, Wednesday, and Friday. Sunday he takes milk, fruits and sweets." For days afterward I'd gone about the house singing "Morarji likes coffee, he doesn't like tea. Morarji likes beet root, he doesn't like squash."

To win his approval the Indian Representative and we had vied to see who could offer him the simpler reception. Friends, thinking of Mr. Manuel, who was always saving our most delicious treats—brown sugar, canned Danish butter cookies—for V.I.P.'s, were mind-boggled by the austerity competition. "Boiled radish weed served on paper plates? Dried turnip greens, nuts, and paper cups?"

The Deputy Prime Minister had startled people, particularly the young Sikkimese nationalists, by his abrasive manner. Although he had publicly said in Montreal not long before that India wouldn't prevent Sikkim and Bhutan from joining the U.N.—although in that case India couldn't be responsible for their defense—now he was evasive and rather brutal about the treaty. "Everything is outdated if you want to make it outdated," he had said to Sikkimese questioners. "Otherwise what is outdated in it?"

Chogyal, however, despite a rather good-hearted difference over Indian and Sikkim drinking habits (Drink Sikkim Gin was the first billboard that greeted the Deputy Prime Minister on crossing the Indo-Sikkim border), respected and liked Morarji—"He's a good man, an honest man with principle." And, indeed, he appeared to be. For, true to his word, when he had returned to Delhi, Morarji had taken up Sikkim's cause, stating that, as Sikkim was not part of India, the Indian government should return the fourteen crores of rupees (as against the twelve crores Sikkim had received from India as aid in the same amount of time) she had been taxing Sikkim for excise duty. The Foreign Ministry was appalled, both by Morarji's outspoken statement that Sikkim was not part of India and by the thought of parting with the money. Quite a bit later, through the Foreign Ministry, with no hint of its being Sikkim's due, we got the money back as an "ad hoc grant," a beneficence.

About the same time, partly from a high of national feeling I'd been enjoying with the young Sikkimese and partly from a growing need to indulge my scholarly bent, which I'd neglected, I took up Chogyal's old idea of writing a research article on Sikkim's grant of Darjeeling to the

British East India Company in the last century. Reading the material, I'd come to the conclusion that the British and the Sikkimese had had a genuine difference of interpretation about the grant, a result of their different cultural backgrounds of legal thinking, the confusion of legal interpretations being heightened by the different languages that had been involved. The first two treaties between the East India Company and Sikkim about Darjeeling hadn't even been translated into English until (and then only very roughly) many years after the transaction first giving Darjeeling to the British. In my article I suggested that the Sikkimese—as their traditional theory of landholding was that all land belonged to the king and one could have "usage" only—gave Darjeeling to the British for use as a sanatorium but had not intended an outright grant. The British, I felt, had simply assumed the grant was outright and had begun to administer the area (as they probably would have sooner or later in any case, with or without cultural misunderstanding) as part of their Indian possession.

The article, printed in the very sober *Bulletin of Tibetology*, of which I was an editor, stirred up a hornet's nest. "Sarah Lawrence girl claims Darjeeling for Sikkim." "America's Trojan Mare in Gangtok." "CIA agent in borrowed plumage." "American wife plans missile base." The Indian reaction was vituperative, and I was remorseful, scared. I'd known it would mildly provoke, pique really, but in a scholarly way. There was no question of a Sikkimese claim on Darjeeling. Even if the *Bulletin of Tibetology* was the appropriate channel—which it was not—the period of time I had discussed in my article was prior to the incontestable annexation of Darjeeling by Britain in 1861.

Afterward, whenever the Indian papers wrote about Sikkim's wish for treaty revision, my article was trotted out as a further damning black mark against the country. The newspaper attacks seemed to be calculated to appear whenever any Sikkimese official was going to Delhi for talks.

After he'd visited Sikkim, the editor of *Blitz*, the sensationalist and widely read Indian paper that had printed the "Trojan Mare" piece, tried to undo the damage and wrote a good, in fact glowing, account of Sikkim and our work. Unfortunately, however, only the first part of a three-part article appeared. A phone call from the Foreign Office, we heard, had intervened. I was fearful. Although generally there was a fund of goodwill in India for us (half a million people turned out to cheer Chogyal and me in Madurai on our visit to southern India, and the

Delhi municipal government had honored us by inviting us to open the new buildings of Mahatma Gandhi's Harijan colony, where he had stayed), the Foreign Office seemed out to get us.

Basically, people elsewhere didn't care about Sikkim, or, if they did, they were mainly curious about Chogyal and me. Even many sympathetic writers distorted Sikkim's nuances. For that matter, Sikkim as a whole, in terms of world power politics, was a nuance—a microdot—easier to interpret through stock musical-comedy or Shangri-la references than actually to look at. The Shangri-la concept was dangerous for us. At every interview I'd given over the years I'd tried again and again to drive the point home that no matter how small and semiexotic we might be, we were real, we existed.

If people didn't credit us with reality, we would perish very soon, the victim of very real power politics. When we tried to explain this to people from big power countries, however, they'd shake their heads—they were fond of us as we were, as their image of us was, and they couldn't understand what we were talking about. The only people who understood, cared, were other little countries, all themselves too weak, or possibly already taken over, to help. It was ironic. When we'd been invited by a senior Buddhist priest, the Gombo Lama, before the flood time, to visit him in Buryat Soviet Mongolia in the U.S.S.R., four pantomimes were going on—two of which, Buryat's and Sikkim's, were a silent cry from the heart. The Soviet Union, to show that they encouraged Buddhism—which wasn't entirely true—allowed the Buryat people to invite us. The Indian government, to show they promoted Buddhism and Sikkim—which wasn't entirely true either—permitted us to go. The Buryats, for their part, had invited us to strengthen their identity, show the outside world they were unique, different from their Soviet overlords. We, for our part, had accepted the invitation to reinforce our own identity, show the Buryats that we were unique, different from the Indians. We understood them, they us, and we had a lovely, cozy time together joking, eating big meals, drinking brandy in the stuffy cooking-odored dining room of the pension where we stayed.

Big countries not only didn't care; sometimes the very fact of little countries seemed to embarrass, even irritate them. "The weakest buckle on the Himalayan belt," National Geographic called us—a wrinkle to be ironed out. One U.S. Information Agency aide from Delhi, when he came up to Gangtok, even brought as a present a book advocating that the little buffer countries—Nepal, Sikkim, Bhutan—along India's northern borders, be more or less merged to avoid a vacuum near China. We were *not* a vacuum. If we weren't acknowledged, however, one might be created!

Like a newly married daughter, afraid her parents would slight, even scorn her new family, and equally afraid her husband would not deserve and win her family's respect, I was defensive, anxious, when American diplomats occasionally visited Sikkim. I realized the Americans were in a somewhat delicate position because of me. They didn't want an embarrassment on their hands when India, increasingly pro-Soviet and anti-American, was by far their greatest priority. Equally, I didn't want to embarrass them—or India. Sometimes, however, I felt they didn't have to bend over so far backward—that something else, aside from diplomatic niceties, was at work, that there was an impatience with something they didn't want to take the time to learn about. What we were trying to do at this rather critical moment was to develop an understanding that in some way might be helpful to Sikkim or at least make the situation less dangerous. Since it was not diplomatic (safe) to talk about Sikkim's problems, and I resented and dreaded our being used as a news peg, it was hard to find ways to keep Sikkim in the public eye. We'd used handicrafts, then jewelry, and, now in 1971, we were concentrating on fashion.

With the help of Vogue in Paris, and Alice in New York—who in the middle of her honeymoon had been running around lining up appointments for us at the American Crafts Council and the Metropolitan Museum, finding ballrooms for shows, collecting accessories, meeting with Bergdorf's, the store showing the clothes we'd made up—the collection I'd been working on for two years with my friend Rinchen Gyatso, the tailor in Gangtok, was finally ready. Bergdorf Goodman had done a good job. There were not only Sikkimese things in their windows but they had coordinated their efforts with those of their neighbors Van Cleef & Arpels and Delman, both of which filled their windows with Sikkimese art. On the night of the opening, Sikkimese flags flew on both sides of Fifth Avenue from Fifty-seventh to Fifty-eighth streets. The next day there was another fashion show, in the ballroom of the Colony Club, and the following day the clothes were shown in the guest-of-honor spot by the Pan Pacific Association at the Waldorf. Our final and most satisfying success—as the space was big enough to show the fashions to full advantage—was the jam-packed show in the Smithsonian's Red Hall in Washington. Before the event began, Alice screened her slides of Sikkim, and the recently recorded Sikkimese music was played as the mannequins walked down the long aisle.

The fashions were doing well—Bergdorf's couldn't keep enough in stock—and, with the help of a wonderfully sensitive public-relations woman, the first we'd ever used, we'd gotten about half a million dollars' worth of free publicity, almost as much as Red China, which had just joined the U.N. Best of all, although, inescapably, we were involved in it, the coverage was mainly about Sikkim's culture, not about us.

At the parties we'd been giving in Delhi and abroad over the years, guests who didn't know us well were always confused. Although gay, the parties were a Sikkim push—they had the earmarks of a fund-raising event—and yet we never asked for money. That would have been very un-Sikkimese. What did we want? The answer was simple and not so simple. Often we didn't dare define it even to ourselves, let alone to the people we were mutely appealing to. We wanted people to have Sikkim in their consciousness. If, God help us, something happened, we wouldn't be quite so alone. We knew they wouldn't be able or willing to help, but somehow the mere fact of outside people knowing of us seemed to diffuse the awfulness of a potential take-over and possibly, magically, keep it in abeyance.

The year 1971 was a critical time: Nepal after years of strangulation had just begun to find its balance vis-à-vis India, to win concessions of transit and other rights due a landlocked country. Bhutan finally was in the U.N. after years of resisting India's exacerbation of local feuding and her attempts to enhance her leverage. A story circulated in Calcutta in which the Bhutanese king, on his return from a long medical treatment in Switzerland, was held virtually incommunicado at Government House in Calcutta for several days and told tales about civil dissension in Bhutan making it necessary to send the Indian Army to restore his rule. "Let them come," he was rumored to have said, "but they'll have to fight their way in." Nothing in Bhutan's treaty with India stood in the way of Bhutan's admission to the U.N., and in the end India had finally capitulated and even gracefully sponsored Bhutan as her satellite in the world body.

Time was going by; almost all nonfree territories, colonies, trusteeships had achieved their independence. The cries in Sikkim for treaty review and possible U.N. membership (while continuing, if India wished, the defense agreement) were becoming more urgent. The National party, which openly advocated treaty revision, won the national election in 1972 by a strong majority. India countered by proposing "a permanent relationship status" similar to Puerto Rico's connection with the United States but without the open-ended possibility of opting out of the connection which Puerto Rico enjoyed. While hanging onto the power, India wanted to get rid of Sikkim's protectorate classification, which was becoming an embarrassment. Despite the fact they were protected by their color—only whites could really be imperialistic—it would be more convenient for the world's largest democracy if a euphemism could be found to describe their stranglehold.

Something was going awry. Mrs. Gandhi, whom my husband and all of us in Sikkim had loved and counted on (she'd loved Sikkim too; aside from her affectionate manner, she'd even furnished her little house in Delhi with our handicrafts), had been acting very strangely, almost bizarrely, since her coup against Morarji, and the Indo-Pakistani war over Bangladesh in 1971. She'd always said she'd help us, but now she was behaving in an extraordinary, furious way when she met Chogyal or any official from Sikkim. When my husband asked her what was the matter, she would say, "You know, you know," and wouldn't say any more.

Even harder almost to bear, although less consequential than Mrs. Gandhi's recent belligerence, was Tikki's. T. N. Kaul—Tikki—had been my husband's good friend from his training days in the Indian civil service and one of Mrs. Gandhi's closest Kashmiri advisers. On almost every trip, between seeing the children in England and visiting the dentist in Switzerland, we'd come back through Moscow, where Tikki'd been posted as Indian ambassador, to ask his counsel and help about Sikkim. Now, mixed with the treacherous affection Stalin's daughter Svetlana described in her book *Only One Year* (when he let her down during her effort to defect from Russia through India), he was showing, after years of friendship, the same new hostility as that of Mrs. Gandhi. Twice he'd come up to Gangtok with a group of Foreign Office officials to press for agreement to Sikkim's reduced status of permanent relationship. (They had brought what looked like a cheap spy attaché case, the kind with a tape recorder in it, which they held near Chogyal when he spoke, and went out periodically to tinker with.) When Chogyal protested the proposals they were pressing on him, Tikki stormed out of the living room shouting, "You'll see."

President and Mrs. Giri of India had been scheduled to come on a state visit to Sikkim, and Chogyal had been deeply pleased, encouraged by the prospect of ironing things out, getting some kind of talks going, forming a new basis for friendship. Everyone had put weeks of planning into preparations for the visit. The Forestry Department had been almost beside themselves, surrounding the palace lawn, where the presidential helicopter would land, with rare plants and orchids. Mr. Manuel and I had been plotting the vegetarian dinner we were giving in their honor as if it was a major campaign. The morning of their arrival Norbu came up early to help me make a bean dish for the occasion. Overhead we heard a roar, then silence again. They'd tried to put down, but the clouds had closed in. They'd left and were on their way back to India. There were not going to be any talks.

Marilyn, our American photographer friend from Delhi who'd been living there so long she was privy to much of the capital's gossip, comes up to stay with us. The mood there, she warned, was getting very tough. Some of the Foreign Office people were saying publicly that they could have Chogyal out just like that—Marilyn made the quick sideward head motion Indians use a lot. Her and Frank's situation too was getting more precarious. Although Frank, in his editorials, had been a longtime champion of Mrs. Gandhi's, her white knight, and was now only mildly questioning her policies, he was already feeling her anger at him and his paper. There was not much one could do. In any case, after the hard work of my fashion show, I felt like resting, not doing anything for a while. Bit by bit, however, I began to learn more Nepali, studying every day with Monmaya, my Nepali secretary. If there was going to be strain ahead, the more integrated everyone was, the better.

14

FEELING DISTANT, sad, I tag along with the older children and their friends from England and America who are spending the summer with them. They're open and affectionate with me. Still, I'm thirty-two, not twenty, and I'm not just a friend; I'm their mother. When we dance —there are a lot of young people's parties this summer—the boys are sweet, making sure I always have a partner. But the dancing does stop.

I'm sad that Norbu is going. All spring he's been reading books from our library, preparing. Through the ethnomusicologist we've gotten him a scholarship in cultural anthropology at Brown. He'll make an excellent student, and his studies will give him the skills of understanding society that Sikkim needs. I'll miss him, though, so much.

The first days he's gone, I lie in the guest room reading the Brown-recommended books he'd been been studying. Norbu had been reading them like a guide, a lifeline of knowledge to this new strange place, the West. I pick up his *Madame Bovary*. Almost every other word is lightly ticked off with a pencil mark—its meaning looked up down in that dimly lit house in Tathangchen.

As a goodbye present he brought a big basket of millet for making chaang (the local beer), some fried-rice biscuits, and a thick wool coat lined with yellowed sheepskin. "I thought you'd like it, Gyalmo," he said, not looking at me. "It's sort of like the things in your fashion show." I don't quite know what to do with it. It's huge and a little smelly, as the skin is poorly cured. I've put it finally in the landing cupboard, doubled up on top of the tablecloth we rarely use. I wanted to tell him before he went that I love him.

At the end of the summer I realized that I hadn't been out of Sikkim, even to India, for almost eight months and really needed a vacation. To my astonishment I discovered Bangkok was closer than Delhi, less than an hour from Calcutta. Wonderful noisy vulgarity. The first day, at the Intercontinental Coffee Shop, waiting for my pastrami (probably buffalo, even if the waitress insists it's beef) sandwich, fingers touching marbleized Formica counter, ears full of piped music, I felt as if I'd come out of the sanatorium in *The Magic Mountain*, dizzy and convalescent. What relief not to have to look up anyone, to be unofficial, to experience, or at least to practice, being a person. The only setback—and that more comical than threatening—came the second night, when, lying back in the big hotel bed, I planned an evening of watching TV (three channels, with a radio switch that allowed you to hear the English original instead of the Thai dubbing) and eating.

With only a little embarrassment, I ordered a room-service supper of two medium-sized cocktail platters of cheese, paté, and roast beef hors d'oeuvres, a ten-ounce T-bone steak with Idaho potato and sour cream, and corn. To my horror, when the waiters came pushing several white-clothed tables covered with serving dishes into my small room, they were followed by a looming maître d' I'd met at the Intercontinental in Hong Kong. "Majesty," he said, indicating the crowded tables, "there must be some mistake." Gluttony proving, however, an even stronger emotion than shame, I managed to say with shaky hauteur, "Certainly there is, but you may leave the things all the same." For the first five minutes of *McCloud* the maître d' continued to stand officiously behind my chair, until I convinced him he could withdraw.

The pulse and variety of Bangkok restaurants and night life were overwhelming, rather like New York's. Even when I finally looked up the Indian ambassador, it was fun. As relieved to find me a pleasant duty as I was to have an attractive escort, he took me around the city's bawdy nightclubs.

I'd missed seeing things, doing things, so much—been more homesick too for America than I'd realized. Now, every morning at nine when I jumped on the sight-seeing bus to visit another temple or excavation site, loving the loud voices, the simplistic opinions about Thailand, the people's basic kindness, I would try to infiltrate the various knots of American tourists. For some reason, though, none of them extended themselves to me, and I sat eavesdropping rather wistfully.

For several weeks after my return to Sikkim, to lessen my regret at ending my short vacation, I threw myself into rehearsals for the Tathangchen School play, the highlight of the school year. Together with the children and teachers, we had worked out the most ambitious concert we had ever put on. All the parents of the children from the village helped make props and costumes. This year's play would be special, as it was the first time it would be held at the school itself. Because it was such a steep climb, many of the Gangtok public had never been down there. Now, perhaps, we would get more support, after they saw what we were doing.

The night of the performance the children are enchanting. They sing, their voices like flutes, and stamp out vigorous round dances. At the end, holding hands, they begin an old Navajo chant that Wendy, the new headmistress, a Sikkimese woman educated in America, has taught them. "Behind me peaceful. Before me peaceful. Under me peaceful. All around me peaceful. Ah, beautiful. Ah, beautiful." We go outside on the bit of flatland in front of the school, the hill dropping sharply away at the edge. Cratered by the high mountains surrounding us, with the moon shining down, we sing the national anthem. The children's voices thunder even in the vast space, and then all of us, guests included, form into circles to dance a *tashi*, an auspicious round wishing luck to all present, the Chogyal and Sikkim. Some of the guests depart. The rest of us and the children, who can't stop singing, go back into the warmth of the school building, where we sing until early morning. Then, exhausted, with the sleeping children borne on the backs of the bigger children, we go home.

The next day at lunch Chogyal tells us what's been on his mind all summer, making him so tense. His intelligence reports have been citing evidence of an Indian intelligence plot to cause widespread disturbances in Sikkim with the help of some Sikkimese Nepalis and Kazi and Kazini in Kalimpong. Apparently the Indian Intelligence Bureau is already stashing arms in Sikkim itself. Part of the plan has to do with dynamiting major installations, including the hydroelectric power plant; there is a contingency plan for demonstrations, and a final shoot-out at the palace. Chogyal's just back from meeting Mrs. Gandhi in Darjeeling, telling her what the Intelligence Bureau is up to, trying to get her to intervene.

"I'm not sure I got through to her," he tells us. "I'm not sure she understands. I tried to tell her that they're playing with fire, that if they play up the Nepalis here they're playing right into the Gurkha league's hands in Darjeeling. They're asking for trouble if Sikkim goes all Nepali; it will certainly enhance the Darjeeling Nepalis' call for autonomy and bring Greater Nepal that much closer. And it won't just affect Darjeeling district either—it will affect the whole Nepali northern belt of India

right along from Uttar Pradesh through Assam. They're so arrogant they
don't understand what they're up against. Even this time Mrs. G. had to
be helicoptered out of Raj Bhavan in Darjeeling because of Nepali demonstrations surrounding the grounds. I believe there even were placards
saying randi Gandhi ["prostitute Gandhi"]. The government of India
doesn't know who their friends are."

Soon after that, in London at the doctor's office, I'm shivering again,
but this time it is the Chogyal's skin that seems literally to crawl on his
face, moving up and down on his brow and temples. His eyes pop out
and he makes little snorting noises in his nose, as he sometimes does
when trying to control a stutter. "Terminal." I've just caught the word
"terminal." Up till now I'd been sort of nodding along, not knowing
what this was about. Nephritis—whatever it is—is mildly serious, I knew,
but I thought the doctors rather odd when I met them, staring at me
that way, sizing me up. The one who started making the graph with the
dots I thought more than a little odd—quite peculiar, infantile—showing
me those dots as if I'd never seen a graph, and never coming to a conclusion or saying anything more. And now this red-bearded man in this
antique, Dickensian hospital room—thick green-painted wooden furniture, machinery not yet installed lying stacked on the floor—is looking at
us, through us, saying Yangchen's kidneys will fail. Yangchen and the
children, whom we've brought along, as we're going shopping afterward
in the minicab, are outside, just on the other side of the door into the
next room. I have no weight, no substance. The doctor is bowing to us,
looking very pained, saying how sorry, how very sorry he is for us.

My husband's moving like an automaton. I'm scared to leave him at
the flat for fear he may have a heart attack. At lunch I leave Yangchen
and the children at the table in a hamburger shop to call from a pay
phone to see if he's all right. I can't look Yangchen in the eye. I try to
look to the side or through her. My legs, when we walk, are weightless
and seem to come up high, my knee near my chin, before, with difficulty, I can make them descend. I have no gravity. I have no skin, no
structure. Only the minicab that we keep getting back into after we've
been in a store is a shell that holds me together. We've been buying
Shetland sweaters for the boys, and the little children are begging to go
to a store where they can buy souvenirs.

In New York, Dr. Rubin of New York Hospital-Cornell Medical Center tells us that Yangchen is going to be okay, that the worst that will
happen is dialysis or kidney transplant. He can't believe it when he hears

what the English doctors have said, sees how upset we are. He just tilts back in his chair shaking his head. It's like a stone being rolled away. Every night since England I'd been peeing and throwing up in the bed of the poor woman whose apartment we'd borrowed. But after I'd asked Alice to buy another mattress in Bloomingdale's and have this one boxed up for me, I got hysterical thinking how weird it would seem if a guest came to stay in Gangtok and then mailed off one of our mattresses for no apparent reason. "Normal Christmas," Chogyal had said. "We should wait to see the U.S. doctors until after we've spent a normal Christmas."

After the Chogyal leaves New York, Yangchen and the children and I stay on for a couple of weeks. Yangchen is delighted with New York and even more delighted that, following the doctor's advice, she will not be going back to the cold, drafty boarding school she has hated, but will be returning home. Amazingly, after her interview with Dr. Rubin she already seems better. To celebrate, we plan a trip that will take us to northern Massachusetts. It's so long since I've been in New England, so long too—perhaps the first time in my marriage—since I've been in America enjoying myself, not doing work for Sikkim.

Squeezed into the taxi we've hired from New York, I feel our bodies next to each other: Joyce, her daughter Danielle, Yangchen, Palden, Hope, Norbu, and Joe, the sardonic driver. I wonder what he makes of us. We've been talking nonstop about the Indian plans to dynamite installations in Sikkim. Norbu is wearing his Sikkimese robe, his village knife dangling from his sash. He's homesick; being back with us has brought out his feelings about Sikkim. I am high with love for everyone in our small space. All of us connected much more deeply than the words we chatter. Our closeness here even more intense than in Sikkim. I am glad of the pressure of their bodies against mine. Outside, the fields around Newburyport, where we've taken the children to see my ancestors' old houses, are sealed with snow.

At a little guesthouse in Gloucester Harbor we stamp the bell for service, squalling for reception like New Yorkers until a dreamy-eyed girl comes down the stairs to clear the cat off the reception desk and register our names. Here we spend the night. Condescending, we agree to the girl's suggestion that we have some singing in the sitting room after dinner. "Beats the Sunday-night sermons on Gloucester TV or profiles on parsons, hah-hah, or whatever is on the other channel." The children have changed into their bathrobes and play, blowing soap bubbles. The girl, accompanying herself·on a guitar, sings in a voice purer, more ethe-real than Joan Baez's or Joni Mitchell's. Norbu joins her in his deep bass, then plays some Sikkimese songs on his flute. I could burst with happi-ness and love.

It is all very brief, but I steal a few days for myself when we return to New York.

"He walked in. He walked in." Carly Simon's song is played repeat-edly on the radio. It isn't the words, which have nothing to do with me, but the strong beat, which resonates to some part of my feeling for Matt, my old friend from growing up who used to write me weekly letters at boarding school. A writer now, he had after years of being out of touch telephoned me on this visit to ask about some travel assignment to the Himalayas. No shyness, no games. Acknowledgment. We acknowl-edge, we acknowledge each other. We are magnificent, loving, funny. It's love. Not just a case of writer lèse majesté.

The last day of our few days together before Yangchen, the children, and I have to leave, he gives me a marked book of Donne's love poems. I do not know how this will end, or continue. It has ended. We have not talked or tried to reason things out or to plan. No point in any of those. It is simple, stupefying. We love each other. We are parting. I must go back to Sikkim.

Leaving / driving past Kent sign / departure squeezed through Tri-boro as through a shredder / one last look over shoulder view of knife-bright skyline / aborting self from self / I'm in New York / this bloody mangle sawing ever tighter on a cord is really not me / maybe it's the other way / it's not important / my body here / myself entrailed in New York.

Oh, Lord, how I miss him. On the airplane Jane Alexander's face, four feet long on the cabin movie screen, bobs up and down making fish-like mouthings. The children, pale and bleary from the junk food and the late nights, watch me nervously. I write and write, trying to make my words touch. We have already entered another time zone. He must be sleeping.

The landscape around the château where we stop over in Switzerland is a white and black negative. Driving to the château through an abso-lutely white countryside, we see a man rehearsing for the winter festival, at which they burn effigies of the old year. He wears a purple jacket and knee breeches and holds a long silver trumpet, bright against the snow.

Matt rings at eleven one night, waking up our hosts, the Von Schultes.

Mrs. Von S. thinks it must be my husband. My husband, sounding somewhat strained, rings the next day. There's not much to say, but the people, or rather a few of the people who lost the last election—which had been held while we were away—are acting up.

I almost can't mail my letter to Matt at the Zurich airport, the Indian Embassy man sent to see us off sticks so close to my side.

I feel culture shock. In Calcutta, Gandhi, my husband's business partner, is giving me advice about astrology—the second Indian to do so today. A few hours ago, when we stopped over in Bombay, the former trade agent, who'd come bearing grapes (even peeling them!) to the airport, trying to reinstate himself in the Sikkim trade agency, chattered on about the stars: how Chogyal's luck was changing for the better. Now here is Gandhi going on about the same thing. "I know you will laugh, Gyalmo," he says, "but for your luck what you must do is every Tuesday feed to your cow chapatis. I know you are thinking it is just Mr. Gandhi's belief [here he pats his forehead], but if you are believing, if you can believe, and you are feeding the chapatis, then psychologically you can feel better." It is a relief when our plane is called.

Usually we follow the long steamy road along the river from Bagdogra, inching our way in jeeps. But this morning Chogyal has requested a helicopter for us, and we skim over the tops of hills, crests rising up under us like waves, dense jungle alternating with winter-bleached terracings, ochre-painted farmhouses in clearings. I've made this trip so often and have always felt that I was coming home. Not, as some writers describe their journey into Sikkim, going into the unknown or secret, but going home.

When visitors had asked me what it was like to live far away, I'd always been surprised—far away from what? This was my nexus, the rivers leading to this territory, drawing me through the circles of hills to Gangtok.

Today is different. For the first time I don't feel I'm coming home. I feel only that I've left America and that it's very far away. The helipad surrounded by mountains seems a bleak nest. The officials who come to greet us are also unusually cold and formal. Maybe it's just the drab overcoats they're wearing. Winter as a rule is so mild here people don't wear them much.

Usually our greetings after a longish absence are affectionate, fun. A time to catch up on projects. The officials and the townspeople come up to the palace and we have tea and drinks in the big sitting room. Lovely homecomings, like good parties with all the friends I want to see.

Today is strained, people are on edge. When I see Keshab, the forest conservator, whom I know well and who is just back from Yale—to which a friend of mine had got him a scholarship—I greet him with mock indignation, and he jumps a mile. Keshab had promised that while we were away he would get the Forestry Department to replace the gravel parking lot in front of the palace with a simple turnaround. Nothing's been done, and when, teasingly, I say, "Oh, Keshab, I'm heartbroken, you broke your word, you've let me down," he starts back guiltily. Then he recollects himself and explains various difficulties that kept his department from beginning the plans.

Even our unpacking is different this time. Usually unpacking after our semiannual trips is festive—our big immigrant suitcases, frames broken from overloading, splayed open on the upstairs landing, spilled contents lying in piles on the floor around them. I've brought mostly things for the children—party decorations, toys, books, shoes. For the house, records and a few craft pieces; for all the palace servants, presents. The children and ayahs ooh and aah as each new treasure is taken out, passed back and forth. This evening everyone is thrilled as usual—except me. The new things I've bought remind me of my distance from New York.

Usually on my return I go to every room in the house and sit down for a time to feel its presence, to rescale myself to its size. I love this house so much—our small daffodil-filled bedroom, the children's room—like a vicarage nursery warmed against the February cold by a fire—my beloved library. Seeing these rooms now makes me less sad to be back. I'm touched by their sweetness, innocence. Even *I* feel more innocent again, and the feeling of purity returning in some ways helps dull the sense of loss. There is no choice. I must somehow manage to go on.

To keep myself from thinking too much about America I plunge into work on old projects. Relandscaping the driveway is the first. One day at dusk Keshab and some of his assistants come over and we map and remap a possible approach road that will join gracefully with the several other smaller roads converging on the palace. The trouble is, if we get the roads together at an acceptable angle, we keep coming up with a peculiarly shaped center island. Some of the shapes arrived at are hilarious, and all of us get the giggles. Using a string covered with flour to chart the directions, the men and I mark the gravel lot in every possible variation. Large blackbirds, cawing noisily, follow on our tail, pecking up the flour from the gravel before we can get a fix on the lines we've laid down. Thank God, Chogyal's away on a short trip, so he's not a witness. Finally, despite the birds and the difficulty of encompassing the feeder roads, we find a solution, and the work is completed by the next evening. Great slabs of turf are unrolled under the feet of astonished palace sentries, and that night the children, their friends, Keshab, the foresters, and I picnic on the center island of the drive.

Tathangchen School has not yet reopened. Palden's and Hope's friends spend all day playing at the palace. The boys work with Palden building Lego fortresses on the verandah, and the girls work with Hope on a puppet show in the big living room.

I'm worried about the school opening. Wendy and I have met with the head of the Sikkim Guards and with the headmistress of the Guards' school, and both have forgotten their agreement to start a joint seventh grade with Tathangchen. It's ridiculous. Before we left, Colonel Gurung, the head of the Guards, had suggested that he would not only give us space this term in their school for the new grade but also that, in the future, if the Guards should make the scheduled move from their present barracks, we might be able to use the barracks for a combined Guards-Tathangchen School that would run right through high school.

I'd been thinking about this new school all the time we'd been away. It would take the load off the overburdened high schools in Gangtok and would mean that the Tathangchen children could go right through and get a good education instead of being forced, as they are now, to enter the boring and acculturating high schools in town. Under this plan we would get all the Guards' facilities and they would get our good teachers and curriculum. Now Colonel Gurung is saying that he doesn't even want a joint seventh grade, that the Guards are going to start their own, and that any available extra space will be needed for army dependents. There are no army dependents. Sikkim is a nonfamily station. I'm puzzled and suspicious. What does the man mean? What are we going to do?

Wendy and I are nonplussed. Our school is already full to bursting with only six grades. Even now, to make space, the children are being shunted back and forth from classroom to classroom. Finally we are saved by the graduated sixth grade, which, determined to keep on in Tathangchen, raises some money to rent a room in one of the village houses above the school. Getting another teacher shouldn't be a problem since there are many college students home just now who I'm sure will volunteer. Also, Yangchen wants to teach, and in the back of my mind, so do I.

No matter how much I try to force my mind to think only of work, thoughts of Matt keep intruding. When they do, I'm torn—half wanting to push them down, half wanting to allow myself to be taken. Even things in my immediate sphere have changed because of him; I see more clearly, more sharply than I ever have. Instead of living here unconsciously, as I used to, I'm like a camera now, recording impressions to write him. Things seem at the same time more detached and more vivid. Some moments are so intense they're almost painfully beautiful. One evening, driving through town, I watch the carpet-weaving girls from the cottage industries walk up the hill from their picnic at the chorten, where I've been with them earlier. As they climb the road they sing. Some carry flowers they've picked, and some have wound them in their hair. Because I'm so conscious of the moment, trying to freeze it in my mind, I'm conscious too of its ephemerality.

I don't know how I'll be able to send out the letter I've been writing. Our letters have always been read, but I've never faced this before. Maybe one of the many guests who are about to descend on us can take it when leaving.

I sleep as late as I can, and, when I can't sleep any longer, I delay getting up by reading European art books in memory of Matt and the West, and working my way through the dwindling pile of *Herald Tribunes* that were saved for me when I was away. The Indian Representative told me about a Somerset Maugham story in which an old British colonial officer is so obsessed with his tenuous homeland connection through ancient newspapers that when a subaltern tampers with his arrangement of the papers he orders that he be killed.

I'll miss Bajpai, the Indian Representative, when he goes. The new designate Representative alarms me. He's a conservative Hindu, so caste-conscious he actually runs his hand down his trousers to wipe it off after I shake it. He thinks I'm an American heathen defiler. When I mention this cautiously to Mr. Bajpai and tell him how invisible, how much part of Sikkim I feel, how I fear, however, that his successor sees me as somewhat of an outsider, an infidel, Mr. Bajpai says it is just shyness. Maybe it is, but I beg him in any case next time he goes to Delhi to reassure the new man about me. I feel so easy with Mr. Bajpai, mostly because I never (this conversation is the second exception) speak politics with him. He never baits me, as some of the other Representatives have done. In fact, he always steers me toward safe subjects, making it a point to save me from myself. Now, in my detached mood, I find local politics less real than ever. Still, I don't want to be drawn into anything by the new man.

15

K. C. Pradhan, the brother of my friend Keshab, the Forestry Department chief, has been jailed for making seditious pro-Nepali-supremacy, anti-Chogyal speeches. He must be about the only political prisoner that Sikkim's ever had. I don't know him well, but he seems immature, egotistical, macho. The opposite of Keshab.

Chogyal says K.C. and some others are making trouble because they're on the outs. The National party, the mainly Bhutia Lepcha nationalist party supporting treaty review with India, and supposed to favor the Chogyal, had won such a thoroughgoing victory last fall, he said, that the other parties had nothing to do but act up.

Yangchen's illness (Dr. Rubin and his family have been visiting, and he says Yangchen seems to have stabilized, in fact is better!) had so thoroughly wiped out my old fears of rumored troubles that I'd more or less forgotten about them. Desultorily, I ask Chogyal's official secretary one day, and he reassures me that it is okay for the kids to run around as freely as they do. In the library, another day, I ask Karma, now back from England and working as Chogyal's deputy secretary, if he thinks that April 4, the day set for Chogyal's birthday celebration, might be a likely time for demonstrations. If people are still planning them, it seems to me the perfect setup for trouble. Karma says not.

On March 20, our tenth wedding anniversary, Mr. Thapa comes to the palace to call on me. I think he's come to wish me congratulations, but he doesn't mention the anniversary, just makes small talk and drags out the visit. Finally he says, "Please, can't you tell the Chogyal he should make peace with K. C. Pradhan and the others? They're wild boys, but I think now we've got no choice." I draw back in apprehension. Any time I've talked politics I've gotten into so much trouble.

I've been warned by Chogyal, ever since Mr. Thapa began his newspaper, that I mustn't talk to him about anything serious. I squirm in embarrassment and regret. "Well, okay, I will, but please don't tell me more." He leaves looking very upset.

Soon afterward a young man who has recently joined the Youth Library as head of the Nepali section of the Textbook Center comes to see me; he has a black eye. Although I'm very fond of him, he's always struck me as a bit young. Now I'm both touched and scornful that he should come up to the palace to complain to me about having been roughed up. "I was beaten up by a hoodlum I've never seen before. He's from Darjeeling, not from Sikkim. There are a whole lot of them floating around town. Your Majesty ought to tell the police." I commiserate with him but am not about to inform anyone.

I dream that we are dancing in the Sikkim Guards' mess. Suddenly, up through Tathangchen comes the Indian Navy. I see faces outside the windows of the mess and know that the men are poised to attack. I run from the room, taking with me my glass of Scotch, and hurry across the bare lot. There is barbed wire slung across the center of the lot, but an American MP waves me through a passageway. On the other side of the concrete I've crossed is a forest with a brook running through it. I put my Scotch in the water to keep it cold, careful not to spill it, and then turn and embrace a stranger, a Tibetan refugee.

Leaving out the parts about the Scotch and the refugee, I tell Chogyal's secretary about the dream and ask him if prayers for Sikkim could be said. He says they're already being said in monasteries throughout the country.

There is a ceremony at the chapel for the swearing-in of the new councillors. For such occasions in the chapel the thrones are always placed according to geomancy. Today the Chogyal sits looking east, facing the newly elected councillors. The children and I sit facing north, across from the gazetted officers. The chanting of the monks is musical and energizing. I always feel peaceful and in tune with the services. The rhythmic prayers calm my nerves. At the end of the service, when it's time for the senior executive councillor of the new ruling majority, the National party, to go up to Chogyal and present him with a scarf, this politician, a man I've never respected very much, heaves his fat bulk upright, trembling in his excitement at being first, before the Kazi, the leader of the losing party. I find his eagerness, in fact the man himself, unfortunate. I wish the National party had a different leader. I look up and see Keshab smiling at the scene. I'm about to grin at him conspiratorially when he surprises me by letting his smile fade suddenly.

Yangchen goes with her father to the official opening of the Council. I feel apathetic, and in any case I don't feel well, so stay at home. There are a few demonstrators outside the Council House, Yangchen tells me later, who are there asking for one man, one vote. A friend of mine, Ramchandra, was out in front like a cheerleader. All day long people tease me about him. "I always warned you," Chogyal says. "Coming round here buttering you up and you making such a fuss over him. It's really you who've built him up. I told you to stay out of things."

In the afternoon a group of thirty or so Nepali Sikkimese men, including Ramchandra, come up to the palace to speak to the Chogyal. They're demanding one man, one vote, and they protest the recent elections—not saying that they were rigged but that the electoral system itself is unfair. Chogyal sits with them on the upper lawn and talks to them with conviction If the parties in Sikkim want one man, one vote, they must pass such a resolution; at present the Sikkim electoral system is based on a joint party resolution that stipulates a parity system between Nepali and Bhutia Lepcha voters. He has nothing against a change in the system, he says, but he's always ruled constitutionally, not unilaterally by proclamation. He has never even exercised his right of veto over the Council; if they wish to change the system, they must approach it as an all-parties problem, and not as something to be ordered by fiat.

Chogyal believes totally in what he's saying. I think he is both credible and incredible, both right and wrong. I know he is a committed constitutionalist, does not allow himself to overstep an inch. To him the idea of upsetting a three-party agreement, even though it's an agreement arrived at to some degree through his influence, is abhorrent. Couldn't he, however, say something hopeful to these people—that he hopes the election system will evolve into a more representative system of voting? I know he does hope this, that he looks forward passionately to the day when the safeguards for the Bhutia Lepcha community can be dropped. His whole working life has been devoted to trying to integrate the different groups in Sikkim, trying to make them all feel Sikkimese, hoping they will evolve politically to national consciousness, when they will vote as citizens rather than as communalists.

The irony is that until this time comes, the system of representational parity that currently safeguards both the integrity of Sikkim as a country and the well-being of the early founders of the country contributes to polarizing the state. There is no easy answer. If the parity system is ended now, the Bhutia Lepchas will be swamped. Worse still, the country's life itself could be jeopardized, since there are those among the Nepali Sikkimese political leadership who have little loyalty to Sikkim and would prefer to see it a part of Nepal. This is changing. The younger Nepali Sikkimese are increasingly patriotic, but Chogyal feels more time is needed. On the other hand, if they want one man, one vote now, isn't it awfully hard to stop? Haven't they already earned it by sheer force of will? The group listens politely, even affably, to the Chogyal and accepts the tea and biscuits that we offer.

Despite the civility of the meeting, some Tathangchen children who have been hanging around are frightened. "We heard them talking. They are going to make a shooting at Chogyal's birthday in the stadium. As they were going away they said so."

Ramchandra has come again to the palace to petition the Chogyal for one man, one vote. Yangchen and I are playing Scrabble on the verandah so we can watch what's going on and who comes in and out. As he leaves, he greets me with his usual self-conscious grin. "Hi, Ramchandra," I say. "What's going on?" Passionately, if somewhat incoherently, he explains their stand. "But, Ramchandra," I say, "we are all working for this. This is the solution everyone wants. You have done so much real work, work with your hands for Sikkim and your village." Only a few months earlier I'd trudged up a mountainside to see a concrete water tank Ramchandra had made. "You've also been privy to Chogyal's thinking and know he wants the same things you want. How can you join a man like K.C., a goonda full of hot air who's done nothing for Sikkim? This is just playing into Indian hands. They're the only people who'll gain. Certainly our Nepali Sikkimese won't. You're just being used to divide Sikkim and to block the demand for treaty review."

Ramchandra looks at me slightly wild-eyed, dry foam above his lips, shaking his head. "No. Chogyal must do this or else."

"Or else what, Ramchandra? Is it true that down at the petrol pump the Congress party is saying Chogyal and Gyalmo must be katum—finished?"

"Oh, no, Your Majesty," he says, eyes shining, "that we have never said."

Now Ramchandra has begun a hunger strike on the upper lawn. I shouldn't be cynical, but I think it suits his sense of drama. He's always been the lead actor in every school play. It's hard to take him entirely seriously. Even he himself, I suspect, sees himself as performing, at least in part.

Ramchandra's and my friend Kirin is back from engineering college and has come up to the palace to see if he can be of any help. First, he shows me with pride a book he has brought for our tenth anniversary, a warmly inscribed art book of gems and minerals, one of his loves. Then, for some time, he tells me his general news. Two things are exciting him: one, an informal tutoring session that he and some of his friends have started during the evenings to help their younger brothers and sisters in schoolwork; and the other, an inspiration about some engineering technique that will make buildings in Sikkim less likely to crack during earth tremors. Though I can't follow his technical points, I always enjoy Kirin's enthusiasm. Today, however, I'm impatient.

"Kirin," I interrupt, "can't you reason with him?"

Kirin's sensitive face is pained. "I've tried. I talked with him about everything. He's just not listening. Something's happened to him. You know, Your Majesty, last winter when his new baby died, I was so upset for him and his wife, but he seemed not to mind, to pay no attention, just continued to act in other people's business. His ego is making him even stranger, and now they're praying to him like God, so he can't stop even if he wants."

"Well, Kirin, tell him in a roundabout way that I used to pray to him. When I prostrate myself to the Buddha image, I need something to meditate on, so I've taken three faces—a Nepalese, Ramchandra; a Bhutia, Norbu; a Lepcha, Mrs. Lucksom—and when I bow, I concentrate very hard on trying to bring these faces into one by an act of meditation, to help bring a unity in Sikkim." Kirin's face is sad and embarrassed as I speak. He nods helplessly.

For several hours afterward we work together silently cataloguing and shelving the stacks of books brought back from our trip which are still on the floor. "I've got a question, Kirin. Some man sent us this pile of books from the States. I was going to send them down to the Youth Library, but several seem propagandist about America. Not too much, but a little. Should I send them down with the others or throw them out?"

He looks at me thoughtfully for a little while, and then, politely, regretfully, he says, "I think, Your Majesty, just now you'd better throw them out."

It is the third day that Ramchandra is out there. I'm reading Camus' *The Rebel* and I don't understand a word about the imperative to rebel that it goes on about. It seems pointlessly abstract. In fact, I'm reading it to put a distance between myself and what's happening. I'm worried about Ramchandra. He's skin and bones anyway. A government official suggests I cook something and take it to him. "He'd never refuse something from the Gyalmo's hands."

"She's enough involved as it is," Chogyal replies. "And, in any case, I gather his chappies are secretly feeding him."

I feel half in the palace, half out there with Ramchandra. It's beginning to rain, and the thought of him out on the ground is disturbing.

It's still raining during the Indian Representative's dinner that evening, and there are sounds of thunder. Mr. Bajpai tenses every time there's a burst. He seems to be listening for them. "Do you think, Gyalmo, we are really going to get a storm, or will it pass over?" he asks repeatedly. He's acting very strange tonight. High and on edge. Everyone is. It's a family party—just the Representative, a couple of his American houseguests, and our family. It should be pleasant, but everything is so charged. Before dinner Chogyal keeps hacking away at Tenzing, telling him that he thinks too much of himself. Tenzing, furious, controls himself, trying not to fight back in front of Bajpai.

The dinner too is unusual. The food, in contrast to the standard curries, is exquisite. Also, every beautiful thing the Bajpais own, most of which I've never seen before, has been put out on the table. Silver ashtrays, Baccarat cigarette holders, cloisonné candy dishes. They all seem new and unused—a wedding-present display.

Bajpai is going on about his current hobbyhorse, Talleyrand, and how painful it was for the old diplomat to lose his grip over his creature Napoleon, how galling it was for Talleyrand when Napoleon's youth and energy overcame the old man's experience and sagacity. Bajpai's so urgent about it. I've already given him Harold Nicholson's *Congress of Vienna* and the few other books on the subject we have in the library, but he begs me to look for more. "I want to write a psychodrama, Gyalmo, about the two of them locked in struggle." He talks about the Greek idea of character as fate.

Suddenly he switches from intellectual talk to manic old-boy high spirits. "Come, Chogyal," he says to the other end of the table, "let us do for luck the old Oxford custom." Rising, he takes four silver quart-sized tankards of beer from the sideboard, keeps one and passes the others to Chogyal, Tenzing, and Wongchuk. Throwing back his head, he drains his mug without pausing. I watch him, astonished. I've never seen him more than sip at a cocktail before. One by one, to applause, Chogyal and the boys drink down their tankards. Afterward Bajpai says, "Now let's dance," and without asking consent, rolls back the carpet in the small sitting room next to the dining room. "Come, Gyalmo"—he seizes my wrist—"come with me. We are going to pick out a record. It will be the last tango in Gangtok." We dance. He dances sideways, slightly on his toes, like a crab scuttling on his claws. I am enjoying the almost sexual energy of his high. Tenzing and Wongchuk watch, amused, and the Chogyal embraces Mrs. Bajpai, who refuses to dance.

"No, no, Chogyal. I'm wise enough not to try what I know I really can't do."

Chogyal gives her a warm embrace, saying, "Never mind, it's good to know one is among real friends."

She shrinks away from him, her petite body very straight, and, looking him coolly in the eye, says, "Some other place maybe, Chogyal, but not here." A truth has been spoken that jostles against the music and the frantic bonhomie of the evening.

On the way home Chogyal and Tenzing resume their arguing. It is more a King Lear-offspring struggle than the Talleyrand-Napoleon tussle that Bajpai had been talking about. Tenzing is upset that he has been put down in front of the Representative. "It doesn't help to do this in front of the Indians, as I'm going to have to take over sooner or later, and what kind of opinion will they have of me?" He is right, I know, but still something inside me stirs with anger and hurt when he speaks of "taking over." He has said this so often to his father, even at a very early age. Although it is not intended as such, it seems a wounding thing, reminding his father of his mortality.

Chogyal is stung by Tenzing's rebuke. "In that case," he says, "why don't you take over? You think it's so easy. You'll see. From this moment I abdicate in your favor. You are now the Chogyal—I am he no longer."

Yangchen and I, believing him, stay up till dawn whispering about what will happen. I am elated at the possibility, as it will mean that we would be less bound to work and sacrifice, freer to be ourselves. I feel such a rush of happiness and anticipation that I am overcome by guilt and force myself to think the opposite, to feel concern about the effect of the drastic change on Chogyal's psyche as well as its repercussions for Sikkim and for Tenzing. In the morning the matter has vanished. Nothing has changed.

*   *   *

Mr. and Mrs. Bajpai come over for drinks. K. C. Pradhan has been released from jail. Chogyal and Mr. Bajpai talk by the fireplace in low voices. Partly to establish my innocence, partly because I'm mildly curious, I ask Mrs. Bajpai if she knows what's happening. "Not really, Gyalmo, it all seems like a story to me, not real." I also feel vacant, a nonparticipant. Underneath, however, in an odd, passive way I understand that somehow we are to be victims.

On the evening of April 3, at the reception at India House for the new councillors, Bajpai sees us off. "Remember, Chogyal, I'm one hundred percent behind you." A flash goes through my mind of the violence rumored to be planned for the stadium the next day. I think: I'll bet you are, especially when they're shooting at us.

At seven the next morning I hear what sounds like shots down the hill in the bazaar. A half hour or so later Karma comes running through the door into our bedroom, where we're still in bed. He touches the floor with one hand in perfunctory obeisance. Even on the run, Karma can do this. Often, when I meet him trundling with files from his office by the chapel to the ADC's office, he shifts his briefcase from right to left hand without missing a beat, bends his knee, touches the ground, grins, says "Morning, Majesty," and jogs off at top speed, his broad shoulders swaying.

Today he's as breathless as ever but full of an added fearful energy. "There's a firing down in the bazaar, La, the police have been holding about five or six thousand demonstrators since early this morning from crossing the line, but the crowd started throwing bottles and stones at the men guarding the checkpoint. After using tear gas and lathi charges, our boys fired to disperse them. Two of the crowd were wounded but not seriously. They're armed, La—they've got kukris and lathis and some of them have guns."

So it has begun. It doesn't seem real.

I'd known that Palden's school friends had been afraid of going to the stadium for the sports events scheduled for that afternoon. "There's going to be a shooting—we heard the demonstrators talking." Nonetheless I'd sent Palden dressed in his official school uniform—a brown cotton robe worn at special functions—to join his schoolmates down at the village for the march up to the palace, where they would present scarves at the birthday reception.

Outside the palace the scarf-giving has started, and there is a great pushing and shoving as about three thousand people try to crowd up the steps onto the verandah. Mr. Manuel comes up to say that more food is needed for the spread on the side lawn. I watch from upstairs. Keshab's face is veiled and smiling. Villagers are carrying orchids and bunches of field flowers wrapped in newspaper. Indian merchants are carrying tinned biscuits on trays, and Tibetans unfurl long silk scarves as they pull up our driveway in jeeps flying multicolored prayer flags.

Inside, Chogyal is receiving scarves in the big sitting room. The carved and gilded screens for the room's French windows have been finished only a few days earlier. It is the first time the public will see them. I'm proud of the effect and hope people will notice how much more cheerful and Sikkimese the room appears now that we've finally done away with the old limp curtains.

We are all in brocades, Chogyal in his gold coronation robe, Hope in her last year's blue silk dress, too short, showing her sneakers, which I hadn't until now noticed she was wearing. I'm in my fashion-show clothes—ivory dress, red blouse, and red-and-blue-flowered tunic. We advance stiffly from the palace to the pavilion by the royal chapel, my mother-in-law, other relations, and officers joining us as we proceed. I'm irritable at having to dress and put up my hair at this early hour. In the bright sunlight my eyes feel sore and scratched by the flakes of yesterday's eye liner, which I haven't had time to cream off.

The Tibetans have now swept up in their prayer flag-decked jeeps and are parked around the chapel. To my surprise they don't get out but remain sitting there. We take our seats on the dais in the pavilion. Hope sits in the back row, behind Tenzing, the other relations, and Bajpai. I watch her and see she's bored, toying with my childhood locket that she's wearing. Palden is standing apart, with the other children of his school.

Karma, stumpy in his bronze dress and gold jacket, is reading the birthday message and honors list at the lectern. All of us are blank. I sit, stiff and straight, trying to keep a business-as-usual appearance. Karma's voice breaks a little with strain when he announces that, although not serious, there has been some trouble in the bazaar, and that as an extra safety precaution the scheduled afternoon sports events in the stadium will be canceled. He adds that the birthday dinner at the palace, however, will be given as usual.

At mid-speech the Tibetan jeeps wheel away, flags waving. Lhanzinla, Chogyal's half sister whispers what we all know: there must have been more trouble at the bazaar.

After the ceremony, as soon as we reach the verandah, all the men start shedding, as they always do, their state robes. The women, more decorously, go upstairs to change.

Palden is back home for lunch, very relieved at the cancellation of the afternoon sports events. During the afternoon he and Hope tag around with me as I supervise putting up the tents outside the verandah and on the side lawn. Knobby-kneed Sikkim Guards in shorts help the carpenters construct the wooden dancing platform. The children thump on the uneven boards, spraying themselves and the platform with talcum powder. Sagging wires with bare bulbs are looped around the tent poles. The garden-party cloths are put on tables, the red bunting hiding the table legs. The garden-party crockery, brought down in tin washtubs, is ready for use. Our customary veg and nonveg tables have been organized, and things don't look bad when the gardeners finally bring down the flowerpots, which have been carried around all day from ceremony to ceremony.

Usually about three hundred to four hundred people come. This evening there are barely half that number. In the outside tent by the verandah I talk to some young agricultural officers who've just joined government and whom I haven't met before. As always, I make it a point to eat at the table deemed the lowest in rank. The Indian officers on deputation have, as usual, pushed inside to the food served in the two dining rooms.

After dinner I chat in the sitting room with a Mr. Vreeland and his wife, who are guests of the Representative. Mr. Vreeland is in the U.S. Foreign Service, and the two men are old friends from some previous posting. It's odd, though. Mr. Bajpai seemed concerned about their coming just now, asking me repeatedly if I thought it was a good time.

The Vreelands compliment me on the beautiful clothes people had worn that morning and are wearing now. I tell them how grateful I am to Mr. Vreeland's mother, Diana Vreeland, then the editor of Vogue, for her help with my fashion show two years earlier. It upsets me that visitors sometimes see just the brocade in our lives, the opposite of our ordinary life and dress, so I also joke with pride about Hope Leezum's sneakers. Soon, though I regret leaving them, I move on. I'm scared to be seen talking too long to Americans.

Outside, dancing has begun in the tent. Floodlights illumine the camellia bushes and the scarlet-tunicked Sikkim Guards' band on the lawn across the driveway. During intermissions the children fool with the brass instruments. Wondering where the Sikkimese are, wondering where Chogyal is—where anybody is, for that matter—I dance with a number of Indian officers. I know I must keep on dancing as if everything is all right.

People leave early, about eleven. I go back into the little sitting room, shocked to find rows of Sikkimese government officials crowding the dimly lighted room. Chogyal is leaning back on a banquette, repeating his story of how, in 1947, during the landlords' uprising, encouraged by India to achieve a merger with Sikkim, he had gone out on a dangerous mission alone. Tenzing and Karma sit forward, impatient. Karma, white-faced, his brow furrowed, is saying, "Yes, but we've got no time, we've got to decide now."

The Indian commissioner of police, a Bengali, says, "Sir, we must make a decision."

Someone briefs me in a whisper. A message has come: the police stations in South and East and West Sikkim have been overrun, looted, arms stolen. Policemen and government personnel have been beaten and held prisoner. The crowds are armed and are adding to their weapons as they go along. They're now about twenty miles away from Gangtok, halted at Singtam, a halfway point from the Indo-Sikkim border to the capital. So this is why Bajpai was so concerned about the rain at his dinner party—the crowds must already have been on their way.

The police commissioner, to keep them out of the capital, wants to meet them at Ranipul, the main junction of East, South, and West Sikkim, which lies below Gangtok. "Get the Guards in here." The Guards, who are usually busy hosing off plates and dismantling tables after a party, come in at a half run. From a cupboard under the side stairs, which I had never seen opened, they drag out long, coffin-shaped boxes full of guns. The boxes as they are dragged scrape the stone floor of the corridor, scrape my heart.

We go to bed. Chogyal's loaded gun is on the mantelpiece next to Clover's little statue and the painting of Buddha.

The next morning the demonstrators are at Ranipul. The police commissioner, very angry, bits of foam flecking his mouth, is in the garden talking to Tenzing. I gather that the troops promised by the commander of the Sikkim Guards, Colonel Gurung, a staunch pro-Indian Nepalese on deputation from the Indian Army, had failed to show up at some bridge where they were supposed to have halted the demonstrators coming from western Sikkim. Although Indian, the police commissioner is furious; his honor as a policeman loyal to the

Sikkim police is at stake. "My boys are there waiting, sir," he sputters. "I can't believe it." Without the Guards the police are helpless.

The demonstrators are putting out in front the women and children they've taken along the way.

In the ADC's office Tenzing and I get through to his friends in Cambridge. The phones are working pretty well, since the Indians want to monitor them. Tenzing excitedly says something that's to get him in trouble later. "We've got enough manpower and ammunition to put them down. The trouble is they're using women and children." Although, in fact, he is saying that we would not even defend ourselves as long as innocent people would be hurt, he will later be accused of implying exactly the opposite. I say in a very measured way, "Please tell Clover to tell Peter the plan is working."

In an effort to counter the troubles—which he had foreseen since the previous August—Chogyal had informed one of Henry Kissinger's young staff members, when we were in America at Christmas, that a plot was being formed in Sikkim: through the Indian Intelligence Bureau weapons were to be brought in from the Darjeeling district and cached; a number of major bridges and institutions were to be blown up with explosives; and at a given time the Nepali work force in Sikkim, Darjeeling, and Kalimpong was to be marshaled as demonstrators to surround the palace and stage a shoot-out.

If enough key people knew of the plan, Chogyal thought, perhaps by some miracle it might be forestalled, perhaps by some pressure put on the Indians. I had felt that even if it was unrealistic to hope that events could be prevented, at least in some ways it was a comfort to know that someone else knew. In a way this gives me now some small measure of sanity. If you are suddenly the target of a massive attack, you cannot help but wonder whether you have caused it, whether it is you and not something outside of you.

The next day I speak to Clover from the alcove upstairs. "The plan is working," I say.

"I know," she says.

"What are you doing?"

"Oh"—her voice sounds scared and stricken—"I don't know what you would want us to do except tell Peter."

"No, I don't mean that, Clover—tell me, what are you and Tom doing? What did you do today?" I must hear something tangible of daily life, some grain to remind me of some other reality.

"Oh, we . . . Tom and I played a little tennis . . . Eliza's got an ear infection"—a small apologetic laugh, Clover's laugh, special to her when she half boasts, half apologizes for talking about her children.

"Okay, Clover, I'll keep in touch with you. Much love to you all—I love you so much."

The demonstrators are on the football ground. Trucks have been coming up all day. The army has been giving them trucks, fuel, tarpaulins for shelter, and food.

The phone rings in the ADC's office. No one is there, so I pick it up. It is Shanti, Keshab's wife, asking if by some chance her husband is there. She is anxious about him, since he should have been home some while earlier. I am suffused with anger and hurt. Karma has told me that Keshab has joined his brother K.C. and is in league with the demonstrators. When they'd been at Yale, my friends in America had looked after them and their children like family. "No, Shanti, he's certainly not at the palace."

The voice at the other end is uneasy, anxious for reconciliation, knowing I know. "Well, I hope, La, that everything will be all right."

"Yes." I put the receiver down heavily.

Some people are still able to come to the palace. Karma, Chopra (the former Sidlon, or Prime Minister, who's returned here on a brief visit for the April 4 celebration), Chogyal, and I sit under the magnolia tree.

"Well, at least it's good to know we've got the ham radio," I say. Maybe we can get a message out on that.

Karma looks at me angrily and then jerks his head at Chopra. "Keep quiet."

A Lhasa relation, Ragasha—smiling, teasing, safe—sleeps at our house. The Tibetans are filled with an energy, born of deep love for the Chogyal and a furious determination that they will not lose their new adopted country. One homeland gone is enough. Here they will make their stand. Our Tibetan nurse Memeh is so angry she stalks the house in a bony scarecrowlike, angular walk.

I first hear the demonstrators coming up the road from the Academy —a vast sigh, long cooing noises. When they fan out along the lower circular road around the palace compound, you can make out the chanted words. "Chogyal murdabad, Kazi ko jai, Indira Gandhi ko jai, Bhutia Lepcha katum. Bharat ko jai." ("Death to the Chogyal, long live Kazi, long live Indira Gandhi, an end to Bhutia Lepchas. Long live India.") Tenzing points a rifle—playing, impotent, angry at them. Friends restrain him. Skinny, listless, carrying jholas full of rice and weapons, the crowd moves close together, ridden herd by their leaders, like press-gangs. The leaders shout orders. It's most frightening when they come along a path adjoining the lawn that is separated from the western side of the palace only by a fringe of bamboos. They come several times a day, each time circling the house for several hours. When they come we run for the Scrabble board. But everyone is too stricken to play. Wendy, the Tathangchen headmistress, plays for all of us.

Dan, Wendy's husband, says that yesterday morning, from their house, they heard the Guards schoolchildren begin to sing the anthem, and then their headmistress' voice stopping them. Furious, he got the Tathangchen children to sing the anthem as loudly as they could.

We sit with Dan and Wendy under the magnolia tree, listening to radio news of Picasso's death and President Nixon's growing beleaguerment. Despite his harmfulness, I feel sorry for Nixon. I identify with his encirclement. Dan says waiting for what will happen next reminds him of *Nicholas and Alexandra*, a movie that's been shown recently in Calcutta.

Sometimes when the demonstrators come, we move outside to the front garden that faces the main gate so we can see them. I push the letter I am writing to Matt into my tunic and pull on a loose turtleneck; if the palace should be burned, the letter will be on me. "Oh, Gyalmo always puts on her turtleneck when she is afraid," someone says. Each time, when I come back in, riffling the pages in fear and haste, I shove the letter under my closet. One afternoon a servant sees me.

Often when I am indoors and the trouble starts, I play Eric Andersen, guitarist and folk singer, really loudly on the new record player I've brought back from America. The song on the band just before the one I want ends with a sirenlike dissonant harmonica noise, then comes the familiar, "Oh, take off your thirsty boots and stay for a while—for you've done a-marching a-many a-weary mile." Small and way back, into my head comes a pinlight of detached irony. We were the marchers, we were the ones with good songs on our side. For freedom, for equality. It is unbelievable. Now we are among those being marched at, a symbol to topple.

Sometimes I go to Yangchen's room. The two of us kneel on the floor coloring Kate Greenaway figures in a drawing book. Anger so great, so exquisitely modulated into coloring, clean brush into purple paint, suffusing steamy clouds of purple paint in a glass of water, painting the barest breath of filmy vapor mauve, just up to the outline of the long puffed dress. Long filament screams thread through my head.

There are guns all over the house. Rifles, their barrels broken, lie on each dining room chair, on the burnt-orange raw silk I'm so protective of. Young men full of animal excitement, urgency, spring double-stepped up the stairs. Despite the incessant music, I hear the pounding. Boys from Tathangchen go in and out of the clutter room opening off the landing by our bathroom door and rummage through the room full of old presents, pictures, lampshades, suitcases, photographs, love letters, boxes of slides—and guns.

About thirty kids, all of them known to me, are out with Tenzing on the front lawn, practicing firing in my rock garden against the embankment that leads to the upper lawn. Young Phurpa, Palden's friend, is there, tolerated as scout and messenger. Phurpa who could make and draw anything—toys, bows, arrows, pictures of comic-book heroes, scenes of mountain villages and children playing. This past year he has grown up and has come to see Palden only occasionally. Now he is out there, accepted as a man by the older boys from the village. In turn they take up positions, lying on their stomachs, rifles outstretched, on the western side of the compound. The demonstrators file by on the path five feet below, beyond the thin fringe of bamboos. There is a cowboy aspect to all this that scares me.

Usually the crowd begins to arrive in the morning, just at waking—the noise of the chanting comes closer, like a wave.

Palden plays out on the verandah that opens off his room so he can watch what's happening. For days he builds and rebuilds the Lego fortress he and his friends had been working on, extending the wing that houses the trucks—the trucks backed in so that they can be brought out quickly. Near the fort, aligned along the cracks in the floorboards, his soldiers are positioned—Germans, English, Japanese. The first ranks kneel or crouch, those in the rear are erect, shouldering bazookas or, arms upswung, are about to throw their grenades. In square towers, which Palden calls "bunkers," separate from the main building, there are more soldiers. Huddled figures keep watch through narrow slits. Outside, cowboy and Indian civilian scouts stand or lie behind bushes. There are more soldiers in battle position along the perimeter of the roof. They kneel, rifles poised, protected by low parapets. Crack! Palden tenses at the sound of a rifle being cocked. Just a moth hitting the paper shade. It's the moth season now, and at night we lie awake listening to the gun noises as big insects bullet into the shades.

In the beginning Palden used to stand by the kitchen side of the palace watching his friends go along the road below until they forked off onto the school trail, down to Tathangchen, his head pressed against the fence palings until the iron made welts on his forehead. His friends had been loyal. Moon-faced, grinning up at him, trying to convey their love. "Hi, see you," they would call. He couldn't really hear the words from the road.

Nothing moves on the upper lawn. Nothing moves on the bleached grass. The tethered flag flaps about the pole. The quietness outside makes us feel more sharply the fears that lie squeezed in our chests. Any action outside on the lawn would be good. Palden has learned since this began that any kind of activity outside takes the fear out of his chest and makes him more of an audience. Still nothing happens. Last evening Hope and he sat in their little wicker chairs drawn up to the verandah railing to watch. Now the chairs, still pulled close to the railing, are like empty theater seats.

Palden knows, however, that the Guards and the older Tathangchen boys are out there and knows where they are. By watching them at emergency drills and at real stand-tos as they scramble to positions in the trenches, he has created a pretty good map in his mind. One of their oddest places, he thinks, is behind the greenhouse, near the willow tree. Odd, he points out, because for months he and his friends have been digging a bunker in the same spot, stealing boards from the carpenter to shore it up whenever it showed signs of caving in, defending it against Hope and the other little children when they came defiantly to urinate there. Tikki, our mongrel dog, had always been with them when they were digging. Now Palden says he is glad Tikki was run over when we were in America. The little dog was a wanderer, and Palden asks, with a stab of fear, what would have happened to Tikki now. He would have wandered out the gate, surely, and been killed.

The trees rimming the lawn darken, and Palden turns, listening to Memeh's steps as she carries his dinner up the stairs, her slow, measured steps signaling the balanced supper tray. Quite different from the pounding feet on the staircase all these recent days.

It all began, Palden says, with the tobacco shop near the palace gate. He and Hope had wanted to go there for peppermints that first night. It wasn't very far, and he and the other children often used to go there. That evening they weren't allowed.

And now, every night, there are the sounds. Not the urgent staircase and bullet-moth sounds of the inside day, but the long outside ocean sounds of the crowd, and the sighing birdcalls that sound like intruders' codes.

16

ONE MORNING I go into the children's room about six. Hope and the nurse are still asleep. Palden is up, in his flannel bathrobe, his bony wrists sticking out, face white and pinched. The Guards outside are running with great urgency and jumping into the bunkers in view of the verandah. There must have been a stand-to. I ask Palden if he is scared. "No," he says quickly, looking away.

"Well, I'm a little scared, sweetie." This son of ours who doesn't talk.

"Do you think they'll take over, Mummy?"

"No, sweetie, not now, not just now."

"When, then—in a couple of years?"

He means the Indians. He says what no one else will acknowledge except perhaps to themselves. "I'd rather be a minister in Nepal than an Indian." This is a fragment of the conversation that has been going on around him. Chogyal has been asking aloud what the people want. Wouldn't it be better to be merged with Nepal, so that at least we might keep some identity rather than be struck into the dominant welter of India?

There are hot cross buns for breakfast, full of raisins and citron. Sticky, white sugar crosses. Our new cook has been expending himself since the troubles began, baking things each day, trying to tempt us to eat. I feel always on the verge of throwing up and live on consommé, bananas, Valium, and cigarettes. Later on, at eleven, I will have beer, and at lunch, whiskey. Mr. Manuel also continues to function. He comes each morning in his old suit and vaudeville-dignity tie clip and asks with a straight face, "How many people will there be for lunch?" The question almost makes me laugh, but the laugh comes out as a twisted inhalation. I lie in bed stoned most of the day and grimly continue to read. Durrell's

Alexandria Quartet, Balzac's *Père Goriot*, Male's *Gothic Image*, anthologies of poetry.

There is a meeting in the big sitting room. I sit with the children outside, on the swing in the magnolia tree. The main corps of Sikkimese government officers has come, including many of Keshab's clan —the Pradhans, who have been working with the Indians in this plan. As they go into the big sitting room they almost all nod and smile. I want them to look in my eye.

They have come to decide with Chogyal what to do about negotiating with the demonstrators—whether to yield to their one man-one vote demand or whether to ask the government of India to restore law and order. A representative is elected from among the officials to go down to the football ground to negotiate, to agree to the end of communal voting. The leaders of the demonstrators will not agree. They are determined to see the Indian government assume power, no matter what political concessions are made. The Indians and the leaders of the demonstrators are one.

Much later that evening the police commissioner bumps into me in the library. "Can't you," he asks, "prevail on your husband to allow the Indians to take over? We are finished and time is running out."

"I would never attempt to influence him. In any case, P.C., are you sure it's gone? What about world opinion?"

He waves bony hands. "What world opinion? Where are the journalists? What's being put out is just the Government-of-India line. No foreign journalists can come; the Indian journalists here are all India House's men. And even if we had the journalists, where would we be? We haven't got all the people, and without all the people we can do nothing."

I agree silently. I know he's right. It's funny how easy it is to come to this conclusion. Maybe it is because so many of my Nepali friends have lent themselves to the movement. Is Dhan Bahadur, my friend whom I helped get a scholarship at the East-West Center, involved? Karma says so. He's down in the football ground with them. I can't believe it. Karma says he saw him in a demonstration wearing his yellow American slacks. Dhan Bahadur has sent word to me that he's being held hostage along with others. He begs us not to accept the Indian terms, says that the leaders are falling out among themselves, that the followers want to escape, that the movement won't be able to cohere much longer. Karma says not to put stock in his message.

There is some revenge in my submission to the idea of Indian paramountcy. This is what people want—let them have it. I, who have always been especially attached to Nepalis, hate them today as much as the most prejudiced Bhutia Lepcha. As for the latter, I am frustrated and resentful. By and large, they're not helping, not even doing small things that wouldn't get them in trouble, such as monitoring the news on Sikkim that is being given out by All India Radio. We have worked so hard, so long, for it to come to this.

Up until now our troubles, although terrible, have been possible to bear because they have been troubles from the outside that, although battering us, have in some ways strengthened our resolve, our character. These troubles, as they are caused, in part at least, from the inside, by ourselves, are impossible to bear. I have a secret too. I want to live. I burn with shame and breathe shallowly through my mouth. Surrender is so easy. I mistrust myself; I must be silent; I am noncommittal to the police commissioner. Much later that evening, in the living room, a paper is signed by all the men, asking for Indian intervention. I think Chogyal wanted it, although earlier he had angrily rejected a threatening note from the Indian Representative offering personal safety for our family in return for handing over power. "Blackmail. I'm prepared to die—who does he think we are?" This new consensus is different; it takes the responsibility away from him. His homespun robe is damp and rumpled. Perspiration beads his lips; his eyes are clouded. We are not talking much.

Later that night Chogyal's official secretary comes up to our bedroom. His head drooping with fatigue, he sits on the floor, his files on the bed. Chogyal and I are both sitting up in bed. They are discussing the paper that will ask the government of India to restore law and order. There is no provision for an end to the Indian supervision. I am appalled. Despite my resolve not to interfere in any way for or against, I ask, "Couldn't you put in 'until the Sikkim government is able to restore order'?" The provision is included, but is rejected by the Indians.

There is a lull, the first since Chogyal has agreed to hand over the government to India to restore law and order. Yangchen and I drive along the short Ridge Road to the Chopras' house, where our ex-Sidlon and his wife are again staying during this return visit. Mrs. Chopra is indignant and full of gossip. "I always wondered what Bajpai had been up to, all those times he was too busy to come to functions. I always said he must be up to something. If you're behaving yourself in Gangtok, there isn't that much to do. I went out last night to try to learn some things and met a wife from Bajpai's staff who said that they'd been ordered to leave their house last night to move into tents at the Residency. Mrs. P. said it was ridiculous, that there was no danger, no need. Bajpai is really trying to make it look as if they're threatened." Her face clouds in anger. To Mrs. Chopra the trouble is an extension of the social and political gamesmanship that the Representative has always practiced with her husband.

I need to stretch and say I'd like to walk back along the Ridge Road. Tathangchen, beloved, familiar, to the left; the bazaar, now unknown, down at the right. She looks apprehensive. "No, Gyalmo—I think you ought to drive. No use taking chances."

When I get home I go to the library and am there for about an hour. Then, for some reason, I go toward the ADC's office and look up. My heart stops. There is a Sikkim Guard by the sentry box in the driveway, kneeling in battle position, surrounded by sandbags, rifle aimed down at the lower road circling the palace. It is obscene, the most shocking thing I have ever seen, this grotesque, surreal violence on our peaceful road. The evening-walk road, kids abreast singing, holding hands, climbing in the nullah, plucking flowers from the mossy wall. My stomach churns with fury and sickness. Looking down the driveway, I see other Guards scrambling to take position behind sandbag fortifications. In the first action of the Indians since they have accepted responsibility for the maintenance of law and order they have let the mob back, they have *brought* the mob back. They have lifted the ban, and thousands of new marchers have been brought up against the palace.

The Chopras come for dinner to say goodbye; they are going back to Delhi. It's now clear why Bajpai worked to get him out of Sikkim last fall. The Indians didn't want an Indian head of government during the take-over. They wouldn't be able to say, as they are saying now, that Sikkim is a badly administered feudal autocracy. It's ironic that they should be back here now visiting during these days.

Chopra, Sandhurst-trained, David Niven-suave, is leaning forward with exaggerated attention to what Chogyal is saying: "It's very important that Mrs. Gandhi hear of what's happening. You must get word to her the quickest possible. She must hear."

Chopra bows his head frequently. "Yes, Chogyal, I think it's the only thing."

I watch them across the library. Fury boils through me. Mrs. Gandhi knows. I scream, "Of course Mrs. Gandhi knows. Mr. Chopra, you know that, why don't you tell Chogyal that?" Two faces turn on me. Chogyal's unfocused, Chopra's masked, angry. As the Chopras leave the library I am washed in fear. Once again I have shown that I know and have known. In a faint, supplicating voice I say, "Goodbye, I hope I've not said anything that will make further trouble—it just seemed—well, you know."

And the Chopras say, "Of course," and Mrs. Chopra says, "Gyalmo, do be careful."

Before they get in their car Chogyal takes Chopra to the ADC's office. He is enraged about the Indians' breach of faith. Today, in town, the army stood by while crowds looted the police station, and our own police, whom they'd demobilized, had to stand by and watch. Tears spring in his eyes. "I will revoke the agreement. If this is their honor. I will take it back." Doesn't he know that it is a chess game, that if he now removes this, they will take us, kill us anyway, and go on to the next move of the take-over? They will do it one way or another.

A visitor staying in our guesthouse insists on taking a jeep out. She is halted and mobbed. The Vreelands have been flown out by army helicopter, doubtless so they will not witness Bajpai's meetings. The Sikkim House architect and his family are to leave this morning. Yesterday they came up from the guesthouse to sleep at the palace. His wife and children are strained and anxious. He is ponderous and careful. In his heavy Swiss-German accent he says, "I think the Indians mean it to be just a cat-and-mouse game, but they are moving the line forward day by day! What bothers me is that the crowd could get out of control. Even if directed, a crowd at some point gets its own energy." Again breaking my resolve not to interfere in any way, I tell Chogyal in front of the architect and his family that if the so-called army protection is removed, I will take the children and walk up to India House for protection. I am acting something out. I don't know why I'm saying this. I want attention, solicitude, to engage his attention. Chogyal, naturally, is exasperated. "Go, then, but you'll have to walk." He is walking around the house saying we will go down together, repeating the Sioux pledge that these black hills where we have shed red blood, site of our fathers' shrines or something, will never be surrendered.

I am happy that my Mary and Joseph statues, which I'd sent as a token to Matt, are safe outside. They are the things I love best in the world, and the fact that they are in America makes it seem in some ways as if at least part of my spirit too is safe and free. I think of the ferry in the bay, spray-capped waves. I think of Matt less and less except in the sense that I want to live—it is a yearning that the memory of loving him gives me. I'm holding on so hard to stalks of survival that any relationship seems too problematic. I have no energy for anything but to see that the children and I survive.

Some nights, though, I stare at the Chinese scroll over our bed of a curving pine-framed bay and force it to be the Cornish coast, where Matt said we might go one day. Some days I see the bay as the cove where Jane lives on Long Island Sound, sheltering and loving, blue sea swell, free sea. Small, loathed painting, crack open this ring, let me be free.

Alice and Clover call me often, whenever the lines are clear. For days after new trouble they'll be shut down, then after some time restored. I hear the White Plains operator talking solicitously to them—"Hang on, dear. Yeah, we're getting through now,"—fighting the Indian operator. "I know they're there." I love that White Plains voice so much. Good, loving. Safe. American. In a way it makes me feel very close and very far away.

A friend gets a phone call from Kalimpong, the Indian border town. "Leave, leave. They're coming over the hill. They've got grenades and guns and mortars." They say the bazaars in Kalimpong and Darjeeling are empty. All the people have been brought here. The crowd in the stadium, someone says, is divided into four categories: the Darjeeling-Kalimpong labor force; the Sikkimese villagers who have been gathered by the marchers on their way up to Gangtok, threatened with the burning of their houses and fields or with beating and murder if they didn't join; some true Sikkimese democrats who are genuinely ready to struggle for one man, one vote; and a last, rather pathetic group of demonstrators—Sikkimese villagers who'd been enticed to Gangtok by being told that the Chogyal's fiftieth birthday was a special occasion that would be celebrated on a grand scale, with much feasting and public festivity. Some of the latter and the villagers who'd been pulled along by the Darjeeling-Kalimpong crowd escape from the football ground, where they're herded under guard, and trot back along the roads until they're caught, beaten, and returned in the trucks going to pick up new people across the border.

Fights break out in the stadium, and a Tibetan is killed. Some say no, that a Tibetan killed a Nepali coolie. A rumor is being circulated that the drinking water in Gangtok is poisoned. No one knows who is threatening whom—each side thinks it is the intended victim. To be safe, we drink Coke for a day; the children are thrilled by the blanket permission to drink soda.

Lhanzinla, Chogyal's half sister, and Ragasha, his Tibetan cousin, are acting like self-appointed marshals. When Lhanzin goes home at night, she does as the servants do—takes a jagged empty bottle under her coat. Since the police have been disarmed, and since the army is just standing by or encouraging trouble, Ragasha and the Tibetans have organized a night patrol, and booted Khampas, from eastern Tibet, stamp around the bazaar trying to keep order. During her patrols Lhanzinla sees border-road officers rounding up coolies to take them down to join the demonstrators.

One day she goes down to the football ground to appeal to the crowd for her Dhaju, elder brother, "as any sister would do." Although fiercely loyal to her brother and Sikkim, she is also on a high with all the drama and recognition she is getting. "Now is the time we must fight—otherwise it will be too late!" I look at her silently. We have fought earlier; it is too late, now we should stop. After some time the Tibetans are threatened with expulsion from Sikkim if they engage in any further political or policing activities. I dream that night that I hear sounds of their boots in the bazaar—then silence.

Seemingly at random, but in fact in an organized way, violence is taking place throughout the southeast and west of the country. A retired elder statesman's house is razed, then dynamited, to make sure absolutely nothing remains but twisted metal of Buddha statues. His wife sleeps several nights in the jungle. An old Bhutia village head is shot point-blank through a window in his house near Rumtek. People's jails are set up in the Hindu temples of the border towns.

Finally news of the troubles reaches North Sikkim. People are saying that all the North Sikkimese, Bhutia Lepchas, about five to six thousand, are trying to come down, that they are coming down the northern roads armed with their long swords to defend Sikkim and the Chogyal. I find it touching but alarming. If there is an embroilment with the people in the stadium they will be decimated. The army is stopping them at bridges along the way; they will not allow a counterdemonstration. One group of about several thousand charges across the bridges and is on its way to Gangtok. In a moment of comedy, Karma steals all the government transport jeeps that are parked outside while a meeting is going on at India House and sends them to pick up those marchers who have gotten through and bring them the last lap. Provisions and some scant shelter have been provided for them on the outskirts of town. Both villagers and the National party are contributing rice.

Carrying pictures of the Chogyal and me, the North Sikkimese circle the town singing. The leaders have bull horns, but some play flutes. The songs are gentle, traditional songs praising the Chogyal and the beauty of the countryside. They are love songs. My feelings are so numbed that I feel only dimly the sadness and poignancy of their efforts. I remark to a visiting Bengali journalist who is with me, watching through the bamboo, "It was odd that the other demonstrators didn't even use drums. I should, I think, if I were organizing people."

"Yes," he replies, "if you were leading villagers, and not bazaar coolies from Kalimpong and Darjeeling who are paid three rupees a day."

Some beautiful old men with snow-white braids come to appeal to Chogyal not to turn away from them, to continue to struggle for Sikkim. More word is beginning to come in from the rest of the country. Dikki, who is married to Kazi's nephew, comes one afternoon with her husband. We had been taking lice off one another. Dikki laughs and we tell lice stories. Dikki, a pretty, pale girl, newly wed, had been in their country house when the invaders first came. Men had come to her door demanding her husband's guns. Each gun that country people owned was on their list, she said breathlessly. They were not people from her village. A leader comes and takes the men from one village to a distant hamlet to terrorize the local headmen and elite. Her kitchen, to which, with new housewife's pride, she was so attached, was ransacked—bags of rice, and grains and chang stolen or strewn about.

One day Bajpai comes and finds me sorting clippings on the dining room table, looking for ones that quote him as referring to Sikkim as part of India. Terrified at being caught, I turn sharply. He rearranges his face.

One late afternoon Yangchen and I walk around the edge of the palace lawn, past newly dug trenches, foxholes as strange as moon craters. It's like a dream, Yangchen says. We lie on our stomachs on a ridge of land overlooking the road by the secretariat. Kesu, the master painter's daughter, and her sister walk by. We wave and greet each other.

"Hi, La," says Kesu, looking up, beaming. "We're just out on a walk to see if there's anything we can do. I get too angry cooped up in our house in the bazaar, so I had to come out. The bazaar is awful. We hear everything in the stadium all night long, so it's hard to sleep. I hear the coolies running away and then the guards running after them, bringing them back."

The drivers, always one of the most powerful political groups in Sikkim, have taken over where the Tibetans were stopped. They are organizing pro-Sikkim, pro-Chogyal intelligence. Some of the drivers have been caught with weapons and arrested, becoming martyrs for the others. It's to little avail. Anything that the pro-Sikkim group does is immediately cracked down on by the Indian Central Reserve Police, who've recently been moved in from India. Meanwhile the murders, kidnapping, arson, and looting by the other side go unchecked. Kidnapping is becoming common, with people being taken at gunpoint from houses and from jeeps, then held in temple jails until they escape or a deal is made. Contrary to what Karma indicated, my friend Dhan Bahadur *had* been kidnapped, along with his sister, a nurse in Singtam, and forced to act as medical aide to the Janta camp in South Sikkim. My uppermost feeling is relief that he had not joined the other side voluntarily.

In the beginning Tenzing plays a major role with the young volunteers guarding the house and with the Sikkim Guards. Chogyal is increasingly worried by Tenzing's impulsiveness. Tenzing is increasingly impatient with his father's indecisiveness. One morning, fairly early in the troubles, he decides to go to a town south of Gangtok to check on the crowds there. Lhanzinla warns him not to go. He drives off with Roland and some other Guards and returns in the evening shaken, afraid, and young-looking. Now very dependent, he trails Chogyal around. "We *had* to shoot our way out. It was the only way. Armed men circled the jeep, shattering the windows, rocking us back and forth. They had us. If Roland hadn't shot, they would have taken us. The alternative was capture—we *had* to charge the barrier."

One man had been shot, and only in the leg, but within hours All India Radio, the Indian government radio station, is broadcasting regularly that the Crown Prince has killed peaceful demonstrators. Tenzing is effectively immobilized. The Indians' propaganda works. Towns in various parts of the country which had been calm break into anti-palace fury. In Gangtok, demonstrators surge around the palace calling for the Crown Prince's immediate arrest and trial. After the experience, Tenzing joins me in being cautious, almost detached. In a couple of weeks a helicopter is sent by the Indian government, as a favor, to fly him out on his first leg back to Cambridge. Watching him take off from the palace lawn, I rage silently, jealous of his easy quitting when I remain—as I've always remained—immured here.

When Tenzing gets to Delhi, still frightened by being the target of Indian anger and propaganda in Sikkim, he gives some interviews that follow the Indian line praising the Indian Government's handling of the situation as "maintaining order."

17

IN THE FLUSH OF POWER lent by the North Sikkimese presence, the Tathangchen village women have revenged themselves on a Nepali Darjeeling girl who had earlier burned the Chogyal's picture on the football ground. Although there is some justification for their anger, Wendy, usually profoundly shy, is shaken and jumps into the fray. Later, white-faced and trembling, she comes up the driveway to where we are sitting under the tree. "It was disgusting," she stammers. "Oh, Chogyal, they tried to tear her clothes off—all she had left was her choli and petticoat—they were like animals. I had to drag them off her." That afternoon, driving up from the football ground, she and Dan are stoned in their jeep by Darjeeling Nepalis who shout that Wendy was the instigator.

A number of Sikkimese students who'd been at college in India have come back to help. Today their unofficial leader, Tashi, a rather self-important boy studying law, has come to the palace, very pleased with himself, bringing a petition he has written asking Chogyal to regain Sikkim's sovereignty. Afterward, when we sit in the small alcove of the big sitting room, I say, yes, it's a fine petition, fine patriotism, but too late. The student elite who have been away to privileged schools all along should have been more responsible to the country, should have contributed more. Compared to the less privileged students in local schools, what have they done? Tashi is irritated, and later I'm sorry. It was senseless to provoke him. Everyone who is helping should be encouraged. It is just that I'm so tired of boosting people's egos, pleasing everyone for Sikkim's sake. Before it was okay, it served a purpose; now when it seems to little avail, I am sick of it.

Despite my impatience with them, the willingness and fresh eagerness of the returned students are appealing. Since there is no longer any police wireless service, they've been acting as runners between Gangtok and the districts. Also signs in English on expensive poster paper are appearing all over town. One says *For King and Country*. I think I know the boy, an Alexandre Dumas enthusiast, who put it up. I ask Karma why the signs aren't in Nepali—they look unrepresentative in English. He laughs and says, well, since the signs are aimed at the Indians anyway, they may just as well be able to read them.

Yangchen is busy among the sign-makers. She kneels on the library floor using a Magic Marker on pink paper. I chide her gently. "Look, sweetie, I saw the security officer yesterday walking up to the palace with rolls of pink paper under his arm. Couldn't you at least have asked him to buy a less noticeable color? Everyone will have seen him buy it, and then the Indians can say all the pro-Sikkim posters were made in the palace." Ignoring me, she proceeds with pride in her disarming schoolgirl manner, stenciling, cutting, and pasting.

I have been working on a picture book for Jane M. I feel so compressed, encircled—it is as if I'm being squeezed and am assuming new shapes. Now a bulbous head, now an airless pinhead and an engorged body. If I do something with my hands, it releases some of this tension. I put my whole self, using spit as a solvent, in the drawings. The story is true. It's about a dream Jane once had after her dog was stolen in which in a nearby factory she found the thief, who confessed to having taken him. Waking, she drove all day to different factories near their town, and finally met a man who said he did have the dog and would take her to him. They drove together through Harlem, down streets bruised like souls. The dog was there in his house, bright as paint, the only beautiful thing the man had.

Hope Leezum and Palden, with pale, drawn faces, are wearing their name T-shirts that someone sent from England in the fall. Palden's is dark blue, with his name in red letters. Hope's is turquoise, with her name in pink. I fear something about the shirts. It frightens me to see my children named, pointing them out as targets.

One day, something unbelievable: it's as if a reel has been put in the wrong place, as often happens at the Gangtok movie house. I'm sitting on the verandah, and suddenly our old butler and the other servants start bringing trays of glasses into the big sitting room.

"What's happening?" I ask.

"Oh, there is to be a drink party," the butler says casually.

"A what? Who's coming?" I demand of the ADC. "Oh, some visiting general from Calcutta, I think, and General Ray and our own general [I note the familiar possessive still used to designate the Indian general in Gangtok] and Mr. Bajpai of course. In all about thirty people."

Here we are in the middle of a siege, and suddenly the enemy is coming right into our house to be entertained? It is preposterous, a parody. I am stunned. During the reception Bajpai and the generals beckon me to be photographed with Chogyal and themselves by an Indian Army photographer to immortalize the signing of the May 8 agreement. Everyone is smiling and holding drinks. An animallike noise comes from my throat. Tears pour down my cheeks, shining in the flash-gun light of the photographer. In embarrassment the group disperses. Indian Embassy wives ask me solicitously, "How is your daughter?" meaning Yangchen. I look at them amazed and say that tension is not good for kidney disease.

The Indian press has asked if after the reception we could be filmed with the children, playing a game in the library or something. The idea, I understand, is to show that we are well and happy, not threatened or dead. I recall a photograph in *Life* magazine of the U.S. POWs in Korea forced by their captors to sit for a photograph in which they'd managed to spell out "fuck" with their hands. Sitting on the floor in front of a Monopoly board with the children and Chogyal, I stick my middle finger straight up and smile hostilely at the cameraman, but gradually, frightened, I gentle it in a curve before they notice. The session concludes with the filming of the senior pressman offering a scarf to the Chogyal and wishing him all congratulations and good wishes for his wise concession to the democratic wishes of his people.

The newspaper coverage of the take-over in Sikkim is looking-glass history. We make almost no effort to tell our side. Our fear of the Indians and our hope that the problem may go away if we avoid confrontation make us accomplices of our conquerors. Sometimes we embellish their lies.

The second morning or so of the troubles I was near the ADC office when a call came to the Chogyal from *The New York Times*. Chogyal belittles the extent of the troubles and says that things are fine, he and I can go anywhere, and it will just be a short while till order is restored. His secretary then takes the phone. When he is asked if the Indian government had anything to do with the take-over, he replies with almost imperceptible irony, "How could they? They are our protecting power." Even when we rise to an oblique accusation against the Indians, it is too subtle for the outside world to understand, although sufficient for the Indians to seize on to berate us.

From the beginning, India House's press conferences develop one theme: despotic, anachronistic, undeveloped state, ruled by myopic, inept ruler and ambitious, adventurous American wife. All the news comes either from the Representative or the Foreign Office in Delhi. Later, newsmen, including Loren Jenkins from *Newsweek* and a Los Angeles *Times* reporter, who're allowed to go to Kalimpong, the Indian border town, get their stories from Kazini, the wife of the Indian government protégé. At first, the Indians deny any role in the upheaval, but gradually, as their vehemence against us and their confidence of success increase, their spokesmen hint of India's involvement and how we had it coming to us.

Although I'm told by sympathizers that it is Bajpai who puts me down personally in the press conferences, one part of me can't accept this. One day when he comes to the palace I show him a clipping and almost beg him to share my hurt, to say he's sorry—more than that, to say he wasn't responsible for what's said there. Tears course down my face. For once he's at a loss for words.

In the past, despite our efforts to keep Sikkim, and not ourselves, in the news, the Chogyal and I had been the chief news peg for stories on Sikkim. Now the gleeful attacks and I-told-you-sos of the foreign press are concentrated largely on us and our "downfall" rather than on the loss of the country. An historian of Hawaii writes me later that he was fascinated by the similarities in the take-overs of Hawaii and Sikkim. Before Hawaii was annexed, the mainland planters had smeared the characters of the king and queen, portraying them as power-mad megalomaniacs to forestall the sympathy they might have received if people had been reminded of their commitment to the islands and independence.

From Hong Kong, Cocoola issues several strong statements to the press absolving Mrs. Gandhi but saying the Indian Intelligence Bureau is behind the take-over. Spokesmen in the palace and Tenzing both refute her accusation against the Intelligence. Cocoola, angered—with some justification—at being out on a limb and subject to Indian reprisals, tells Clover on the telephone that if it is just a question of a local uprising, with no Indian involvement, and that Chogyal could not keep order, then he deserves to lose his throne.

No one asks my opinion, and I take refuge in a kind of obtuseness. When, however, Clover tells me on the phone that they have lined up press for Norbu to speak to, I say, "Please, Clover, don't do anything that would hurt us, we are still surrounded." Norbu writes me that he is choked with frustration.

One odd journalist incident involves me. It is inconsequential, indeed irrelevant, but it is blown up in a nightmarish, crazy way. In an effort to save my life, which people in the States believe to be in some danger (partly because they feel that the character assassination we are receiving may be a prelude to our removal as king and queen by either duress or death), friends give *Newsweek* excerpts of letters I have written since returning home. The excerpts are intended to show my sensibility and devotion to Sikkim. One bit says something about still living a daffodil, garden kind of existence, but that the shadows of violence are beginning to close in. (When the children and I had returned to Sikkim from America, all the daffodils I had planted in our rock garden were in bloom. Although unhappy, still I had taken comfort in the physical innocence of my surroundings and, in fact, the innocence of our *being*—our flower-bright virtue.) The shadow of violence was a phone call that Kazini had made from Kalimpong a week before the upheavals threatening to have Karma shot. Another quote says something to the effect that, as a small country with no possibility of worldly defense, our only hope for survival is a pure flamelike devotion to the cause—the only problem being that a flame consumes one, a candle dies. Tenzing has called from London to say he is distressed by the article.

I've not seen the article and have no access to it. Is all the furor because it contains one of my many references to Matt? What might my friends have done? My mounting terror, my childish terror of being found out, and my apprehension that my last, my only precious thing, my love for Matt, which I had put away during this time, will be dashed and broken are even greater than my fear of the crowd encircling us. What had been said? What was included? For two weeks I go about the house stiff-legged with fear.

I have to wait for the arrival of a family friend who, even in the face of disaster, insists on visiting us. In an agony of suspense on the day before she is due to come, I organize, with Yangchen's help, a treasure hunt for the Tathangchen children. I put prizes all over the garden and verandah. Later, when the children have found only a few of them and Yangchen asks me where the others are, I just stare at her dumbly. They are never found.

The next day the woman goes straight to the guesthouse, and I, too guilty to greet her, wait in the palace in exquisite fear. When we finally meet we sit in the round alcove in the small sitting room, I staring at the bulging string bag next to her thigh. I take the letters and *Newsweek* magazine to the bathroom and, sitting shakily on the john, begin to read them. Matt is short and direct: he loves me. The *Newsweek* article, to my astonishment and relief, merely includes innocent quotes. What could Cocoola have been so exercised about? I am angry and weak thinking of the wastefulness of the two weeks of extra fear I have been through and because of the fact that Cocoola, while we have been living here in real danger, has caused an enormous stir over nothing.

After having seen the harmless *Newsweek* quotes, I am amazed that Cocoola will not let the matter drop but aggravates it by writing a letter to *Newsweek*—which they print—castigating me for my garden hyperbole, saying Sikkimese actually work very hard and in the mud. This I know, as I have been staying here all the years she has been in Delhi and abroad. The daffodil metaphor is one of my few flowery images of Sikkim. In the past, both publicly and privately, I've tried hard to turn aside gush about Sikkim as Shangri-la.

Cocoola's public attack pulls tighter a strand in my head that says, "What's the point? Leave." A subsequent *Newsweek* article (written as a senior Indian official said later "on orders from up"), however, marks my conscious deciding point to leave for an indeterminate time. I get the unexpected article in my packet of clippings from a service.

SIKKIM:
Queen of the Mountain
She was given to describing Sikkim in such phrases as "silvery gray and magical," and since few foreigners were allowed to visit the isolated Himalayan kingdom, Hope Cooke's burbling letters back home made being queen of the mountain sound like every little girl's dream come true. It was, as the former Sarah Lawrence debutante told it, a storybook land where orchids grew like weeds, oranges were the sweetest in the world and everybody lived happily ever after. Everybody, it turned out, but the Sikkimese. Last April, thousands of them revolted against their 300-year-old monarchy, and since then, that rarest of species—refugees from paradise—have been pouring into India. There last week, free from the fear of palace reprisals, the exiles talked openly to NEWSWEEK's Loren Jenkins about Hope Cooke's reign as a Himalayan Marie Antoinette. Below, Jenkins's report:
They have gathered in the mist-shrouded Indian village of Kalimpong and the tale they tell is the classic tragedy of a dull man pushed beyond his depth by a scheming, ambitious woman. Before Hope came along, the royal tradition in Sikkim did not amount to very much. The

rulers, who called themselves Maharajahs, were little more than no-madic Tibetan chieftains—an earthy breed who only 100 years ago were running around barefoot. As heir apparent, Palden Thondup Nam-gyal's ambitions in life, they said, didn't go much beyond wine, women and Mah-Jongg.

Then, at the age of 40, he married Hope. It was her influence, many Sikkimese believe, that launched Namgyal on the pursuit of the trap-pings and appurtenances of monarchy. When his father died, the title of Maharajah—which underlined the fact that Sikkim is not a sovereign nation but a protectorate of India—was not good enough for Namgyal. He had it changed to Chogyal, the ancient Tibetan title for "ruler." His modest bungalow officially became "the palace." As for Hope, one fre-quent palace visitor told me that she set out to be more of an Oriental queen than ever existed this side of Siam. In speaking of herself (which she invariably did in a Jackie Kennedy whisper), she affected the regal "we" and demanded that visitors and servants treat her with the defer-ence due royalty.

While the pretensions and the required kowtowing were hard enough to swallow, Sikkimese refugees said the royal family's profligate spending in a land of poverty was a bitter pill indeed. The Chogyal and Hope seemed to be dashing off to Europe or the United States almost constantly. On each return, the palace-controlled Sikkim Herald would make a big thing of announcing just which kings and queens had enter-tained the Sikkimese rulers—a not very subtle attempt to imply parity between the royal houses of Europe and the rustic court of Gangtok. "We are a poor people," a Sikkimese journalist told me, "but we are not fools, and we know how much money it takes to travel like that."

Still, the Chogyal and Hope probably could have continued to live the life of imitation royalty indefinitely except for one problem: Hope, Sikkimese refugees said, was obsessed with the desire to be a *real* queen —of an independent nation. Under her guidance, history was rewritten in Sikkim's schoolbooks to establish the kingdom's validity as a sover-eign land. As the Chogyal pressed India for increased independence, New Delhi—which views Sikkim as vital to its defense against China—grew increasingly concerned. The royal couple were playing with fire, and when 20,000 rioting Sikkimese converged on the palace to demand the Chogyal's abdication, Namgyal had to ask India to step in to re-store order. India, as a result, is more firmly in control of Sikkim today than ever before, and the Chogyal and Hope have been stripped of all power. Namgyal, I was told, has ventured out of Gangtok only once since the uprising, to try to rally support. Indian troops escorted him unceremoniously back to the palace.

"It was so stupid and so ridiculous," a Sikkimese politician said. "It did not need to have happened this way. But they kept flaunting this monarchy thing until it blew up in their faces." The explosion left Hope's delusions of grandeur shattered and the future of the ruling house of Gangtok very much in question. "How long," a prominent

Sikkimese asked me last week, "can we go on putting up with this sort of mediocrity?"

Newsweek, July 2, 1973

I am stunned, too astonished to cry. It's the most extraordinary thing I have ever read. They are describing me. I am dumbfounded. I run down the hill to Dan and Wendy's house and stumble up onto the porch. "Dan, can I talk to you?" The ADC has called to tell them that I'm coming. Dan has put out some glasses of iced tea and a plate of cookies. Wendy says, "Oh, hello, Gyalmo," and retreats into the house, banging the door. She looks as if she's been crying. I am too preoccupied to ask her why she won't join us.

Dan reads the article and tries to comfort me, saying, "They have to pull you down because you've done so much. They wouldn't bother otherwise."

I forget to ask him if I could or should leave. Soon after I get back to the palace, Wendy comes running up the road and into the big sitting room. She throws her arms around me and says, "Oh, Gyalmo, I didn't know. I'd been quarreling with Dan, and when you came down, I felt even more shut out. I didn't know what you had come about." The two of us, holding each other, cry and cry and cry.

Chogyal orders his secretary to copy the article and sends it with his card to all our friends he believes have betrayed us.

Shanti tells Karma, "How could he do that? It is not worthy of him. We are just little people and have nothing to do with it."

Dhan Bahadur, genuinely hurt, comes to the tent at night. He has tears in his eyes. In the light of the bare bulb our shadows loom large on the canvas wall. "Chogyal, I was amazed when I got this paper. When I got it, I had to come straight here. I never helped in the take-over. I respect and love you and Gyalmo." I believe him. I love him. I'm frightened, though. What if I'm wrong—shouldn't love him, shouldn't trust him?

The Indians have done their work well; as in judo, they have used our strength against us. They have set out to destroy Chogyal and Tenzing in Sikkim and India, and me—since I'd received the most coverage outside—abroad. Accused of being a reason for the take-over makes me feel scared and guilty and alone. It makes it more necessary for me to go, so as to provide no extra incitement or target for further ravages of Sikkim, and, at the same time, it makes it harder to go. In my heart I know I have worked hard enough for Sikkim to earn my passage out, but this new attack, saying I am to blame for the hurt done to Sikkim, adds to my guilty feelings about leaving.

Clover organizes a letter-writing campaign to *Newsweek*. Many important people respond. In reply they receive snubbing letters. Finally one from John Kenneth Galbraith attesting to our character is printed. Years later I am to hear that the reporter apologized to Chogyal.

At the same time that we are being discredited abroad, efforts intensify to discredit the Chogyal among his own people. While I'm sitting upstairs reading and the Chogyal, not feeling well, is wrapped up in a blanket reading in bed, a servant runs in with the telephone. (Calls usually came to the ADC's office first, and then everyone dashes around looking for the Chogyal with a phone trailing at least three hundred feet of cord.) The Chogyal, listening, exclaims, "What statues? What on earth do you mean? Smuggling? He says I'm involved?" More frenzied telephone calls ensue.

I gather, piecing it together, that the state trading agent of Sikkim in Calcutta has been caught by customs trying to send abroad a valuable South Indian temple deity, a Nataraja, I think. The package was being sent in the Chogyal's name and the agent had told the police that he was doing it for the Chogyal. Within hours it is being talked about in the Gangtok streets. It is preposterous. The Chogyal is a profoundly religious man with a deep veneration for Hinduism as well as Buddhism. Profaning religious images is the last thing in the world he would ever do. I'm outraged. Then a little smug. After so long a time of being vilified, this is one time when not a word has or could be said against me. Then realization hits me. *The statues*—my little Mary and Joseph. In the phone conversations with my friends I've been using the expression "the statues" as a code for Matt. At least a dozen times I've asked Alice, "How are the statues? They are the most valuable thing to me. They are priceless." Oh, my God. They will say I've exported a warehouse of Natarajas.

After the Indians have clear control the siege lifts. It is the third week of May. We have been indoors since the fourth of April. There's no real signal for the end of the incarceration. The end is almost as desultory as the beginning. Karma, I, and a few other people are hanging around in the ADC's room. Karma (he and I were always exchanging movie intelligence) says, "There's an English picture, La." Today's English picture, appropriately called *Rage*, is the first one since the troubles. Seven weeks ago Yangchen and I, bored and restless, had been walking down to the movies when we met Karma running up the palace hill to report the first trucks of demonstrators.

We drive out the palace gates for the first time. It is a gray-green evening—giving a feeling of being under sea—moving slowly, warped and wavering. Sandals, shoes, and broken, spread-eagled umbrellas litter the road. All the Gangtok intelligentsia are at the movie house.

After that I take the children to every Russian and English movie that comes. There is *Fra Diavolo*, a Laurel and Hardy version of a Mozart opera. The children love it. Before the film there is a chance news short of me meeting Marian Anderson in Calcutta. The people in the orchestra draw in their breath as they always do when they recognize someone, then they begin to clap. I am puffed up and look down at Bajpai and his wife to see his reaction.

I have wasted so much of my life going to unspeakable movies in Sikkim. Worse still is the fact that I have grown to value them, depend on them. The thing that finally influences me to leave is Scrabble. For the past weeks we have been doing nothing but play that game. I realize suddenly that, although I've been working all these years for Sikkim, all I've done for myself, for my life, has been to kill time.

When I realize that I'm intent on leaving, I call Alice to ask her to make arrangements for the children's school. (I know that during the winter she has been looking over various schools for her son.) I will put them anyplace she suggests. Amazingly, Alice's mother, on the strength of her Bank Street connections and Yangchen's impressive list of courses taken at school, is able to get Yangchen into a college in New York despite the fact that she hasn't finished school or taken all her precollege exams. I am very pleased. Yangchen's life seems on the upswing. Now, although she has dropped out of her boarding school, she will not be just keeping pace with her classmates but will be ahead of them. As amazing as the jump into college is Yangchen's health. Despite the horrors of the past weeks, there has been no recurrence of her kidney trouble.

The date has been set. But a final irony: I've been advised to stay through Indian Independence Day. We're to leave the afternoon of August 15. To leave before might be taken as anti-Indian. I pull myself toward this date with bleeding hands and knees.

When Chogyal and I go up to North Sikkim with a young English houseguest at the end of May, I realize that I must not believe in my decision to leave or trust my ability to effect it. I am drenched in jealousy of our guest's young mobile life, her freedom to choose what course she will take, to go from crest to crest. Meaning to be kind, she tells me that, although maybe I can't have the freedom of big choices in my life, perhaps the limitation will help me sharpen my consciousness in small choices.

The troubles don't seem to have touched North Sikkim. The school celebration in the district headquarters is as usual. Only one young Indian teacher stares aggressively, acting restive and peculiar. I give a short speech to the assembled scouts and guides and schoolchildren, praising the peace we find here. Afterward, at their small fair, to my astonishment, I guess the number of jelly beans in a jar almost exactly, winning a Chinese alarm clock with a very loud tick. I have never won anything before. My children say it goes "Chop stick, Chop stick." All along the wet road back to Gangtok, villagers come out to greet the Chogyal and tell him of their love and loyalty. Chogyal is looking a little better, a little more alive.

His pain and loss are racking. The country is in ruins; it is obvious that soon India is going to complete the take-over. He is dumb with grief. My leaving is too painful to bear. I lie, my guts molten in a cast. I am forever trapped here. My brain and heart burning in this prison. I cannot leave this man. I make myself like stone. I have no feelings. I am leaving. I am leaving like an automaton with no feeling. My only impetus is a cunning streak of determination that my children and I will survive. To survive, we must go.

The Gangtok general comes one evening to "take his leave" as he is going on posting. Insolent, jeering face. He has done his job well. In his piping voice he unctuously invites us to visit him in Assam or wherever he is assigned. They will never let us out. I look at him, straight through to the middle of his skull. "If we live," I whisper.

One day the demonstrators are brought back again. Hope and Palden are walking toward the Academy playground with their friends. To my horror, from my bedroom window I can hear the sound of the mob coming up the hill from the bazaar. I race to the gate and start running along the road to the school. The children are racing back along the road, Hope's heart pumping wildly, her body quivering. "I lost my shoe, Mummy," she says. "I ran so fast I lost my shoe."

Smallpox has hit the town. There are twenty reported deaths in Gangtok alone. We have scarcely had an instance for twenty years. It was virtually wiped out in Sikkim, and has been only now reintroduced by the thousands of demonstrators brought here from across the border. The children have shots at the palace, but I'm appalled that Hope, along with the other children at school, is given an adult dose of the strong Russian vaccine and comes home with a purple, angry eruption on her arm the size of a half dollar.

Since the siege has lifted the children have gone back to Tathangchen and I have resumed teaching to kill the torturingly slow time until my departure. Each day I drink a large mug of brassy green sweet beer and go down the hill, down the dirt rabbit-hole path, sliding to the bottom, banking, retrieving myself on ledges and river hollows. The mica in the soil shines brightly, hurting my eyes.

In Tathangchen I breathe and come alive—small bear cubs, restive, tumbling, loving children—bowlegs, runny noses, acrid smell, smoke in their hair. Bright eyes. Fourth-grade social studies. Seventh-grade English class. Walking back up the steep hill, I feel like a penitent carrying stones, expiating, doing penance for leaving these children I love.

The day before my birthday Wendy and Dan organize a party in the big hall of the school. Bright walls, paper flowers, teachers' charts, library shelves, science corner. The children give me photographs of the various classes in a gold frame. Tea with milk in thick cups. Everyone sings. They all chorus "Happy birthday, miss," to me. "Miss," meaning "teacher," is my highest accolade. "Gooda morning, miss!" Thunderously. Along with other townspeople, the whole school comes up to the big sitting room the next day to give scarves. I'm cocky, bright, feeling good. These children have a spirit, a pride not found in other Gangtok schools. A good number of people have come with scarves, a thousand or so—many more than usual. My birthday was never official, people weren't particularly expected to come. Today the people who've come are indirectly trying to show their support to the Chogyal.

My children run amok and play in the piles of scarves, streaming, rolling, billowing—a haystack.

Yangchen wants to give me a party that evening. I don't know whom to ask. No one knows any longer who is safe. Finally all the Tathangchen teachers come, along with some relations and youngsters who used to help me shelve library books. We make a bonfire and dance. Cocoola's daughter Sodenla and Lhanzinla, both of whom, independently of each other, are trying to organize resistance to the take-over, quarrel about ways to proceed. I'm relieved when the evening is over.

Grateful for the love and understanding I receive when I'm with them, I've abandoned myself to Dan and Wendy. In the past, outside of official dealings with them about school affairs, I've tried to be careful about seeing too much of them, as it made people jealous and laid me open, as

Dan is Swiss, to accusations of favoring foreigners. Now it doesn't seem to matter.

Dan has been wonderful, particularly with the Chogyal. He comes up every afternoon. Of all things, they are baking together. Chogyal has always been proud of his ability to bake scones, and Dan, who worked one summer as a baker, has just learned of this. They make the scones in batches in the small kitchen, one of the tent poles holding shut the broken oven door, each claiming that the batch he's made is the best, demanding appraisals from Wendy and me. The two of them are a sight —clothes, faces and hands dusted with flour.

Most of the friends I work with, except for the Tathangchen people, are changed. Giggly Monmaya, my secretary, is now tight-lipped and noncommittal. I try to corner her into reflecting on the troubles, but she says nothing, her expression shut down, clamped. She is depressed and quiet when taking dictation, and it is impossible to make her loosen up even on topics that have nothing to do with the troubles. Only Mr. Thapa is as candid and loving as ever. Even now, although he is stricken, a mischievous grin lights up his face. "Well, we had a good try." Some Indians, including the education director, professing sympathy and dismay, come to call to gauge my opinion on the involvement of the Indian government in the upheavals. Presumably acting as *agents provocateurs* of the Representative, they comment on the participation of the Indian government in the troubles. To their surprise, I am for once mute and look baffled by such a suggestion. Not much for them to report there. My whole personality is changing, or rather seeping away, leaving me bone-dry and brainless. One day, at dusk, I sit on the upstairs verandah and do something I haven't done since kindergarten—knit! Karma walks in, sees me, and gives a great shout of astonished laughter. "Your Majesty, this is too much!"

I do mechanical jobs. For weeks I sort the hundreds of photographs I have kept stashed away in paper bags in the library. I sort my letters, which have been filed the same way. I pack the letters. They are part of me and I don't want to leave them. The suitcase lies for days in the middle of the library floor. Lhanzinla keeps peering into it to see what's there and what isn't. The tailor Rinchen Gyatso comes to the library to take in a few long dresses I will take with me. Chogyal's secretary watches as Rinchen makes tucks around the waist. "I don't think you ought to go, Gyalmo. You'll get swallowed up there."

"Oh, rubbish, I've said I intend to return in April." April. It's so arbitrary, so absurd, it is like saying never. My mind is empty, poised between knowing and not knowing.

One day I receive an anonymous letter signed "Black April" threatening to tear my children and me to pieces. I am sitting at the dining room table thinking about it, waiting for the Representative and Chogyal to conclude their talks in the sitting room. Bajpai comes in alone and, seeing me, says oddly, "Oh, Gyalmo. You look so beautiful." I look at him—a death's head.

The Representative and his wife invite Chogyal and me for dinner, the first time since the troubles. The meal is served very late, as Bajpai, who is doing the cooking, waits until we come to begin the preparations for the soufflé. We sit drinking for a long time. I feel depressed and dizzy watching his fine bony wrist endlessly whisking the eggs. It is a torture— he is talking on and on. I want to be home. I want to be looking after Chogyal, who is slumping over with fatigue and depression.

The dining room has been changed again. Bajpai—sometimes with great effect, as he is an aesthete and has appreciated the structure and feeling of the old Residency—is always exploring to see if he can find the true heart of the house, always changing things about. The current choice is not a success. He has put the dining table in a small, windowless, rather cell-like room. Chogyal is mute, staring at his plate, beads of perspiration filming his face. I'm about to get my period and feel a rising hysteria. Suddenly something snaps in me and I dare ask Bajpai something that's been long on my mind. "Excellency, remember once you said to me you always hid behind your quotes? Well, the last thing you quoted to me at your party the evening before the troubles was a Mallarmé poem about *mensonge*. *Mensonge*," I repeat, looking right at him.

"What, Gyalmo? Are you saying that I've ever lied to you or lied about these recent events?" Getting out of his seat, standing taller and taller, his oval skull-white face peering down at me. Dark eyes getting large, furious. "WHAT ARE YOU SAYING!" he screams.

He strides out of the room to the library next door and returns with a French dictionary, which he crashes down on the table splayed open to M words. " 'Lies,' " he reads, his voice thunderous, " 'deceit' . . . 'illusion.' "

"Oh, yes. Oh, yes. That's what I meant."

"You mean that you and Sikkim had been living in an illusion all these years all along?" He looks at me, not quite ready to believe that's what I meant.

"Oh, yes, that we had been living in illusion," I echo, trembling. He is still shaking with anger when he sees us to the door.

The next evening I see him again at a dinner party given by one of his staff. We play Scrabble with a set that they must have bought on their last posting, in South America. It is full of Q's. I keep getting C's with cedillas. I sit next to the Representative at dinner. I'm anxious to mollify him, afraid of his power over my departure and even fearful of his power over me abroad. "Mr. Bajpai," I say, dropping the "Excellency" that he abhors. "I just wanted to tell you that I won't be involved in any politics abroad. I'm just going, I'm just going. . . ." I falter. He, smiling, exquisitely graceful as ever with words and their tone, steps in to rescue me.

"For a breather," he concludes. I nod in relief. Underneath the table I see his fists are clenched so tightly that his knuckles are white where the blood has drained away.

The night before I leave, the Siliguri general invites us to the local mess for drinks and dinner. It is madness. I don't want to go. I want to stay home with the Chogyal and the children and feel the house I love so dearly. "Oh, please," I beg him. "I want to stay home."

"But Chogyal is coming, definitely," he says.

"Well, then, I want to stay with my children. I'm leaving tomorrow."

"Well, you're taking them. You'll be seeing them. What's the point?"

I want to impale myself into that house, to sit down, as the Russians do, before leaving, just to remember. I go, as bidden, to the cocktail party and sit on a hard sofa talking inanely to army wives. The general looks at me, gauging what I'm up to. "You shouldn't leave the Chogyal, you know," he says, his eyes narrowing.

"Oh, General," I say, laughing gaily. "Look at you now, always off in nonfamily stations." They are afraid I will tell. I ask the general for an army escort for our drive down. He looks surprised. I insist. This way they can't stage an accident. It will be their responsibility.

The next morning we dress for Indian Independence Day. Chogyal wears the white cotton Gandhian cloth dress he is so fond of. Ironic to be wearing the cloth of India's great man of peace to this event of our conquerors. We walk to our chairs. It has been arranged so that we have to walk past the newly appointed (by India) Sikkim advisory councillors, who stare insolently and remain seated as the Chogyal passes. Chogyal stands on the reviewing stand with Bajpai, taking the salute. The anthem is played and the Indian flag unfurled, spraying Chogyal's and Bajpai's heads and shoulders with confetti. Bajpai gives a murky talk referring to

the troubles and how pleased he is at their resolution, finishing by calling
for people to come to him if they have problems. I find the speech odd
and think he is arrogating powers to himself, but Chogyal is relieved
that he has not announced any further overt steps to integrate Sikkim. At
the outdoor reception that follows, Karma informs Kazi that I will be
leaving that day. He responds with the understatement and graciousness
still typical of Sikkim. "Oh," he says, "I didn't know. Will she take the
children? It will be a big change for them."

At the palace, Kesu, who has gotten a scholarship to a college in Virginia, is waiting to see me in the library about her visa to America and
travel plans. I sit on the edge of the sofa, staring at her face. Her features
begin to flow together. In the middle of advising her how to get her
health card arranged in Calcutta, stumbling from the room, I dash upstairs to the children's room, where Aiyee and Memeh are getting the
last things in order. I have cried only once before. Aiyee and I had been
putting the children's clothing and toys in their suitcases. I was holding
Palden's brown oxfords, bought too large so they'd last him for the year,
the new shoes still stiff, untried, the tongues sticking out, when an
animal howl tore from my stomach, shocking myself and Aiyee.

Bajpai comes with a scarf to say farewell. He comes with his sister,
whom I have never met, so the moment is diffused, untraumatic, spent
in pleasantries.

I go to find Chogyal. "Please," I say, "let's all go down to the chorten
and pray."

"If you want." He is spent of emotion, numb with sadness. He drives
us down the road in the jeep, brown beautiful hands on the wheel, and
we pull up the long, steep dirt driveway to the chorten. Keeping the
remaining chorten to our right, we file around the small chortens. Encircling tangle of trees, cheep of crickets and birds. Kneeling on the stone
path in front of the central Buddha, touching my head to the ground, I
pray that we, our family, will always be together.

At the palace there is a big gathering. Even the very elder statesmen
have come, an unusual honor. I sit with my mother-in-law and my husband on camp chairs in a little tent put up near the driveway. Chogyal's
eyes are damp with tears. No one speaks of anything important. Norbu's
aunt comes to bring me a shirt and woven bag she has made to give to
him. Gyalyum, my mother-in-law, has, according to custom, given the
children some rupees, spending money for the trip, in envelopes. The
children are comparing how much money they got from other relations.
The ADC comes and says it is time to go and receive scarves. I go out to

the driveway—crunch of gravel. Among the hundreds of people gathered are Dhan Bahadur, standing, sad, shy, under the magnolia tree, his scarf held out awkwardly; Mr. Thapa, wearing the bright blue-and-yellow tie I'd given him one Christmas; round Mrs. Lucksom smiling in her plaid shawl; Tenzing Gyatso, who is only just now returning my guitar; Kirin, back from engineering college; all the Tathangchen children, for once still and serious; and some Indians who laugh mockingly and say, "Oh, Gyalmo's always going on trips to foreign lands."

I go up on the verandah to take scarves from the servants and Mr. Manuel, and start forward to hug Memeh, whose body shrinks as she wrenches away from me, crying, "Ah, no." I embrace Chogyal a final time and the children touch their foreheads to his. We wheel in the car up to the chapel, where we put rice in the silk scarves, tie a knot, and then throw them up to the images on the high altar. We have a superstition in our family that the trip will be all right if the silken scarves lodge with the statues and don't slip back down. This time the rice scatters downward as the scarves fly up, but they settle and there is no anticipated unlucky thump of their hitting the floor.

Returning from the chapel, we drive past the people, who still stand in little knots in the driveway. Past the fishpond and the avocado tree and the azalea bushes, past the Sikkim Guard, down the driveway where almost every evening I have walked hand in hand with children, joking, singing. Not looking back. Through the geranium-ringed red-and-yellow gate.

18

FORTUNATELY our car is full of Tathangchen children who are traveling down with us to see us off, so we laugh and talk and I am relieved
that we've gotten through the actual farewell. The Sikkim Guards' pilot
and the Indian Army pilot I had asked for precede us and several other
jeeps follow behind. Thubden, a palace servant, and Banjor, an ADC,
ride with the baggage, Thubden perched precariously, leaning out from
the back, holding onto a suitcase strung to the jeep with rope. I have
requested that Thubden come to New York for some time to work for
us, as it will make it more like being at home. He will be an extension
of our life here and a balance for me and the children; his maleness will
lend us the semblance of a family. Also, he will buffer my unfamiliarity
with household work. I have requested Banjor to accompany us so that
we might make our entry into America as Sikkimese, which is important
to me. He will be our persona. I've been for so long part of an institution,
with no individuality, that now I'm making Banjor my portable traveling
institution. He will also be—in case, God forbid, the press accosts us—
our spokesman. I fear the worst. We will be besieged on our arrival.
Banjor will know what to say and will give a Sikkimese construction to
our trip, show us to be Sikkimese.

Wendy and Dan bring up the rear in their jeep. Dear, wonderful
friends. Thank God, they are coming to spend the night with us at Siliguri. I do not think I would survive otherwise.

Through the Ridge Road past the bandstand, past the road sign bris-
tling in all directions which the general had made for me, past the
Academy and the cottage industries, past Tseten Tashi's shop and the
Espresso Bar, the last glimpse of the girls' school and the soccer ground,
down beyond the chorten where the road falls away from Gangtok. I

have not been down the road since the troubles. Ghosts of the marchers pass us coming up the road.

The children, Tashi, Tobgay, and Karma Thinley, excited by their trip to Siliguri, where they have never been, sing and sing and sing. Palden shyly joins in.

We cross the border at Rangpo along the rattling bridge. A man from the Sikkim liquor distillery, out of old habit, arrives breathlessly at the bridge carrying a scarf and an enormous box of Sikkim liquor samples. "Please, Your Majesty, distribute these among your friends. It will help us." Before we cross, the Sikkim Guards' jeep draws away, the Guards saluting, and starts back to Gangtok. We are joined by a West Bengal pilot and start off through the thick, dark forests of Bengal, down the spiraling road leading into the sticky, humid lower hills that fringe the plains. Finally we get our first view of the plains, stretching away horizonless like a hazy sea. An hour or so later we have left the hills and are barreling along the first straight piece of road. The car's speed picks up to fifty as we drive through the rows of newly planted teak, the children and I squirming in fear. On our corkscrew mountain roads we hardly ever move faster than a crawl. Ironically, now that we are in real India, the speed we've acquired starts the Sikkimese car flag flying with a crackling flutter. Up until now it has clung limply to the mast.

We reach Siliguri at dusk. The drivers of the ox-drawn wagons have already lit kerosene lanterns that hang swaying under the carts, lighting up an immediate pool of road. Bicyclers and pedicabists interminably ringing their bells buzz away from our cavalcade. Over the jute fields surrounding the town, flocks of white herons circle in the dark sky. Behind us in the hills we have left, village lights are coming on.

When we arrive at the new Sikkim National Transport branch near the railroad we meet Cocoola in a jeep, pulling out of the compound. I have not seen her for a long time, since well before the troubles and her letter to *Newsweek*. I bow and compose my face in the rictus of a smile. I am so afraid of her, it seems to me I rattle like a cup in its saucer and she must hear it. She is looking very rested and soignée in bright yellow slacks. Her jeep is already loaded up, but I ask her deferentially if she would like to use the car going back to Gangtok. "Oh, no, Hope La," she replies, giving me a dazzling smile as she starts off up the road to Sikkim.

Banjor has ordered a Chinese dinner to be brought to the Transport Bungalow—a treat—from an unspeakably bad local restaurant. Wendy, Dan, Yangchen, and the children have settled down on the floor in the living room to a game of cards. I shut the door to my bedroom and take my old letter into the bathroom. I have not looked at it since May, since I wrote the last entry about the troubles. Even this morning when I took it out of the slipper from under my cupboard, I didn't look at it but just wrapped it quickly in an old purple scarf. Now, under the greenish fluorescent lights of the bathroom, I flatten it out on my lap to read it. The pages are damp from the months in its musty hiding place. The first page is stained with sweat it absorbed when I used to hide it on my body during the siege. Then I see there is something else. I am paralyzed. I look and look and stare, my eyes horrified, fixed on the paper. On the top edge are the clearly defined, slightly rust-stained marks of a paper clip.

My letter has been read and undoubtedly copied. I sit on the toilet aghast, willing the marks away. The implications well up in my mind. It is difficult to breathe. My heart is pumping. They have read my letter and they know I know about the troubles—what they've done. And they know about Matt and may tell Chogyal to destroy him. He has lost his country, and now they might tell him he has lost me. When will they tell him? I must get back before he knows.

I go back to the living room, my body like stone. I can't tell anyone, even Dan and Wendy. The fans churn sickeningly overhead. Lizards are beginning their evening prowl around the walls. One of the children has knocked over a glass of orange juice, and flies lap at the thick stain of liquid on the floor.

I remember that I haven't separated the things we will be needing for the week before we get our air-freighted baggage. All our bags, according to custom, owing to the rough jeep journeys and the cardboard quality of the Indian containers, have been stitched into burlap cases. On the verandah of the guesthouse we rip them all open, ploughing through the odd collection of clothes for something that might be useful to take with us.

Banjor somehow rounds up a team of Siliguri tailors to stitch the boxes back into the cases. The West Bengal Police guards around the bungalow give up any pretense of professional indifference. Leaning on their rifles, they gather in knots around the suitcases, looking with suspicion and envy at our few belongings. A small crowd of idle townspeople have collected and peer at our activities from over the compound wall. My children are naturally delighted and take the occasion to pull everything they can from the boxes, claiming they must have it with them.

The paper-clip marks have slightly receded, but when I am finally able to sleep, I dream of them. The next morning, as we drive off in the jeep, Aiyee, the nurse, runs after us, laughing and crying and holding out her arms. "Semola, semola [little daughter]," she calls to Hope Leezum.

The first thing I will do in Calcutta is to telephone Chogyal that I will come back.

In Calcutta we have several hours to spend before our connecting flight to Bombay. Our apartment is still depressingly full of artificial silk bought for our fashion show. Pretty soon the white ants will get at it. There is no quiet place to sit down. The place is full of security officers, and Mr. Gandhi and his sons, and the new Sikkim trade agent, who is still working out some problems about our visas. I have a new fear that someone might plant a statue or other contraband in our air-freighted baggage in order to frame us. Apparently Gandhi has the same idea. In stentorian tones, rolling his eyes at the Indian security officers in the apartment, he says, "Gyalmo, better, much better you take all with you." He makes such a scene that I blush with embarrassment and am sure the police think my bags are loaded with national treasures.

Mr. Chattergi, from Oxford University Press, the invaluable supporter of our textbooks, comes to say goodbye, bringing with him several containers of pistachio ice cream. "Gyalmo, I wish you were stopping longer in Calcutta. I would take you to Park Street for a really good sundae. Anyway, when you come back." I feel very sad and embarrassed at the gentle inopportuneness of his gesture. I am going to the land of ice cream. I love Mr. Chattergi so much.

We talk about the textbooks. Neither of us says what we both know— that they will not continue. I brighten a bit. Ashi Kesang, the former Queen of Bhutan, widowed a few years earlier and now queen mother, is coming to the flat later. If the work could continue in Bhutan, it would be something; in some way our work would not be snuffed out. Mr. Chattergi says, "Gyalmo, if we get a contract in Bhutan, I will provide you with ice cream every day of your life."

Ashi Kesang comes with her daughter Dechen, the development minister of Bhutan. I sit, clenched with shyness, on the sofa, strained and unnaturally polite. I have always greatly loved and respected Ashi Kesang and value her esteem. Today her graciousness and gallantry in coming to the flat, undaunted by the risk of upsetting the Indians, overwhelms me. She is very loving and direct.

"Hope La," she says, "you have been through so much. We are very much alike. They have tried to destroy you, as they did us. I admire your courage." I want to cry. I wish I could be like her and make the sacrifices she has made since her brother Jigmie's death and the ensuing troubles in Bhutan.

At the airport Mr. Gandhi shakes his head, disapproving. "It is wrong to go, Gyalmo. Very wrong."

"I am coming back," I whisper. "I'm coming back in a few weeks."

In Bombay we are in a movie-star hotel by the sea. The furniture is Hollywood Moorish. The walls, carpets, and fabric are done in decorator colors; it looks like the West, a world away from Sikkim. We pull aside the heavy curtains and open the window. There before us in the moonlight is the sea thudding noisily on the long beach. Thubden has never seen the ocean before. He is spellbound. I wonder what is going through his head. The next morning the children and I run along the gray beach tracking zigzags around scuttling crabs. After so long, the sea.

Mrs. Karanjia, wife of the *Blitz* editor, comes over to the hotel and spends all day with us. It is ironic—in a way some of the troubles seem to have begun with an attack on me by the *Blitz* so many years ago—the Trojan mare of Gangtok, all the missile-base nonsense, and so on. Now here is Aileen, lovingly mothering us, helping me get calls through to Gangtok. I call several times during the day. It seems so very far away.

"I will come back," I say. "We won't go."

"Well, if you like," Chogyal says, "but it seems, now you've got this far and have made all the school arrangements, you might as well drop the children."

We are flying.

In Switzerland, certain that we have arrived at Zurich, our destination, I insist that we get out at Geneva. We pick up all our hand luggage, including Yangchen's guitar and Palden's little book bag, with his name stenciled on it, the letters piquantly upside down when he holds it, and carry everything into the airport; then, forty minutes later we carry it all back onto the plane, clumsily blocking the aisle. The other passengers look at us strangely.

At Zurich we are met by our Swiss friends the von Schultes and a member of the Indian Embassy from Bern. I am afraid to leave my captors, and to the surprise of the official who has been sent from the embassy, I attach myself to him, insisting that he drive back with us to the von Schultes' château for breakfast. I am afraid of his leaving. I am afraid if he is away from me he will suspect me.

The château by the lake in Cham is a dream of luxurious calm. It doesn't seem real. We spend the day rowing—the children, Banjor,

Thubden, and a young monk from Sikkim who is on vacation from Cambridge, all crammed into a rather small boat. None of us can row. The oars flounder uselessly in the oarlocks and the boat spins in circles as we double up with laughter. Those of us who can, swim. The afternoon sun dappling the reeds around the lake. Feathery grasses in the water tickling my legs. Amber cool water. Floating on my back. Free.

At tea that afternoon on the terrace I look up suddenly to see the children scampering up the stairs to the château. Palden's head is turned and he is smiling. I am about to leave my children. Tears spring into my eyes. All evening, each time I look at them it is like a knife in my heart. We walk around the lake to a small park. Tables with checkered cloths have been laid out under a grove of pines. People are drinking beer and eating, an evening picnic. A man is playing an accordion and several couples are dancing. I cannot believe in their happiness and stare, uncomprehending.

In London we stay with Marilyn, in the house she and Frank Moraes, the previous editor of the *Indian Express*, had bought less than a year ago, only a few months before his death, when Frank, the first journalist to bear the brunt of Mrs. Gandhi's anger, had been forced out of the editorship of the paper and exiled to England. It is good to be with someone who knows what happened in Sikkim, even predicted it. For several years Frank had been counseling Chogyal, unsuccessfully, to temper his idealism, provide for himself against a possible Delhi-inspired coup. Marilyn too had warned us long before the troubles that there was talk in the Indian capital that it wouldn't be hard to overthrow the Chogyal. There is no need now to talk.

At night, surrounded by Frank's lifetime collection of books and Marilyn's collection of Sikkimese folk art, I go to bed in the den. Somehow the idea of freedom and friendship is affecting me, making me crumble like old mummified bodies exposed to air. I cry in a high keening scream that will not stop.

The next morning I ring up Alice in Greenwich, where she and Bill and their children are spending the summer. I forget that it is very early in America. Please go to the elevator people, I beg. (I have been calling her from Europe at her next-door neighbors', who happen to work for the Otis Company.) I am sure that by now their house is bugged. I am terrified about our arrival in America, that we may not crash through the barrier.

"They're waiting," I say, "they're waiting in the wings."

"Who's waiting?" says Alice carefully.

A Pan Am aide meets us at the Pan Am terminal at Kennedy Airport. "Come this way," he says. In an enclosure beyond customs are Clover and Alice and Norbu, also some Indians from the consulate. "Hi," I greet Alice and Clover and Norbu, feeling a glass pane separating me from them. Finally being here with them, I'm blank and cannot feel any emotion except surprise and guilt at my blankness. We shake hands all around with the consulate officials and thank the guard who has allowed my friends to come into this part of the terminal as well as park just outside.

"We wanted to divert you this way," Clover says. "There are two Indian photographers at the other exit." There are no newspaper men around, at least that we can see, so we don't have to deliver our contingency speech.

Alice's father is at the wheel of the car outside, like someone waiting in a getaway car. We all pile in and start toward the city. Hot late-August night. Hope Leezum, sitting on my lap, says conversationally to no one in particular, "They put the little children in front so they would get shot first."

Palden asks where we are going. I say, "To Andrew's apartment." (Andrew is Alice's son.) "Oh," he says, "does it belong to the government? Are you sure?" He repeats the question several times as if afraid the apartment will be nationalized by the time we get to the city.

Through Flushing, through underpasses, over the Triboro Bridge to Alice's apartment. Hot, airless, summer-abandoned. We have the place to ourselves, as Alice and Bill are still in the country. Clover spends the night, before returning to Washington. The next morning she gives me two Western dresses. "I bought you these because I didn't think you'd have any." I haven't worn a short dress for eleven years, and when I put one on, my children are embarrassed. They've never seen my legs before.

The next morning, so that we can talk out of doors, unbugged, Clover and I take the children to the park for a walk. We go to a playground near Sixty-eighth Street. A man saunters into the playground after us and peers around in a desultory way. Calling the children, we leave and walk, talking rapid-fire, slowly through the park. The man is following not far away. We reach the bronze statue of Balto, a childhood favorite of mine, the dog that rescued an Alaskan village. My sister and I often sat holding his ears, glossy from handling, straddling his back. Now, as we linger, waiting for the man to depart, he stands, slowly reading the plaque underneath the statue. Suddenly he veers off and waits across the road, watching our progress. We choose not to cross the street to the Mother Goose playground but continue on down to the Alice in Wonderland statues by the boat pond. The children are climbing up and sliding down the figures when suddenly the man is back with a zoom-lensed camera aimed at the children. "C'mon," I say sharply, and we walk rapidly home. It may be nothing, but it is curious.

At home again, Clover and I go up the fire stairs several flights above Alice's floor and sit on the landing, talking for hours. I tell her of the troubles and my need to return. Our backsides are aching from the metal stairs, and after that I take Alice's pillows with me when I go up to talk with friends.

Alice and Bill are coming back from the country in nine days. We must find an apartment right away. In the afternoon we go to look at furnished apartments that could be rented for a few months. Alice has lined up several. The first one is rather large, with brocade sofas and a great expanse of pale-gray carpet. I know we will wreck it. My Scaramouche children swinging on the chandeliers. Also something else is ticking in the back of my mind. Our orange carpet—the only thing other than a few clothes that we have brought from Sikkim—will not go here. I do not quite want to live with the possessions of this polite man who is opening all his cupboards now for us.

But we can't get an unfurnished apartment; we won't be here for long. We look at two more apartments, one covered with antique mirrors, one, although it is in a very respectable building, covered with drug-influenced graffiti. We laugh and laugh at the unexpectedness of this discovery until on the parents' door we find the yearly penciled measurements of the children's height. The last markings, dated this year, are about shoulder-high to me. The children taking the drugs could have been no more than twelve or thirteen. We leave, sobered.

I am just beginning to feel again, to feel a wave of love for my friends, to allow their love to touch me, I am enjoying rushing through the summer streets with them, laughing, woven in friendship.

Joyce comes for supper that night, welcoming us, like Mr. Chattergi, with ice cream. Mint chocolate chip from Baskin-Robbins. "Hi, Yang-chen. Hi, Palden. Hi, Hope." She loves them so much. Aside from Aunt Mary, our friends are our family. I have made a plan to ask Joyce if the children can stay with her for the winter. Her face clouds over, troubled. "Well, the thing is, Hope, I'm going out with someone, and we may get married. They could stay just now, but later I don't know what would happen." I don't know what to do next. None of my other friends is free to take the responsibility.

There is an ad in the paper that sounds promising, an apartment near the East River and a children's park. Outside the building a small blond boy is selling lemonade, with which he gives away free Hydrox cookies. Older children are playing handball against the wall of the doctors' offices. Upstairs I'm irritated to find I have mistakenly looked in the wrong column. The apartment is unfurnished. It has a view spanning out over low rooftops to Lexington Avenue, and at the back is a small, squeezed view of the river. Whitecaps from tugs. My heart leaps, but we say we are sorry and leave. "I like it," Yangchen says. We couldn't furnish it, however. We couldn't ever furnish it.

Our orange carpet will fit there perfectly. In my mind it is getting larger and larger and will almost fill the big living room of the apartment.

Opaque air. A week of 102-degree temperature. Every morning we leave the apartment and set out for Korvettes. I remember Mrs. Sayyid going every day to Korvettes to add a gadget to her daughters' dowries. We, in contrast, are shopping for bare essentials. A decorator friend has given us a list of everything one needs for a lifetime—twelve glasses, six pots, four kitchen towels, etc. I enjoy the innocence of the purchases— pot brushes, potholders, stepladder, canisters! Somehow they make life seem secure, understandable. The Labor Day sales are on, and Korvettes is running a special event, an election for the mayor of Korvettes. Banjor, running from aisle to aisle collecting mops, buckets, kitchen towels, is more like a candidate for this office than a spokesman for our little band. Poor man, baffled and afraid of New York and his role here, he's anxious to get home.

Since I have left behind my own loved belongings, there is a perverse pleasure in knowing we are getting our new belongings from the commonest denominator of stores. An extension of this feeling is a joy in accepting cast-off furniture that people give us. A kitchen stool, a prim child's desk, a high table that can serve as an altar. The ultimate extension is to use found objects. One evening, walking Jane Milliken back to Grand Central, we pass a giant garbage container in front of the Biltmore. She pulls my arm. Shining among the refuse in the bin is a long teakwood panel. "You must have it, it's perfect for a table."

"Mmh," I agree, "but how can we ever get it down?" A businessman hurries by us swinging his briefcase. I know exactly how we are going to get it down. We call our thanks after his fleeing back as, afraid of further importunement, he races toward the station. At a 69-cent store we buy coils of rope, and, tying our trophy to a cab, we taxi it away and deposit it with the horrified doorman of our new building.

I am impelled to be part of this city, to belong, to embrace. We spend our nights at block festivals or square-dancing on the South Street pier. Old buildings of downtown New York, schooner rigging, lacquer-black river, bridges. We form our own set. None of us is very good. We improvise, mixing exuberant snatches of Sikkimese folk dance with American reels. "Will you, will the set over there," says the man with the loudspeaker, looking at us annoyed, "please square up."

I don't know what I'm going to do. Jane and I have a long discussion. "Don't be a fool. You can't leave the children, Hope." Now that my days are not swept up in the rush of getting our apartment together, I have more time to think and worry. Hope Leezum is wary and anxious. I shut my feelings against her need, her stubborn loving. She follows me every place. She complains all the time of an earache. I tell her not to make up illnesses, that she is making a lot out of nothing, that she should be more grown-up.

Our apartment is bare and incomplete. Our orange carpet does not fill the room. I am astonished at how small it is. The dining table is still legless. The mattresses that will be our sofas are uncovered. We have, though, an earthenware teapot, a steam teakettle, and there are flowers in a jug. Thubden has made an offering of fruits on the altar in the children's room. Hope Leezum plays "I'm Really Rosie" on the children's record player that Clover has given her. When everyone has gone to bed at night I sit in the living room and gaze out over the city lights. For the moment we will just carry on.

The children and I go to the ASPCA to get a cat. A cat will be our center, our domesticity. We choose a little calico kitten that stretches its forepaws out of the mesh cage in an effort to connect. Friendliest cat I've ever seen. I'm ambivalent. She will be our heart, hearth, but she, like us, is orphaned. We'll call her by no name, just Cat. I am hesitant to give the ASPCA our real name or telephone number for their adoption files. I use Alice's name. For the next few days she receives phone calls from ASPCA caseworkers asking after the kitten's well-being. Alice, naturally, is evasive, and they are suspicious.

I can't get over how happy everyone is here. Men and women walking down the streets carefree, laughing. They have no awareness of trouble, of fear. Possibly partly it is summer, but everyone is so open, available. Hope has made a friend in the building, Duncan, the little blond boy who had been selling lemonade the first day we came. She met him on the back stairs. Everyone in our building visits from floor to floor. His mother says I must come down to an eleventh-floor party they are giving.

We have been in our apartment only for a few days when I receive a telephone call one morning at 3 A.M. It's Cocoola's son. "Hi, Aunty," an English voice says, "I'm here at the airport with Kesu and Yuden." I can't believe it. I've just gotten my own place together, I'm not a hostel.

"All right," I say gracelessly, "come stay here, but it's one hell of a time to call."

I am back to being Ethel Kennedy and Ma Kettle, and on top of everything I don't know how to cook. I don't even know how to shop. Last week I asked a man at the deli for three pounds of thinly sliced salami. I thought it would be just enough for one lunch. We have had it now every day for every meal. Tonight I'm all alone in the kitchen, with no cookbook, making scrambled eggs and chicken livers. They're supposed to be cheap. No one is helping me. They all suppose me to be the grown-up. I need a mother. Anyone's mother. I call up a friend's mother. "Sorry to bother you, Mrs. Kittle, but how do you cook chicken livers? Hang on just a minute, they seem to be burning."

The heat is subsiding. The evenings are turning cool. Banjor has left to go home to Sikkim, and the students have gone to their colleges. Our days are settling into a rhythm. Yangchen takes the downtown bus every day to her college. The children go on the crosstown bus to their school. Palden has made a friend in his class, Oliver, who gives him some Indian corn. We hang it on our door to celebrate fall.

Before the onset of cold weather, I drive up with Matt along the Connecticut shore. I don't know what will happen to us. I have not seen him till now. We swim together in the cool, familiar water of the Sound.

One afternoon the children and I are out on the Hudson River with friends who own a boat. Sunlight plays on choppy waves. Small sailboats billow past. Spinnakers full. Spinnaker happiness. Suddenly I know. I'm certain. We are going to stay. I am going to stay. There is a chance here to be happy, to make a life.

I'm stunned by what has occurred to me, troubled by fear and guilt about its implications for Sikkim. I telephone my old friend from Iran, John Bowling, who is now retired from the foreign service. He says in his Will Rogers Oklahoma drawl, "Hope, for good or bad, you've never been more than icing on the cake. It won't make one bit of difference to Sikkim whether you're there or not, or to India when they take over."

I tell Clover my decision when she comes up from Washington. "I'm so glad, Hope. I think it is dangerous there. Just from a safety point of view for you and the children, I think you should stay." Her response startles me. In the short weeks I've been here I've almost forgotten the danger. Danger is not the only reason for staying. I will stay because here if you know you're free, you can be free. You can be happy.

We spend our first Thanksgiving at Jane's house by the Byram shore I have dreamed of for so long. Before we eat, Jane asks each of us to give thanks for some special happiness. Thank you for the water, the ocean, the river, thank you for being free.

First Epilogue

When we came home, when we came back, we had to do everything from scratch—make up our life, make up our habits, ceremonies. Finding a general practitioner, pediatrician, lawyer, dentist, money manager, school, dry cleaner, bank, apartment, weekly housekeeper, the nearest post office wasn't hard; what was hard was learning one hour succeeds the next, one season another. We had no guarantee. No accumulation of dailiness to prove this. At a party I went to soon after returning, I stood mute and terrified. I couldn't discuss my old history and had no new history to respond with when people asked me what I did. Each moment, partly because it was fragile, was precious, to be cherished, to be lived consciously.

All of us champed to learn more—fill ourselves up, make use of possibilities. I scoured the city's streets and museums, Yangchen rehearsed for a college dance recital to be given in the coming spring. Thubden attended English-language classes and a hotel-management cooking course, and the children adjusted to their big coed school.

For a long time I'd avoided visiting the school because I'd been scared to meet a class mother, a former schoolmate of mine with many journalist friends. Inevitably Hope became her son's close friend, and through them we became friends too. When I finally started going up to the school, it was like going to Tathangchen. Already, as in Tathangchen, my children had carved out their own niches. In the lobby, children pointed at me. "That's Palden's mother—you know, the soccer-player's mother."

Known in the school as Palden's mother, in our apartment building I became known as "Big Hope"; the little boy downstairs began it to distinguish me from little Hope. To my delight, I felt like a Mafia matriarch—everyone including the doormen began to use it.

269

When, after three years, Thubden finally left, it was an enormous relief. For months I'd been getting back into my Sikkimese crouch, as Matt called my shoulder-hunched stance of tense politeness. During the last year he was with us it had seemed as if he'd increasingly taken up the air in our apartment. The nervous, shallow breathing I'd had in Gangtok returned. "Should we go to the supermarket?" I'd smile brightly, conciliatorily, as he lay glowering in his room. He was having an identity crisis. Although twenty-six, he was just becoming a person, an individual, which America allowed you to be—in fact, demanded that you be. A tough process. After he'd gone, even the first day, I was amazed to realize the children and I were as fine as we were; we had no need of his weight as ballast or anchor. In fact, I realized that for some time his presence had been confusing the identity we were making for ourselves.

Afterward I learned to cook, to be pretty good. Nothing before had made me feel as capable, as grown-up. I also learned to drive, and received a license to add to my growing collection of cards: museum membership, Blue Cross-Blue Shield, Social Security, even a credit card. The first year I'd been here my only ID had been a card from the public library.

For the first year of my return I'd had no real belief in my ability to remain in America. Our first fall, as a kind of magic charm to bind me here, I'd bought tickets to a music series which I carried around in my purse. I had written down the spring dates in my engagement book—as old people write down distant, future dates as a lien on being alive—with little confidence I would be here to use them. Even after I had passed through four seasons here, I was unsure of my entitlement and strength of will to stay.

In 1975, when Yangchen, on a year's sabbatical from college, went back to be half in, half out of house arrest with her father in Sikkim, she wrote me letters full of anger, condemning my departure. I was shaken by her accusations and the love that broke through the anger. Aside from everything, not wanting to see things as they were, she was scared that my decision to stay was a rejection of her. I wished I could do what she wanted. Sometimes I even wished I could do what Chogyal wanted. I knew that in his own way he had loved me. His letters, in which I read the devastation of Sikkim and his soul, were heartbreaking.

My sensibilities were selective, however. At the same time I went around whispering, afraid to upset the Chogyal and Yangchen, I could be selfish as hell to some people. To Emile, my old friend from college days, for example. Since our return Emile, again a friend, not a beau, came often. With almost saintly patience he would listen endlessly to Hope's worst jokes, to Palden's word-for-word recap of that week's *Time*, and afterward, when the children were asleep, to all the fears and anxieties I'd accrued since I'd last seen him. If it had been a bad week either in my head or in reality, I used to almost gibber in relief at dumping my moil of fears.

I had given myself more to Chogyal than he to me; Emile gave himself more to me than I to him. Matt was the only man I'd ever loved equally, and that, with much pain, I'd let go. When I first came back it had been such a strain to put pieces of myself back together, to provide, to be strong for myself and the children, I couldn't long afford, even on an equal basis, to surrender myself in love to anyone.

When I came back, partly because everything I'd tried to do had turned to ashes, partly because I'd become a media target, I was too unclear, too scared, to define myself, or to oppose strangers' definitions of me. Once, sitting with Hope and Duncan in a coffee shop for lunch, I'd eavesdropped on a couple at the next table having a rather heated argument over a girl. The woman occasionally had been quite virulent in her denunciations. "Why didn't she speak up, then, if she'd nothing to hide? I'll bet she took plenty." Reason clearly was on the woman's side, and the responses of her lunch partner (a man) grew feebler as he tried to defend the girl.

As at a tennis match, my head wagged back and forth as I weighed the points. Suddenly the woman said "Sarah Lawrence" and then "Sikkim." They'd been talking about me! Blood rushed to my head, my heart thumped. I was terrified that my daughter, wearing her name T-shirt, would get up from under the table, where she'd been collecting napkins with Duncan, and reveal me to these strangers. Shaking, I pulled the children out, put on their jackets, and left before we were noticed.

I didn't want anyone to see me, to know who I was. To avoid being noticed, I'd wear dowdy clothes and sit in the back of buses, ready, if someone seemed about to recognize me, to pick my nose—a technique recommended, by the way, as an antirape measure. In my case this act, and also chewing gum in a vulgar, slack-jawed manner, was designed (successfully) to hold attention riveted to the mechanically repeated action, thereby diverting recognition.

A year or so later I had a clearer picture of myself and stopped being so defensive. If I'd met that woman again, I'd have spat in her eye. Ironically, when I'd begun to learn to stop pleasing, begun to learn to be myself, I'd had to step back into role-playing long outgrown, had had to start convoluting to please a few extremely conservative men in Congress.

Until two years after my return to America, anxious not to do anything that might hurt Sikkim's identity or morale in her last efforts to resist India's annexation, I hadn't begun applying for restoration of citizenship through Congress. In the spring of 1975 things looked so bad in Sikkim I'd begun to seriously realize I must line up sponsors in the House and Senate for a special bill appealing for citizenship, and sounded out old friends Senator Mike Mansfield and Congressman James Symington to see if they would sponsor me. With Mansfield's patronage, a bill for citizenship easily passed the Senate but got bogged down in the House. Not only were my citizenship prospects dashed but it even seemed possible that a resident-alien status would be denied me. The official alternative was deportation.

I was mortified that my much beloved country was doing this to me. I felt that in Sikkim I'd upheld some of the best traits of Americans, and since returning I had been almost reverently grateful for our asylum.

Saying one had to dress for Congress as if for church, Clover bought me a Diane Von Furstenburg dress, a chiffon scarf, a patent leather pocketbook and matching shoes, so I would look ladylike as I lobbied against my deportation. The dress began to blear under the armpits and the shoes killed me. Finally I took to running the lengths of the congressional corridors in my democratic shoes, carrying the republican ones with my bag of testimonials.

It was the Bicentennial year, and the congressional steps and rotunda were full of high school girls wearing strapless evening gowns and singing patriotic hymns around upright pianos. Marble corridors echoed with sopranos. One day I was almost knocked over in a revolving door by a horde of stampeding girls, beauty princesses as their labels designated them, on their way, no doubt, to sing.

Part of my problem was both past and present poor communication. I had never spoken up against the articles libeling me. Although extremely painful, in the face of the other problems confronting us, it hadn't seemed important enough. Now I was finding out that it had been important, that I really did have a debased image with many people. Even when I was lobbying I was handicapped by feeling unable to say as clearly as I would have liked how tough India had been, how impossible it was for my children and me to go back. I was scared that if I said too much that was bad about India, I might cause more trouble for myself. The Indians, even here, might get after me, or possibly—though unlikely—the State Department, to keep the peace with Mrs. Gandhi's government, might deny my account of the troubles we had been through and deny me compassionate grounds for being here—offer me up—back! —a pawn. It was hard to take a middle road, to speak with enough urgency of my need to remain here and at the same time not be too extreme in badmouthing India.

Curiously, it was not politics as much as offended morality that seemed to bother the one or two congressmen who had been having "problems" with my special bill. I'd never thought before in terms of feminism, but gradually I grew more and more convinced the real reason they blocked me was not that I had had to renounce my citizenship when I went to Sikkim. The real reason was that I was a woman who had sinned by going abroad to marry an Asian; worse still, despite mitigating circumstances—such as weeks of armed siege—I had come back independently, without him. That, along with my usual misleading newspaper description as a socialite, and perhaps the fact that I was from New York City, was what troubled them.

It was curious. When I noticed the chauvinism in these few congressmen, I began to notice it in some of my supporters. Slowly I realized that my lawyer had been infuriating me all along. "I hope, dear" (always "dear"), he sometimes said, smiling malevolently, "you continue to feel free—just as free as a bird—as long as you"—he would pause, eyes glittering—"realize the consequences."

All along, the immigration thing had been hard. Scary to be on the other side of the form, the other side of the desk along with hundreds of frightened people—numbers, thumbprints. Once when I'd gone down to the Immigration Bureau about some problem late on a Friday afternoon, the official dealing with me admitting that he wanted to catch an early train to the suburbs, abused me just short of calling me a wetback. There were exceptions, however. One man in particular had been great. "Well, do we deport de lady today or tomorrow?" he'd said to my expensive lawyer in a gravelly Bugs Bunny voice. A tease in this frightening bureaucracy. I'd wanted to hug him.

"Don't—I'll chain myself to your flag." (There was one behind his desk).

"That's no good, lady. Ya gotta drape yourself in it, drape yourself, lady. Remembah Bahbra Fitchie. Shoot if you must this old gray head."

"Then"—getting further into the swing of it—"I'll take the bigamy route," I'd cried. My lawyer, his mouth clamped shut, his eyes furious, rose abruptly to go.

"Never," he'd chided me as we left, "never, never make a joke like that." For two hundred dollars an hour he was a drag to go around with.

I was curious to know how Immigration made its rules. There was a statute that stipulated that one couldn't acquire citizenship by expedient marriage to an American. When I asked the nice man, my friend in the Immigration Bureau, how they knew whether or not a marriage was expedient, he replied with certainty that they had a way of knowing. For a moment I was baffled. Then I realized he was talking about sex, sleeping together, "whether the act had occurred"—that was their criterion. Very strange, very topsy-turvy, that intercourse, reduced in many circles at least to the cheapest currency between married or unmarried couples, should be a criterion by which the Justice Department gauged the validity of an immigration candidate.

Despite our troubles, after some time I began to sense that we were slowly emerging into a new life. Often moments of happiness made me feel that we had not only survived but were ataunt with possibilities. Sadly, at the same time we were saving ourselves, Sikkim was dwindling under India's assault.

Ever since the siege of April 1973, step by step Mrs. Gandhi's government had been taking over Sikkim by measures similar in paralegal veneer to the later imposition of emergency rule in India. After the first agreements leading to Sikkim's loss of national identity had been forced in April and May 1973, India had waited until April 1974 to further the annexation. Then, under the supervision of the Indian government, elections were held which led to a 90 percent + electoral victory for the Sikkim National Congress, under the leadership of India's chief ally in Sikkim, Kazi Lhendup Dorji. The election was based on the same electorate polls, that, a year earlier, had led to a smaller but more credible victory for the Sikkim National party, supporters of Sikkimese integrity and treaty review with India.

The Sikkim National party, prevented by the mob rule that eventually resulted in India's assumption of power, had never taken office. Now, with a handpicked and essentially powerless Assembly, headed by an Indian chief executive, India was ready to do more. In June 1974, although almost all the townspeople of Gangtok turned out in an unarmed attempt to prevent the Assembly from meeting, the assemblymen, under Indian armed escort, entered the Council House and in forty-five minutes adopted an Indian-drafted constitution that called for "associate status" and Sikkim's representation in India's Parliament and other political bodies. The resolution was read out once, in English, which 80 percent of the members did not understand, and passed with no debate by a show of hands. Indian police used clubs and tear gas against demonstrators outside the Assembly House, who, if they had voted for the assemblymen inside, presumably hadn't voted for them to give their country away.

Sikkimese at the time were assured by the Indian Representative, Mr. Bajpai, that there would be no question of actual membership for Sikkimese in the Indian Parliament, that the bill only meant that Sikkimese could watch the functioning of Indian democracy as "observers."

In September 1974, after a summer of turmoil in Sikkim, the Indian Parliament was informed by Mrs. Gandhi that the Sikkimese demanded representation in the Parliament and that such representation was the natural outcome of the Government of Sikkim Act and the Assembly resolution. The Indian Parliament, Mrs. Gandhi said, must vote to amend the Indian constitution to confer "associate status" on Sikkim. The ruling congress, ignoring the demand of the Chogyal and the Sikkimese public for a neutrally supervised referendum to see if Sikkimese really wanted to become associated with India, steamrollered the bill through their Lok Sabha, or lower house, in one day. Shortly afterward it passed the Rajya Sabha, the upper house, and was sent to various Indian states for ratification before being sent to the President for his assent.

Though he pleaded with her, Mrs. Gandhi would not meet the Chogyal. The Indian Foreign Minister sent a message to the Kazi saying that the endorsement by the Indian Parliament of the aspirations of the people of Sikkim, as expressed through freely elected representatives, opened a new chapter in the history of friendship between the people of Sikkim and India.

There were protests to this new "arrangement" throughout India as well as in Sikkim. Many Indians viewed the annexation as not only violating the protectorate treaty but also as undermining India's stand against colonialism, and were outraged. The editor of the *Hindustan Times* printed three editorials. "Only the most blind or cynical will derive any satisfaction over the sorry progression of the Indian presence in Sikkim from that of friend to master." He was fired shortly afterward through pressure put on the board of the *Hindustan Times*: the first editor officially sacrificed to Mrs. Gandhi's regime. Many more followed in the Emergency: the take-over of Sikkim was a dry run.

All the little countries around India were terrified by the example that had been set, but only Nepal, which felt her own self-interest vitally affected, had the temerity to speak up officially. Nepalese demonstrations in Kathmandu protesting the take-over continued for weeks. Instead of taking a long-range look at their frontier policy and their need to win and maintain the confidence of their Himalayan neighbors, which several Indian newspapers urged, India's response was to stop all aid, trade, and transit rights to Nepal and to withdraw their ambassador. Little countries were powerless to help, big ones, including America, too preoccupied to care.

In October 1974 a letter from a stranger appeared in *The New York Times*. After Vietnam, the author suggested, the United States was unwilling to involve itself in foreign affairs that had no direct bearing on U.S. self-interest—hence its dismaying "nonpolicy" with regard to the Indian annexation of Sikkim, despite ample evidence that the action contravened both the U.N. Charter and the Indo-Sikkim Treaty of 1950. In consideration of principle, the matter should be brought before the U.N. Since India was not likely to introduce it and Sikkim, a nonmember nation, could not, it was incumbent upon the other member nations to initiate an inquiry. The author concluded by calling upon the United States to take the lead and reaffirm its commitment to the principles of international security.

No one here did anything. Just before Christmas 1974 an appeal was received from Sikkim. It was too late to do anything; only a few people would oppose what they considered a de facto power situation, particularly when the offender was not white but brown. An idealistic few tried. Senator Claiborne Pell, of Rhode Island, and his cousin John Train began a Friends of Sikkim committee. The International League for the Rights of Man called on the United Nations to investigate Indian acts of aggression reported against Sikkim and violations of the principle of self-determination. The league urged Secretary-General Waldheim to use his good offices, and, in a separate request, it urged the United Nations Decolonization Committee to act on the "new colonial situation."

Although both the Friends of Sikkim and the league extended themselves to fight Sikkim's cause, nothing substantial was going to happen. It couldn't; too much else in the world was at stake. Those approached by the Friends were regretful but impotent to do anything except make public statements of concern. The committees at the United Nations were sympathetic. In fact, the Sikkim issue got surprisingly far with the U.N. Human Rights Committee in Geneva before being knocked out; still the end result was negative. "We know what happened," delegates told friends, "but how can we oppose India?" Sickened by the self-interest and self-congratulations that went on inside, I found it increasingly difficult even to take a bus past the U.N.

The students from Sikkim gathered, as they always did when there was trouble. Neither they nor I were allowed by our immigrant status—and, in my case, by my association with the Chogyal, who had to stay aloof from resistance movements—to engage in this last battle. This lack of authentic spokesmen hurt what was left of Sikkim's cause here. Frustrated, not allowed to join, we stayed with the volunteers preparing mailings.

On April 9, a couple of weeks after my trip to Washington to investigate the possibility of a special bill for citizenship, the Indian Army, under Government of India orders, attacked the palace and at gunpoint put the Chogyal and Tenzing, his son, under house arrest. Within the week Sikkim, by a referendum held under Government of India aegis, had become India's twenty-second state. My children and I were now virtually stateless; the Chogyal and Tenzing were prisoners—protective custody, the Indians called it.

Later, a letter reached New York written by a boy I had known fairly well—a tough, inarticulate young man—his words, because he had so few, all the more affecting.

"I don't know how to begin this letter," he said, "so much has happened these last few days." And he went on to describe it. Telecommunications had been severed, letters were confiscated, travel within the country was restricted. The Central Reserve Police were everywhere, one of them for every two Sikkimese. There had also been a build-up of Indian Intelligence. All this had taken place before the disarmament of the Sikkim Guards on April 9.

On April 8 heavy troop movements had been reported on the Gangtok-Siliguri national highway. A whole military division, complete with a regiment of paratroops, was moving out from the Indian Army base at Siliguri, in North Bengal. By that evening Indian troops were seen melting into the area around Gangtok.

The next morning—two hours before the Indians were to mount their surprise attack on the Sikkim Guards—Chogyal, in some alarm, had phoned the Political Officer, Mr. Gurbachen Singh, to ask for an explanation. "Military exercise," the Political Officer had answered. Unconvinced, Chogyal had phoned the Political Officer a second time, and for the second time was given the cool reply: "Military exercise."

At twelve-thirty, while the Sikkim Guards were having lunch, the Indian Army attacked. The Guards' barracks were overrun. At the main gate of the palace the sentry was shot dead at point-blank range. When the unarmed Guards tried to block the palace gate another was shot and wounded. "Please note," my friend insisted, "the first gunfire was drawn by the Indian Army."

Indian troops then swarmed the palace compound and at gunpoint arrested Chogyal and the Crown Prince. Despite the guns pointing at him, Chogyal had walked down to the palace gate to pay tribute to the dead Guard. He had dipped his fingers in the man's blood and smeared a bloody tika across his own forehead swearing over the dead body that he would never, never repeat the May 8, 1973, agreement, even if it meant giving up his own life. It was said that some high-ranking Indian officers wept when they arrested Chogyal. Meanwhile the remaining Sikkim Guards were put under arrest and heavy mortars were trained on the palace. There was no possibility of escape. The Guards were taken to a concentration camp, where they remained. Chogyal's relatives in other houses were also seized and arrested at gunpoint.

The leading force in the Sikkim Guards, a young captain had been arrested well in advance, on April 5, on a trumped-up attempted murder charge. The Central Reserve Police had whisked him off to an unknown place in western Sikkim, where he was subjected to mental and physical torture. Nonetheless, contrary to concocted reports in the Indian press, he did not confess.

Ballot boxes were set up in the open air, with no enclosures. Illiterate peasants were terrorized and dragged from their homes to vote. Resident Indian businessmen, though not Sikkimese citizens, also voted. Loud-speakers directly instructed voters to place their ballots in the pink box —pro merger, anti Chogyal. Those who did so were allowed to cast as many as fifty ballots. Those who chose the white box had their names noted down and were subsequently beaten by CRPs and professional hooligans smuggled into Sikkim by the Indian government.

On April 15 the Sikkimese were forced at bayonet point to raise the Indian flag. Indian thugs, enjoying the protection of the CRP, kid-napped prominent Sikkimese, including three ex-executive councillors and a former adviser to the Darbar, and subjected them to public humili-ations. The Sikkim Prajatantra Party, a nationalist organization, dis-solved under a campaign of violent suppression.

Sikkimese now were forbidden to enter Nepal, but my correspondent had managed to smuggle himself across the border and had mailed his letter from there.

Sikkim's annexation was complete. Of the hundreds of newspapers here that reported the "referendum," only a couple, one the Boston *Globe*, made any point that Sikkim had been taken over, erased. The rest of the papers all headlined the wire service reports (from New Delhi) with banner print—"SIKKIM DUMPS MONARCHY." A few weeks earlier, when a petition signed by ten thousand heads of households (representing almost half of Sikkim's population) had been presented to the Chogyal begging him to halt further Indian encroachment on their country, the news made only one U.S. paper in my clipping service, a journal in Miami.

When Mrs. Gandhi's "emergency" period began in the summer of 1975 I was pleased she'd shown her hand. I was sorry for the people of India but found her open avowal of repression an enormous release. Every morning of the summer after the Chogyal's arrest I would dash down to the sun-stippled porch in Old Greenwich, where we were staying, look fondly at the cove, its waters red at this time of day, sailboat masts gravely swinging like metronomes, grab the paper, and flip through quickly to find the latest outrage. Finally people would understand what we'd been talking about—or hadn't dared to talk about. In my mind—even though our story hadn't been told and none of the papers suggested that there was a connection between the extinction of Sikkim and the present abrogation of rights in India—we were vindicated.

I had little hope for Sikkim's restoration. Friends were writing that there was irretrievable social breakdown: farmers leaving the land, their fields undersold forcibly to the government; Gangtok teeming with army, like a military camp; the townspeople depressed, no one going out, even to the bazaar, if they could help it; young people leaving for jobs in Nepal. The only feeling I had left about Sikkimese national identity was a permanent ache in my chest.

Although part of me respected Chogyal's refusal to acknowledge what had happened, his dedication to Sikkim's cause, his capacity to endure a lonely, suffering life, part of me felt angry, threatened by the danger in which he continued to put himself. No matter how happy and ordinary I made our life here, I couldn't compensate the children for that, take away the strain. We'd sacrificed enough. There should be no more.

Sometimes, with Chogyal over there trying to keep the memory of the flag flying and I here looking after the children, single-parenting, hardly going out, dipping into capital, I was reminded of the old joke about the husband making the major decisions—Should we go to war? Should the currency be devalued?—while the wife was responsible for the minor decisions—How should the children be raised? How should the rent be paid? Damn it, was this my prime?

Over the years, politics in Sikkim still continued to brew. Many Sikkimese, including some of the Nepali Sikkimese who had initially joined the one man-one vote movement that paved the way for the Indian take-over, had in the fairly early stages of the annexation begun a resistance movement. In late 1977, Kazi Lhendup Dorji's adopted son, a young Nepali Sikkimese politician, in a documented account repudiated India's claim that she had merely responded to a popular demand for integration, and, appealing to Morarji Desai's conscience, demanded restoration of Sikkim's freedom.

In the spring of 1978, Morarji Desai, Prime Minister since Mrs. Gandhi's extraordinary electoral defeat a year earlier, publicly confessed penitence and declared that the annexation of Sikkim under the previous regime was regrettable. At the same time he added that, although wrong, the situation could not be undone.

A week or so later, three days before he would have been twenty-six, Tenzing was killed. He was driving the palace car down to the gas station below Gangtok. On a road built for one-way traffic he was hit by a one-ton truck coming up from the unexpected direction. The car went three hundred feet down the hillside. They say he must have died right away. Twenty thousand people in Sikkim went to his cremation. There was no inquiry into the accident.

In the five years he'd been home from the university, through all the troubles afflicting the country and his father, he'd been there helping. I hadn't known him since he'd taken on this responsibility, had grown up. Since his return to Sikkim I'd heard from everyone how fine a young man he'd become, how selflessly, all youthful pride stripped away, he'd worked for his father and the people of the country. He was the most vital, the most alive person I'd ever known. It was unimaginable that he was dead. I kept seeing him going over the cliff over and over and over. Wongchuk, having finished his business studies in England, went back now to take his place.

Yangchen, although very ill (Tenzing had been going to come here in a month to donate a kidney for her transplant, which was almost due),

returned to Sikkim with her English fiancé for the funeral. We held
services, with many monks in attendance, in New York. The night before
the ceremonies the children, Norbu, his American wife, Helen, Emile,
and I cut and folded white gauze scarves for mourners to place on the
altar and wrote out the gist of what the prayers meant. No photocopying
place was open at that hour, so all of us—Hope in her big wobbly writing
—made as many copies as we could describing the core of the ceremony
—a prayer for Tenzing to attain nirvana, enlightenment or a rebirth that
would help all sentient beings.

After the service, home again in our apartment, the leftover para-
phernalia—carpets, butter lamps, cartons of Chinese food—still not put
away, we sat together talking. Norbu, his voice husky with feeling, told
of his parents' deaths within a month of each other, remembering the
sound of the old monk grating bits of their bone into reliquaries. All our
losses, the loss of Sikkim, the loss of idealism, of loved ones, blurred into
one.

Yangchen's continuing kidney condition and her need for a transplant
operation made it now imperative that her father come out, no matter
what the consequences in Sikkim. There could be no more consequences.
The country was gone. A *fait accompli*. Five months after Tenzing's
death, two months after Yangchen's successful transplant (her cousin
Sonam came to New York to offer a kidney), Chogyal signed a paper
recognizing the application of India's constitution to Sikkim, and was
given permission for the first time to travel abroad.

When he came I left Martha's Vineyard, where I'd been spending the
summer, met the kids in Boston, where they'd come from camp, and
took them down to New York to greet their father. There, Thondup
(I'd never called him that before; it would have been better if I had) and
I arranged to make our separation official in the fall. Grateful for the
ferry crossing, the finality of a passage by water, I left the children to
visit with their father and returned to the Vineyard.

Martha's Vineyard, Massachusetts, 1978

We have given enough, often heedlessly. No more. Now we will be coarsened, dull our imaginations to horror, to honor, become like the ice cream-eating August people who amazed me when I first returned here. I can't believe what I have endured, yielded in both personal and public matters. Was it I who put up with the bafflement of my marriage, was it I who was thinking of leaving the children here with Joyce, was it I who was thinking of returning to Sikkim after the troubles had begun? Was it I who sent the kids back that first summer when the palace was besieged again? I'm appalled. Our life's going to be so little, so shining, so safe. Thank heaven, we've come back here in the self-centered seventies, when everyone is wandering about doing his or her thing. I should have hated to have come back in the sixties, to have been surrounded by feelings of hope and idealism.

I feel very female—a hard will, a determination to survive, have my children survive. Perhaps all along, a cause is a male principle we've been seduced into upholding. I never did understand personal honor. Now, when it's in conflict with subsistence-level well-being, I even question the concept of honor in a general sense. There's a twelfth-century Madonna from Spain in the Metropolitan Museum that I go to see each time I'm there. Primitive, bulky wood, parts eaten away by insects. The Madonna holds the baby stiff, frontal, her eyes looking out over his head, staring into space. In her face is the sad knowledge, the apprehension in the face of every mother. I would like so much to tell my children to look outside themselves, to serve some greater purpose in life. I can't afford it. They can't afford it. It's dangerous.

Small moralities are better. The large outside kind are too complex, too daunting. Better just to be responsible to oneself and loving to friends. "What's come over our Hope?" my friends puzzle, as, against polite resistance, I jump up to help with the dishes. She's just working off her private morality, that's all.

Although *The New York Times* reports I live reclusively, I have a hundred-plus real friends, people I love. Last fall I gave a party, with a jukebox, and an open fire, a view of the East River, and basins of food that I'd prepared for several days. People from all times of my life— kindergarten, Iran, college, Sikkim, the present—came. Even then I missed quite a few. When they were all together, there was a hum of energy so great, I thought I'd burst. All of us support each other—help if we're in trouble, rejoice with each other if things are going well. We're an extended family. Some of us are closer friends, siblings, than others. Our close friends are like our brothers- and sisters-in-law. All of us continue to bring in new friends, who begin as honored guests and then too become family. It's hard work and time-consuming. We work at keeping in touch, telephoning, visiting, following the rhythm of each other's lives. Often some combination among us get together to celebrate a ritual—Jane Alexander's upstate Labor Day feast, Mrs. Milliken and Jane's Thanksgiving dinner, my midsummer birthday. We are of all generations—old, middle-aged, young, and children. Our children are friends of our friends' children. When we visit one another's houses, it's like being home—pictures of our own kids dot the walls and tables of our friends.

I see Kesu, Yuden, and Norbu, my friends from Sikkim, often, even though Yuden now lives in New Orleans and Norbu and Kesu live in Providence, where Norbu works at a small Buddhist Center run by the Rinpoche from the Gangtok Chorten. In some ways we remain Sikkimese with each other. Norbu and Helen, his wife, always keep the Sikkimese custom of bringing food—brown rice, honey, fruit—when they come for visits. In some ways we're American. At their house I'm expected to empty the garbage or do whatever share of chores need doing. In all ways we're ourselves, accepting and loving each other for what we are. Love has enabled the wound in me to heal, my life to come together.

At first, when I came back from Sikkim, I was so angry, so hurt and frightened, I wanted nothing to do with my life there, even memory of it. By force of will I wanted to throw away half of myself, make America and life here my only reality. Norbu, Kesu, Yuden stopped me, insisted by right of friendship that the children and I keep our Sikkimese history, remain whole and grow from whole, not torn, selves. We've all changed

and grown. Although they still call me Gyalmo, sometimes—not always
—I'm a private person, separated from their king. Although I first knew
them as students, they're now adults. Without forgetting our old ties,
we've moved on to a new perception, made a new contract.

This summer has been good. I'm ready to go back from this island to
my everyday life of children, writing, jogging, job-hunting. I've been to
see so many TV and publishing people about possible work that Yangchen has given me a T-shirt with my résumé printed on it, which I wear
to appointments. My former celebrity status seems to confuse prospective employers as much as it attracts them. In any case, although sometimes I feel I would like colleagues and the structure of a job (the Water
Cooler Principle), increasingly I realize that I'm a writer and am never
happier than while working in the warm sanctuary of my neighborhood
library.

I'm ready to go back to my apartment, though I'm beginning to want
more. I want someone to celebrate, commiserate, see with, wake up with.
Sometimes I want this man so badly I have to go out running to keep
from going crazy. One day last fall, when Jane M. was busy in a play and
hadn't as much time as usual to extend to me, I went down to her
Greenwich Village house, where she lives with her daughter Cordelia
and Dick, her beau. All around her were familiar, beautiful things collected during their lives. A bag full of Balducci's croissants was on the
hall table. Dick had bought them for the breakfast he was making for
Jane's birthday the next day. "How're you?" Jane asked, as she always
does, but this time, I knew, in a preoccupied manner. Without answer-
ing, struggling to keep my mouth shut, my eyes dry, I walked hurriedly
past her. Suddenly, to Jane's and my consternation, I began to howl. I
was mortified. I'd never been envious, not of someone I loved. I couldn't
stop crying.

I want some material things too. Although sometimes I'm glad to be
free of things—we've only a TV, bookshelves, and mattresses—increasingly I want some lovely things around me. As a start, I want my own furniture back from Sikkim. Even though I accept Rinpoche's interpretation
of the impermanence of life, I've a new wish to live in a committed,
fleshed-out manner. Last year we bought our first dining room table, a
round butcher block that Hope picked from a store window. Since then
our meals have become ceremonies. Even when there are no guests, the
children never think of having supper without candlelight. On each birthday and Christmas that has passed since the table was bought they've

given me something—napkins, napkin rings, decanters—that shows how they value it. The roundness, the ritual.

Maybe I should have ended the book as I first intended, with our first Thanksgiving. I can't. Life didn't end there. In fact, the more I think about it, the more it seems that life, in terms at least of my own development as an adult, began then. Another thing, I'm a little scared to end the book.

"Oh, Hope, you're so stupid," says a friend. "Just go out and get some more life experience." Actually, I don't want a whole lot more—not, at least, of an epic kind. In fact, one thing bothering me is the stir publishing this book—however proud of it I am—will possibly cause. What I want are the small repetitions and dailiness of life. Touches, gestures, connections.

The drunken boat that adventured beyond the stupid eye of light-houses returns. Close to here, on Nantucket, is Sankaty, the first lighthouse you see coming back to America.

PICTURE CREDITS